First published in 1993 by
HEADLINE BOOK PUBLISHING

10 9 8 7 6 5 4 3 2

British Library Cataloguing in Publication Data

Bannister, Jack
   Innings of My Life
   I. Title
   796.358092

   Hardback ISBN 0-7472-0905-7

   Softback ISBN 0-7472-7853-9

Book interior by Design/Section
Printed and bound in Great Britain by
BPC Hazell Books Ltd
A member of
The British Printing Company Ltd

HEADLINE BOOK PUBLISHING
A division of Hodder Headline PLC
Headline House
79 Great Titchfield Street
London W1P 7FN

THE
INNINGS
OF MY LIFE

COMPILED BY JACK BANNISTER

 LEUKAEMIA RESEARCH FUND

FOREWORD BY IAN BOTHAM

HEADLINE

CONTENTS

FOREWORD BY IAN BOTHAM

I have been associated with many cricket books, but none as exciting as this one. The format is like my cricket - simple, straightforward and, I hope, one which will give great entertainment to the public. It is a brilliant idea to take a cross-section of 40 or so cricketers from the great Sir Don Bradman to Graham Gooch, and get them to decide on their best innings.

I am flattered to be part of a cast which includes 30 cricketers who captained their countries over 700 times. Almost all of them have such a wide choice of great innings, often played against the world's best bowlers, that I know how difficult it must have been to pick one and say: 'That was the innings of my life.'

I know I did, because I have managed to affect the results of a few games for every side I have played for, but pleasure in doing the unexpected has always meant a lot to me. That is why I ignored my hundreds for England in making my choice and settled for an innings for Somerset when I deliberately played a maiden while on 96 not out to ensure we won a NatWest semi-final against Middlesex.

Many of the choices will surprise the reader, but half the fun is in reading the reasons why batsmen like Dexter, Gavaskar and Ian Chappell among former players, and Graham Gooch, Wayne Larkins and Chris Broad, who are still playing, have picked innings in which their score was well below their career best.

What I find especially interesting is that 13 of us have chosen an innings played at Lord's, whereas no other ground has more than a couple of entries. In a way, we are actors, and I think this book proves that Lord's offers the best centre stage in the world. I worked there as a youngster on the MCC Groundstaff, and I bagged a pair against Australia in 1981, a few minutes before I resigned the England captaincy, so I have mixed memories about the place, but it is Mecca to overseas cricketers.

I am pleased that a couple of bowlers have got in, because they get so much enjoyment from a decent innings. I played in the Sydney Test which Eddie Hemmings has chosen and it was a great effort, because the Aussies went at him full bore. I only wished I could have played in the other game featuring a bowler, because I would have loved to have seen 'Boycs'' face when he got out sweeping, with 'Stevie' 115 not out at number eleven batting at the other end. The times he's told me to cut the shot out!

The book has everything. Attacking innings like those chosen by Bradman, Graveney, Azharuddin and Lamb. Rearguard actions like Russell in Barbados and Gavaskar at Old Trafford, where they both gutsed it out against really quick bowling, and genuine captain's innings from Ian Chappell, 'Goochie', Mike Smith, Dexter and May.

My other involvement is with the charity for which I have done all my walks - the Leukaemia Research Fund. I have done what I can for affected kids for around 15 years, and I am thrilled that the fund will benefit every time a copy of this book is sold.

Many people will be surprised that I passed over my two hundreds against Australia in 1981. Perhaps, by the time you read this, I will wish I could have waited for the recent Ashes series in England, because I would love to stick one more past the Aussies. No matter, you've got over 40 of the best to read.

This is the third book I have done with Jack Bannister, and I rate it the best. Enjoy it.

INTRODUCTION

Give a cricket fanatic the chance to talk to some of the great cricketers, past and present, and he will jump at the opportunity as eagerly as will any journalist who is afforded the same chance, with the promise of a good story to write. When the two come together, it is a once-in-a-lifetime fusion of work and play, and I feel privileged to act as the middle man between the public and their heroes. The 43 cricketers whose choice of their best innings appears in this book include most of the all-time great living players from Sir Donald Bradman to those of the present day.

The only cricketer who was not alive at the time of writing was Walter Hammond, but I was also asked to sound out two of the best-known non-playing cricketing names in the world - Brian Johnston and Harold Bird - for their choice of the best innings they ever watched. The doyen of 'Test Match Special' unhesitatingly chose Hammond's 240 at Lord's in 1938. Not quite so unequivocally, Bird settled for a defensive exhibition he has never seen bettered, by John Edrich on a rain-affected pitch at Edgbaston in 1975.

I spent many hours talking to the other 41 players, and the reasons for choosing a particular innings were, at times, even more fascinating than the final choice itself. Sheer weight of runs was not always the criterion, although nobody who saw either innings could argue with the choice of Bradman or that of Peter May. Both innings are established as part of history, as indeed are the innings chosen by Sir Garfield Sobers, Graham Gooch and Allan Border, with Gooch's performance winning a Test match, and the other two saving one.

The meticulous attention to detail which most top batsmen have, made their final decision a challenge to ensure that full justice was done to something so special to them. The first hint I got that I was on to something out of the ordinary was when I spoke to my first subject - Sunil Gavaskar in December 1992. I had to push him for days for the innings of his life, but the delay was well worth enduring. When the most prolific scorer of Test hundreds can throw all 34 out of the window and choose a modest 57, then clearly a treasure trove of batting recollections lay waiting for me to explore.

Or was Gavaskar to be a curious exception? Within two months, I knew better. By then, he was one of a dozen famous names, all of whom had scored Test hundreds, who did not choose one of those hundreds as their best innings - nor did most of them pick a three-figure innings.

The character of the men came through strongly as they talked with no little enthusiasm about how they were still impressed by one particular performance above all others. There is a thin dividing line between boasting and as near an objective self-analysis as is possible by great batsmen, some of whose talents were touched by genius. Yet none of them crossed that line.

Recall was variable, and the accuracy differed according to the personality. Bradman could even remember the time King George V was presented to both teams a few minutes before he took guard for his greatest innings, and he cites his score of 191 when he played his first and only false stroke. Ian Botham, typically, remembers some, but not all, of the crucial details surrounding his decision to bat out a maiden in a NatWest Trophy semi-final at Lord's with the scores level, when Somerset had lost eight wickets, compared with nine by Middlesex. Sir Colin Cowdrey made a December morning in 1954 at the Melbourne Cricket Ground come alive, as he described one of the greatest fast bowling spells in history by Keith Miller, while Ted Dexter has different memories of the same ground eight years later.

My trail led me to cricketers from all over the world who talked about great innings in historic Test matches from Sydney to Lord's, from Bridgetown to Bangalore where, in November 1974, Alvin Kallicharran and Gordon Greenidge were involved in a run-out about which they still have totally different versions.

For some, like Javed Miandad and Botham, it was not a Test match which inspired them to the heights. For others, like the ever-lasting Border and the equally durable Ian Chappell, it was not a hundred which earned the rare accolade of self-praise. Pick where you will - each chapter tells the reader something different about a cricketer - both as a batsman and as a man.

The bowlers are not forgotten, with Eddie Hemmings and Graham Stevenson providing perfect examples of why comedians love to play Shakespeare. The twin pleasure for me was to research each subject and then to try to do it justice. Talking to players from different countries brought to light one or two phrases peculiar to that country, such as when Richie Richardson's bat 'started to sing', and when Ian Chappell, believing that one of his bowlers was over-estimating his ability, told me 'I thought he was having a lend of himself'.

Each of the chapters taught me something about that player in particular, and the game of cricket in general. It opened up horizons that few cricket nuts ever see and, for that alone, I am grateful to all the players concerned.

If asked, like I asked Messrs Bird and Johnston - a tactful, but possibly necessary, reverse billing this time - for my favourite innings, I am pushed to go outside these pages, because it would not be possible for me to say that I have seen anything better than, for example, Mohammad Azharuddin's brilliant innings at Lord's, or Gooch's epic performance at Headingley.

I bowled to 14 of them and saw the rest. Of the 14, Dexter was unquestionably the hardest batsman to bowl to, and Cowdrey the most difficult to get out. At least he was after I trapped him caught and bowled off a full toss in his Oxford days.

I will exercise an author's prerogative and pick 'the innings of my life' about which I got most enjoyment to write. It has to be that of Ian Chappell, for the nature of the innings, the historic match in which it was played and, above all, for the background detail of boyhood and career, which was given in typically salty and earthy fashion.

And finally, the one out of the 43 who would be my ultimate choice to play an innings for my life, with the fingers of the firing squad twitching? It is one of the 14 against whom I bowled and, despite getting him out at Hull, I choose Geoffrey Boycott. The title of this book might have been coined for him. After all, he played one every time he went to the crease.

BIBLIOGRAPHY

The Greatest Since My Time by Trevor Bailey, published by Hodder & Stoughton.

Jack In The Box by Jack Bannister, published by Queen Anne Press.

Don Bradman's Book by Don Bradman, published by Hutchinson.

England Test Cricketers by Bill Frindall, published by Collins Willow.

The *Wisden Book of Test Cricket, Volumes I and II* compiled and edited by Bill Frindall, published by Queen Anne Press.

Rhythm and Swing by Richard Hadlee, published by Souvenir Press.

It's Been a Piece of Cake by Brian Johnston, published by Methuen.

A History of West Indies Cricket by Michael Manley, published by André Deutsch.

The Wisden Book of Captains on Tour by Don Mosey, published by Stanley Paul.

The Centurions by Patrick Murphy, published by J.M.Dent & Sons.

Australian Cricket by Jack Pollard, published by Angus and Robertson.

Tangled Up In White by Peter Roebuck, published by Hodder & Stoughton.

DENNIS AMISS

262* on the fourth and fifth days of the second Test between West Indies and England at Kingston, 20 and 21 February 1974.

Amiss batted for the last 9½ hours of the match to ensure a draw. This result meant that England avoided going 2-0 down in a series which they subsequently squared by winning the final Test in Trinidad. His score remained a career best, and it was the fifth of his 11 hundreds for England, coming in the 23rd of his 50 Tests.

Dennis Leslie Amiss, MBE, was born on 7 April 1943 in Harborne, Birmingham. After playing at Edgbaston at the age of 14 in a Schools final, he joined the Warwickshire playing staff in 1960 to begin a career in which he played 658 first-class matches. He made slow progress in county cricket, and did not score a Championship hundred until his eighth season, by which time he had already played for England at The Oval in 1966 against the West Indies.

For the next 21 years, he was one of the most prolific of post-war batsmen, with only Boycott and Graveney exceeding his aggregate of 43,423 runs, which makes him the 11th heaviest run-scorer in history. His final figures are remarkably similar to those of Colin Cowdrey, although the two men had completely contrasting styles. Cowdrey was the archetypal touch player, who almost caressed the ball to the boundary, while Amiss developed a powerful front-foot technique based on strong forearms, together with unrelenting concentration.

Both men were great theorists, forever seeking improvements in grip and stance. Their respective records are:

	Matches	Inns	Nos	Runs	Avge	100s
Amiss	658	1139	126	43,423	42.86	102
Cowdrey	692	1130	134	42,719	42.89	107

The consistency of Amiss brought him 1000 runs in a season 24 times - only Grace, Woolley, Cowdrey, Mead, Boycott, Hobbs and Hendren bettered this achievement - and he topped 2000 in 1976, 1978 and 1984. In 1978, he was under threat of the sack from Warwickshire when most of his county colleagues forcibly expressed their criticisms of his association with Kerry Packer's World Series cricket circus. The Warwickshire Committee told him that he would not be offered a new contract until he could guarantee his availability for England. It says much for his strength of mind that he was able to concentrate on his batting so successfully.

The most disappointing feature of the events which followed the rapprochement between the world's authorities and Packer was that Amiss never played for England again, even though many inferior players were selected, and other 'rebels', such as the Kent trio, Knott, Underwood and Woolmer, were welcomed back. What is not common knowledge is that Amiss was the catalyst in the final settlement that returned the 'rebel' cricketers to Test cricket. Only when Warwickshire reluctantly agreed to offer him another contract did the World Series authorities consent to negotiate a peace treaty, which made it ironic that he was never to play Test cricket again.

He played for Warwickshire until 1987 and, as recorded in *Wisden*, 'he broke every Warwickshire batting record, and more than an era ended with his retirement.'

Amiss was the 21st batsman to score 100 centuries, which he did in July 1986 after a sequence of 15 innings in a seemingly endless period of six weeks following his 99th against Glamorgan.

Batting never came easily to him, because of his unease against fast bowling, particularly in the 1960s. True bravery is the ability to conquer fear, and while it would be unkind to say that Amiss was afraid of pace, he nevertheless had to learn, like Barrington before him, how to cope without having the ability, or the inclination, to hook.

His career is studded with dozens of innings played 'against the collar', especially after he moved up the order to open the innings for his country in 1967. He opened for England for the first time at Delhi in his tenth Test in 1972 at the age of 29 - six years after his debut. He may have been a slow developer - he scored only one fifty in his first 21 innings - but what a strong finisher!

Which performance does he rate as 'the innings of my life'? His list of Test hundreds is more impressive than most, because in only two of his 11 centuries was he dismissed before he reached 150 - a sure indication of a steely quality, combined with natural talent, that enabled him to score heavily once he was in.

> It must be my double hundred at Kingston, for two reasons. It saved the Test and, as things turned out, the series, and by batting for over nine hours, it proved that I could sustain an innings physically and mentally, despite the growing pressure of the situation.

Amiss had played a full part in England's bid to draw the first Test in Trinidad, after they trailed on first innings by 261. This was the game in which his Warwickshire colleague Alvin Kallicharran scored 158 and was at the centre of one of the most controversial incidents the game has known. The little left-hander was 142 when the last ball of the second day was bowled to Julien, who played it safely. Kallicharran moved out of his crease to leave the field, and Tony Greig promptly threw down the bowler's stumps to gain a run-out decision. The appeal was subsequently withdrawn off the field, and West Indies went on to win their first Test at home in 22 attempts, despite Amiss's 174 putting England into a good position before another of Amiss's Warwickshire colleagues, Lance Gibbs, took six for 108 and started a collapse which saw the last nine wickets fall for 64.

It was against this antagonised background that the Kingston Test started two weeks later, and again England were in deep trouble after each side's first innings. England brought in Jameson for Fletcher, and West Indies replaced one spinner with another, Barrett for Inshan Ali. Skipper Mike Denness must have hoped for better things when he won the toss on a good pitch than a total of 353, particularly as eight England batsmen passed 20.

West Indies replied with 583 but, other than an explosive 66 from 58 balls by Julien in a partnership for the sixth wicket with Sobers of 112 in 75 minutes, the main England bowlers - Pocock, Underwood and Greig - contained the powerful home batsmen well enough to raise hopes of a draw when the England second innings began after lunch on the fourth day. Amiss remembers the start of that second innings:

> We had two sessions and most of the last day to get through, so it was important for Geoff Boycott and me to get off to a good start. It could hardly have been worse - Geoff, who had top-scored for us in the first innings, was caught by Deryck Murray off a Keith Boyce bouncer, and we were in real trouble.

Amiss was then joined by Jameson, one of seven cricketers in the match who had played for Warwickshire - the other five were Willis, Kanhai, Kallicharran, Gibbs and Murray. Chris Old would make an eighth in 1983. Jameson was caught off leg-spinner Barrett for 38 and then came the sort of dismissal that seems to happen to a side in trouble. Amiss again:

> Frank Hayes came in before tea, and it was vital we didn't lose another wicket before the break. So what did I do? I ran him out for a duck [a direct hit by Lloyd], so now I had got even more responsibility to bear. It was my fault, but I made a huge effort to put it out of my mind and try to make amends by playing a long innings.

Amiss, like many others, often had differing and firm ideas from his colleagues about the merits of a run - few more so than his opening partner at Kingston. Both batsmen were considered to be equally fireproof when it came to a decision about who stayed and who went. Suffice it to say that Boycott was run out just seven times in 193 innings for England, including the famous occasion by Ian Botham in Christchurch, while Amiss perished only once - in company with John Edrich at Lord's in 1971 against India. Contrast their record with that of Jameson, whose eight Test dismissals included three run-outs.

Wisden's summing up of the position at the end of the remarkable fourth day was that 'it seemed unlikely that England could survive. By the time the score was 217, five wickets had gone and Amiss only had Knott and the tailenders left for company, and they were still 13 runs behind.'

The start of the fifth day could have brought the end of England's faint hopes of saving the match. Amiss was 123, and he played the third ball of the day straight to Sobers at backward short-leg, and the all-rounder dropped the catch.

Amiss was partnered by nightwatchman Derek Underwood, who set the tone for the day of inspired defiance by surviving a barrage of bouncers, which *Wisden* deemed 'too numerous to be acceptable', for 75 minutes, before he was caught by Murray off Sobers. Amiss recalls:

> When 'Deadly' was out, we were 258 for six, 28 ahead, and there were nearly five hours to get through. Alan Knott was really our last hope, so what did I do? I brought off the double - pushed one to Lloyd in the covers and ran him out, no trouble, to make us 271 for seven.

Anyone who cannot understand how cricketers can make basic errors of judgement when running to brilliant fielders should study the 1965 Test at Lord's between England and South Africa, which included Colin Bland, one of the best overseas fielders ever seen on English Test grounds. He used to give exhibitions before games of throwing down a single stump on the run. So England's pre-match team-talk concentrated on eliminating the chances of a run-out by agreeing to consider his patrol in the covers and at mid-wicket as definite no-go areas. A good idea - except Barrington and Parks were both thrown out by Bland.

Amiss must have been in despair, but his indomitable spirit pulled him through, and he received

WEST INDIES V ENGLAND (2ND TEST)

PLAYED AT SABINA PARK, KINGSTON, JAMAICA, ON 16, 17, 19, 20, 21 FEBRUARY 1974.
TOSS: ENGLAND. RESULT: MATCH DRAWN.

ENGLAND

	FIRST INNINGS		SECOND INNINGS	
G.Boycott	c Kanhai, b Sobers	68	c Murray, b Boyce	5
D.L.Amiss	c Kanhai, b Barrett	27	not out	262
J.A.Jameson	st Murray, b Gibbs	23	c Rowe, b Barrett	38
F.C.Hayes	c Boyce, b Sobers	10	run out	0
M.H.Denness*	c Fredericks, b Boyce	67	c Rowe, b Barrett	28
A.W.Greig	c Fredericks, b Barrett	45	b Gibbs	14
A.P.E.Knott†	c Murray, b Barrett	39	(8) run out	6
C.M.Old	c Murray, b Julien	2	(9) b Barrett	19
D.L.Underwood	c Fredericks, b Sobers	24	(7) c Murray, b Sobers	12
P.I.Pocock	c Gibbs, b Julien	23	c sub (V.A.Holder), b Boyce	4
R.G.D.Willis	not out	6	not out	3
Extras	lb 7, nb 12	19	b 10, lb 11, w 1, nb 19	41
		353	(for 9 wickets)	432

	O	M	R	W	O	M	R	W
Boyce	19	2	52	1	21	4	70	2
Julien	18	3	40	2	13	3	36	0
Sobers	33	11	65	3	34	13	73	1
Barrett	39	16	86	3	54	24	87	3
Gibbs	40	16	78	1	44	15	82	1
Fredericks	4	0	11	0	6	1	17	0
Lloyd	4	2	2	0	3	1	5	0
Kanhai					3	1	8	0
Rowe					2	1	1	0
Kallicharran					3	0	12	0

WEST INDIES

	FIRST INNINGS	
R.C.Fredericks	b Old	94
L.G.Rowe	lbw, b Willis	120
A.I.Kallicharran	c Denness, b Old	93
C.H.Lloyd	b Jameson	49
R.B.Kanhai*	c Willis, b Greig	39
G.St A.Sobers	c Willis, b Greig	57
B.D.Julien	c Denness, b Greig	66
K.D.Boyce	c Greig, b Willis	8
D.L.Murray†	not out	6
A.G.Barrett	lbw, b Willis	0
L.R.Gibbs	not out	6
Extras	b 16, lb 18, nb 11	45
	(9 wickets declared)	583

	O	M	R	W
Willis	24	5	97	3
Old	23	6	72	2
Pocock	57	14	152	0
Underwood	36	12	98	0
Greig	49	14	102	3
Jameson	7	2	17	1

FALL OF WICKETS
1-68, 2-104, 3-133, 4-134, 5-224, 6-278, 7-286, 8-322, 9-333, 10-353
1-32, 2-102, 3-107, 4-176, 5-217, 6-258, 7-271, 8-343, 9-392

FALL OF WICKETS
1-206, 2-226, 3-338, 4-401, 5-439, 6-551, 7-563, 8-567, 9-574

Umpires: H.B.de C.Jordan and D.Sang Hue

unexpected support from Old. Not that the Yorkshireman could not bat - he scored six first-class hundreds - but England already seemed doomed. Old was not a renowned player of fast bowling but he survived a hostile attack for 100 minutes to add 72 runs for the eighth wicket.

Lunch came and went, and so did the various landmarks for Amiss, who was by now mentally stretched to the limit:

> All I knew was that I had to keep going. I was physically tired, but the mental fatigue was much worse. Each interval, the other players tried to keep me going - I even had a brandy at tea. The day seemed endless, but somehow we were hanging on.

Magnificent though his effort was, the contributions of Underwood, Old and then Pocock were priceless. Underwood averaged 11.56 for England, and Pocock 6.24, but they fought it out for just short of three hours between them on that tense, final day when they had to contend with everything that Boyce, Julien and Sobers could hurl at them with pace, as well as the wiles of Gibbs and Barrett.

Pocock, who had done a similar job in the first innings of the Guyana Test in 1968, repeated the heroics with four singles as his contribution to a ninth-wicket partnership of 72, with Amiss ever conscious of a time and runs equation that, by the tea interval, was beginning to tilt England's way. When Pocock was caught by substitute Vanburn Holder off Boyce 20 minutes after tea, Amiss had taken England to a lead of 162, and the game was virtually safe, with 90 minutes left. If last man Willis had got out first ball, West Indies might have had a faint chance, but he did not. Amiss says:

> He said he didn't fancy bowling again, and he wouldn't get out. I suppose it would have been nice to have carried my bat, but the most important thing was that we saved the match. I remember the cheers and applause we got from some Warwickshire supporters who were out there, and I have never had such a feeling of relief and satisfaction when it was all over.

Knott, despite the run-out, is full of praise for Amiss's performance: 'The thing about Dennis was how he played the short ball. He didn't hook or pull, so he simply dropped his wrists and let the ball hit him on the body and the arm. It was a terrific exhibition of guts, and yet he never missed a chance of runs, because total defence would probably not have saved the game. He scored 139 out of 214 runs added on that last day, and we were able to hang on in the series and then square it by winning in Trinidad.'

Any hard feelings about the run-out? 'No, although that wasn't the end of it. I was struggling for runs, so I could have done without taking Lloyd on, but it happened again in the next island game in Antigua. Dennis did me again - this time he picked out the young Viv Richards to gamble with, and I was run out by miles again.'

The Kingston Test was notable for the opening partnership of 206 between Fredericks and Rowe which remained a West Indies record against England until Haynes and Greenidge put on 298 in Antigua in 1990 - a partnership that was ended by ... a run-out.

Amiss hit a six and 40 fours from 563 deliveries faced, and it gave him a Test aggregate of 1356 within a period of 12 months. Had Willis got out, he would have been only the fourth batsman to carry his bat through a completed innings for England, and it would have been the highest score by anyone achieving this feat in Test cricket.

Anyone who doubts the rock-solid nature of the Amiss method should note that he was bowled remarkably few times in Test cricket - 11 times in 88 innings, compared with 18 in 96 by Fletcher, 15 in 78 by M.J.K. Smith, 20 in 93 by Greig, 16 in 91 by Bailey, and 14 in 70 by D'Oliveira.

Wisden's final comment sums up an innings which ranks among any played for England in living memory: 'His was the hero's role in a classic escape.'

MOHAMMAD AZHARUDDIN

121 on the third and fourth days of the first Test between England and India at Lord's, 28 and 30 July 1990.

In India's first innings, their captain, Azharuddin, hit a brilliant century to help his side to score the 454 they needed to avoid the follow-on after Graham Gooch's massive 333 in an England total of 653 for four declared, Azharuddin having won the toss and fielded.

Mohammad Azharuddin was born on 8 February 1963 in Hyderabad, and established a world record by scoring hundreds in his first three Tests in Calcutta, Madras and Kanpur against England in 1984-85. He was appointed captain five years later against New Zealand. A devout Muslim - the only one in Indian Test cricket - he has often attracted criticism that he is too nice for international sport, but his boyhood gave him a level-headed outlook on life available to few.

He prays five times a day, and his softly spoken conversation is a delight - his views on life in general, and cricket in particular, are invariably generously balanced:

> I was brought up by my grandfather, who taught me the proper values in life. I was the first grandson of 12, and we only moved back to live with my father when I was 12 and he agreed to accept rent from my grandfather. Naturally, he did not want to do this, but knew that his father was so proud that he had to agree. My grandfather helped me with my cricket in many ways. He never stopped me playing but, so that I could maintain my studies, he would keep notes for me for my exams, and he was especially good at mathematics.
>
> The only cricketing advice he gave me was not to play defensively, but it was his teaching on life that made the biggest impression. He would often tell me: 'Whatever you become, always think of what you had and what you were before.' I still believe that.

I spoke to Azharuddin in South Africa towards the end of India's disastrous tour there in 1992-93. In as sincere an interview as I have ever conducted, he expanded on his philosophy: 'I was brought up to respect people, and I always will, especially my parents, which is why, when I go home for the tour of India by England, when I stay with them and want to go out at night, I shall ask them first.'

Commenting on his first three Test hundreds, he said: 'My big regret is that my grandfather died on 16 November 1984, just under seven weeks before my first hundred in Calcutta.'

I wondered if he was leaning towards that debut hundred as his choice or, perhaps, his 137 two Tests later in Kanpur, where his second fifty came off 38 deliveries, or any of the other six centuries he posted before he arrived at Lord's in 1990 to captain his side for the first time against England.

I choose my hundred at Lord's for several reasons. Before the game, my father called me from Hyderabad and said he wanted me to score a century on that wonderful ground. He always showed great interest in my cricket, and saw me score a hundred in Hyderabad against New Zealand in 1987, but he was anxious for me to score one at Lord's. Then, of course, I had put England in and Graham Gooch got that wonderful 333. It was only my fourth game as captain and, although the pitch was good, there was cloud cover and I thought our bowlers might swing it.

'THANK YOU.' *(PATRICK EAGAR)*

It was not just that my decision was wrong - I wouldn't have minded that because that is part of leading a side. But I was hurt when there was public criticism of me from my own dressing-room. That should not happen during a match, and it distressed me a lot that the manager, Bishen Bedi, who should have kept other players quiet, actually appeared to encourage them to speak out. Accepting criticism is part of captaincy, and I never mind it if it is done in the proper way and at the right time. That was not the case at Lord's in 1990.

My match report for the *Birmingham Post* said: 'Mohammad Azharuddin suffered the slings and arrows of an outraged cricket public in England and back at home, for the first two and a half days of the Lord's Test. Yet never did his head drop throughout the traumas of his opposite number's record 333, and never did he fail to try to maintain his players' spirits.'

I was then unaware of his resentment concerning criticism from the dressing-room, and wrote: 'A non-drinker and non-smoker with a religion devoted to peace and pacifism, pre-meditated violence seemed the last thing the 20,000 Lord's crowd on Saturday would see from the tall, slim Indian captain who had the extra burden of leading a side containing two former captains in Kapil Dev and Dilip Vengsarkar.'

What Azharuddin would not put in so many words to me was that he came close to going in to bat, on

THE INNINGS OF MY LIFE

what was to be a magical Saturday at Lord's, full of temper. Certainly, his normal desire to do well was fuelled both by his father's request and by a determination to prove something to his players. Normally, a score of 191 for three is not a crisis point for number five, particularly when an opening batsman, Ravi Shastri, has just fashioned a stylish hundred.

A capacity crowd had watched a good, if relatively low key, first half of the day, but Azharuddin's dazzling exhibition of attacking play lit up Lord's as effectively as do giant floodlights in other countries. He dominated play to such an extent that his unbeaten 117 at the close came out of 185 scored while he was at the crease, and he did that with partners like Vengsarkar, Sachin Tendulkar and Kapil Dev.

> Devon Malcolm hit me when I was about 20, and I got away with a bit to start with, but I knew that if my Allah was with me, I would play a big innings. Rain stopped play for a while, but I still scored 48 in an hour before tea, and when I reached 50, I had hit 11 fours.

Azharuddin was breathtaking. He did not need faulty length or direction to stroke the ball all over Lord's, but the analysis of three of the England four-man attack illustrates how demolition can be an art. Excluding the admirable Angus Fraser (39.1-9-104-5), Malcolm, Lewis and Hemmings had combined figures of 69-7-323-4. Kapil Dev spoiled Hemmings' figures on the fourth day with four successive sixes to save the follow-on, but it was Azharuddin who put the pace attack to as sharp a sword as they are ever likely to try to parry.

Of his display, *Wisden* had this to say: 'A capacity crowd was treated to a rare exhibition of audacious, wristy strokeplay which took him into three figures off only 88 balls.'

England team manager Micky Stewart is more effusive: 'It was a typical Azharuddin knock. If you pitched a fraction outside off stump and short, he would hit it on the up through the covers. The same line, if pitched just a further 12 inches up would be whipped past the square-leg umpire. The pitch was good, and the Lord's square boundaries are short, but it really was a magnificent display. He needs the ball to come on to the bat, because his biggest asset is that he is such a wonderful timer of the ball. His hitting area is so short, and that makes batsmen like him difficult to bowl to. You will never see a better innings, and it must rank with anything ever played for aggression and sheer mastery. If someone had to get those runs against England, I am delighted it was "Azhar", he is such a smashing bloke.'

I wrote at the time: 'In came Azharuddin to blaze one of the dozen or so quickest Test hundreds in history. It was a phenomenal innings of sheer brilliance, especially in the context of a match he would dearly love to draw after that dreadful first decision to give away the first use of a perfect batting strip to Gooch. He hit 20 fours in a barrage of square cuts, cover drives and flicks through his favourite mid-wicket area, and his determination to impose himself on the match produced one of the most spectacular counter-attacking innings ever seen at Lord's.

'It was an innings of genius but, more important for the Indian captain, the speed of it probably pleased him most, because there was consequently less chance of interruptions to his prayers.'

Despite losing Vengsarkar and then young Sachin Tendulkar for 52 and 10 respectively, his onslaught became ever more furious. At 288 for five, still 166 short of the follow-on target, his side was in deep trouble. In 19 overs before the close, he went from 69 to 117, scoring 48 out of 88. It was his ninth Test hundred, and his fourth against England in seven games. As for the speed of his hundred: the fastest in history is by Viv Richards (56 balls), while Ian Botham's historic hundreds in 1981 against the Australians at Headingley and Old Trafford were in the lower 80s of deliveries faced, and it is not stretching a point to say that Azharuddin's innings deserves to be bracketed with those two performances.

His first action when he returned to the dressing-room on Saturday evening? 'I called my father and told him he had got his wish. I told him "I got it for you," and he was so thrilled.' From most players, remarks like that are usually made with one eye on their public image, but Azharuddin is different in that he genuinely does not believe that this is important.

What you see is what you get: a simple, gentle man in the nicest sense. Nobody who was at St George's Park, Port Elizabeth, during the third Test in December 1992 will ever forget the reaction of the Indian captain when he was the victim of a poor decision which cut short his first innings of any note in the four-game series against South Africa. He was given out for 60, caught at the wicket - one of several poor decisions which provoked so much feeling among players of both sides that it was curious that match referee M.J.K. Smith thought it necessary to fine only one player, Manoj Prabhakar.

When Sachin Tendulkar was given out, also caught at the wicket, his partner Ravi Shastri appeared to hurl his bat to the ground. Tendulkar indicated that the ball had hit his thigh before, after a long delay, he departed the crease in tears.

Youth might be an excuse, but Azharuddin has never been any different. He walked off without a

ENGLAND v INDIA (1ST TEST)

PLAYED AT LORD'S, LONDON, ON 26, 27, 28, 30, 31 JULY 1990.
TOSS: INDIA. RESULT: ENGLAND WON BY 247 RUNS.

ENGLAND

	FIRST INNINGS		SECOND INNINGS	
G.A.Gooch*	b Prabhakar	333	c Azharuddin, b Sharma	123
M.A.Atherton	b Kapil Dev	8	c Vengsarkar, b Sharma	72
D.I.Gower	c Manjrekar, b Hirwani	40	not out	32
A.J.Lamb	c Manjrekar, b Sharma	139	c Tendulkar, b Hirwani	19
R.A.Smith	not out	100	b Prabhakar	15
J.E.Morris	not out	4		
R.C.Russell†				
C.C.Lewis				
E.E.Hemmings	did not bat			
A.R.C.Fraser				
D.E.Malcolm				
Extras	b 2, lb 21, w 2, nb 4	29	lb 11	11
	(4 wickets declared)	653	(4 wickets declared)	272

	O	M	R	W	O	M	R	W
Kapil Dev	34	5	120	1	10	0	53	0
Prabhakar	43	6	187	1	11.2	2	45	1
Sharma	33	5	122	1	15	0	75	2
Shastri	22	0	99	0	7	0	38	0
Hirwani	30	1	102	1	1	0	50	1

FALL OF WICKETS
1-14, 2-141, 3-449, 4-641
1-204, 2-207, 3-250, 4-272

INDIA

	FIRST INNINGS		SECOND INNINGS	
R.J.Shastri	c Gooch, b Hemmings	100	c Russell, b Malcolm	12
N.S.Sidhu	c Morris, b Fraser	30	c Morris, b Fraser	1
S.V.Manjrekar	c Russell, b Gooch	18	c Russell, b Malcolm	33
D.B.Vengsarkar	c Russell, b Fraser	52	c Russell, b Hemmings	35
M.Azharuddin*	b Hemmings	121	c Atherton, b Lewis	37
S.R.Tendulkar	b Lewis	10	c Gooch, b Fraser	27
M.Prabhakar	c Lewis, b Malcolm	25	lbw, b Lewis	8
Kapil Dev	not out	77	c Lewis, b Hemmings	7
K.S.More†	c Morris, b Fraser	8	lbw, b Fraser	16
S.K.Sharma	c Russell, b Fraser	0	run out	38
N.D.Hirwani	lbw, b Fraser	0	not out	0
Extras	lb 1, w 4, nb 8	13	b 3, lb 1, nb 6	10
		454		224

	O	M	R	W	O	M	R	W
Malcolm	25	1	106	1	10	0	65	2
Fraser	39.1	9	104	5	22	7	39	3
Lewis	24	3	108	1	8	1	26	2
Gooch	6	3	26	1				
Hemmings	20	3	109	2	21	2	79	2
Atherton					1	0	11	0

FALL OF WICKETS
1-63, 2-102, 3-191, 4-241, 5-288, 6-348, 7-393, 8-430, 9-430, 10-454
1-9, 2-23, 3-63, 4-114, 5-127, 6-140, 7-158, 8-181, 9-206, 10-224

Umpires: H.D.Bird and N.T.Plews

gesture until, close to the pavilion gate, a rueful smile appeared and he cast one glance at the skies, presumably to his Allah, and allowed himself one tiny shake of his head.

Back to Lord's, the stage chosen by 13 batsmen in this book as the one on which they played their best innings. Azharuddin was out early on the fourth day, and India eventually lost the match by 247 runs, but over 20,000 spectators, were they connoisseurs or not of cricketing artistry, were treated to the rare sight of a touch player performing at his best.

No other modern player has such a wristy method. Few work the leg-side with such facility and, although his strengths can become weaknesses on certain pitches where the ball seams around, he can bat like an angel. Humility can be daunting, when seen from close quarters, but not with 'Azhar', the most open-handed of modern Test captains. Perhaps not the best, but certainly the nicest, and one in whose hands the good name of cricket is safe.

RICHIE BENAUD

97 on the third and fourth days of the second Test between England and Australia at Lord's, 23 and 25 June 1957.

Benaud went in to bat with his side in trouble at 112 for six - an overall lead of 226 but, with opening bowler Pat Crawford injured, the Australian attack was in the hands of Keith Miller and Ron Archer, with Ken Mackay, Ian Johnson and Benaud in support.

Australia badly needed at least a hundred more runs, and Benaud obliged with a magnificent attacking innings against one of England's best-ever post-war attacks, comprising Trueman, Statham, Bailey, Laker and Wardle. His 97 included one six and 14 fours, and came out of a seventh-wicket partnership with Mackay of 117. Benaud batted for 143 minutes, while his passive partner constructed one of the slowest Test innings - 31 in 264 minutes, which remains the slowest progress to that score on record.

Richard Benaud, OBE, was born on 6 October 1930 in Sydney, and learned his cricket at Parramatta High School. He and younger brother John were sons of Louis, a descendant of a French family who migrated to Australia in a sailing ship from La Rochelle. His schoolteacher father achieved statistical perfection seven years before the birth of Richie, when he took all 20 wickets for Penrith Waratahs against St Mary's. He was a successful first-grade leg-spinner, so a future Australian captain was virtually destined to deliver from the back of the hand.

Possessing an analytical mind and a bottomless well of talent, Benaud's graduation to the top in separate careers of cricket and journalism always looked inevitable. His debut for New South Wales came at the age of 18, and he went on to take 945 wickets in a career which also produced 11,719 runs at an average of 36.50 and included 23 hundreds. He won his first Test cap three years later, when he made the most modest of starts to a career which was to end with more Test wickets for him than any other Australian until Dennis Lillee overtook him. He scored three and 19, and took his only wicket thanks to an understanding captain, Lindsay Hassett. With the match all but safely won, the tyro was brought on for his first bowl in Test cricket with four tailend wickets up for grabs. They all looked like going to Ray Lindwall until Benaud bowled number eleven Alf Valentine, and Australia had won by 202 runs to take the series 4-1.

That was on his home Sydney Cricket Ground in January 1952, but although he was dropped for the first Test later that year against South Africa, he played in the remainder of the five-game series in place of Ian Johnson. The Australian selectors are to be praised for the patience they showed with an all-rounder whose batting they thought enough of to bat him at six or seven in formative years that were almost worryingly unproductive.

His first authentic top-order victims were Russell Endean, John Waite and Ken Funston at Adelaide in his fourth Test, but wickets were relatively scarce until his triumphant tour of South Africa under Ian Craig in 1957-58. Lindwall and Miller had gone, and Benaud and Davidson were given much more front-line responsibility.

The now-mature Benaud took 106 first-class wickets on the tour (only Maurice Tate and Ijaz Faqih took more in a season outside England, with 116 in India and 107 in Pakistan). This included 30 wickets in the Test matches in which he bowled the equivalent of 320 six-ball overs for 655 runs, with five or more wickets in an innings in each of the last four Tests. He also scored 329 runs in six completed innings, including a century in both the first and fourth Tests in Johannesburg. The second one, exactly 100, is one to which he gave an honourable mention when asked to pick his best innings.

That series was the prelude to a golden run in the late 1950s and the early 1960s in which he took 31 wickets against Peter May's England side at home in 1958-59, 18 against Pakistan and 29 against India on tour the following year. To underline how his hard work and attention to every detail of his cricket paid off, of Benaud's 248 Test wickets in 63 Tests, 175 came in his last 36 games, beginning with his phenomenal tour of South Africa. He missed only two Tests through injury from debut to retirement, and was dropped three times in his first 2½ years in the side. Thus he could have played only 68 times for his country.

Although Benaud always looked captaincy material, he ascended to the throne only because of Ian Craig's illness and the fact that Neil Harvey had just moved states from Victoria to New South Wales. While the decision was being considered, Benaud led New South Wales in a Sheffield Shield match with some distinction, and so he was appointed. It was particularly fitting, in view of his later career in the media, that he led Australia for the first time against England in Brisbane in the first Test in Australia to be televised. He led his country 28 times in seven series, never lost a series, and won 12 Tests while losing only four. Blessed with flair, kissed with charisma, and not short of the sort of luck the best players make for themselves, he introduced a new dimension into captaincy.

His refusal to let any situation drift without trying something different was perfectly illustrated at Old Trafford in 1961 - his finest hour as captain and bowler. Needing 256 to win the fourth Test and go 2-1 ahead, England were 150 for one when Benaud switched to bowling round the wicket into rough caused by Trueman, Statham and Flavell, and produced one of the most spectacular spells ever seen in Test cricket. He took five for 12 in 25 balls, bowling Raman Subba Row and Peter May, and having Ted Dexter, Brian Close and John Murray caught to change the score from 150 for one to 171 for seven, with Mackay taking the other wicket. The match was won by a high-quality combination of spin and captaincy from one man, whose innovative tactic came from an ice-cool brain that always seemed ahead of the game.

Colin Cowdrey was one of his most distinguished contemporary opponents, and assesses him thus: 'He was the complete captain, an inspiring leader, thoughtful and adroit in the field and a tough competitor. Yet no one has tried harder to make Test cricket an interesting and attractive spectacle.'

When I asked Benaud to decide on the innings he valued most, I knew that his choice would be extra special, and I was not disappointed.

I thought about two of my three Test hundreds, because the first one was scored at number eight in Kingston, and the other one in Johannesburg when I was promoted to number four to attack Trevor Goddard who had been tying our fellows down. At Sabina Park, it was not exactly a crisis when I went in to bat at 597 for six, but I hit well and got my 121 out of 161. In Johannesburg, I got my runs out of

158 for the third wicket with Jimmy Burke, and we won the game by ten wickets.

I saw the match, and remember Benaud hitting Goddard for 38 in three eight-ball overs, despite which the nagging left-hander returned figures of 43-10-136-1. Benaud was the only batsman in the game to break a bowling stranglehold which restricted everyone else so effectively that, even including Benaud's rapid hundred, the match produced an aggregate of 803 runs from the equivalent of 447 six-ball overs.

A GOOD EXAMPLE OF CLEAN HITTING BY BENAUD IN HIS LORD'S INNINGS IN 1956. HE WAS ONE OF THE BEST STRIKERS OF HIS TIME.
(TOPHAM PICTURE SOURCE)

(RIGHT) BENAUD WAS 90 NOT OUT AT LUNCH ON THE FOURTH DAY. PARTNER MACKAY HAS OTHER THINGS ON HIS MIND, AND MAY AND LAKER DISCUSS THE CRUCIAL IMPACT OF BENAUD'S INNINGS ON THE MATCH.
(SPORT AND GENERAL)

I have to pick my 97 at Lord's, because it influenced the result, and it was also the first time I had made a decent score against England. I reckon the game was one of the best Test matches I ever played in, and Keith Miller was magnificent. In England's first innings in reply to our 285, Crawford broke down in his fifth over, and 'Nugget' bowled 34 overs out of the 82 we took to bowl them out for 171. He took five for 72, including Richardson, Graveney, Watson and Bailey in the first six, and I chipped in by bowling May and having Evans stumped.

Then Trueman got into us with three quick wickets and when we were 79 for five, we couldn't hold Keith back any longer. He went in to score 30 out of 33 for the sixth wicket with 'Slasher' Mackay. I was next in, and hoped I would not get in until Monday morning, but Fred had Keith caught by Godfrey Evans and I went in at 112 for six. 'Slasher' was nine and I was three at the close, and we had the Sunday to think about what we would try to do. I hadn't bargained for a John Arlott special. He held a wine and cheese party near Lord's, and there was plenty of red wine and Stilton soaked in port.

I wanted a net next morning, but missed it because I was too late arriving. It was nothing to do with the wine and cheese, but we used to travel by chauffeur-driven cars from the hotel to Lord's, and I was in the last one. We were delayed by an accident, and I was too late for nets when I got to the ground. I remember walking out to bat and, as 'Slasher' went to the other end, he turned and growled out of the corner of his mouth, 'Don't let's get run out, eh?'

Fred bowled the first over from the Nursery End, and I went for a leg-side pick-up, only for it to lob into the covers. Then I got a bouncer and hit it for four, but it was a stroke off Brian Statham which really set me going. I pulled him for four to mid-wicket right off the middle of the bat, and I remember thinking: 'This just might be my day.' I hit Trevor Bailey for a couple of fours - one was lucky over gully - but I kept going while 'Slasher' just drove them all crackers. He was a great leaver of the ball, and many times he would look as though he had played and missed when he had left one alone. I had hit Fred for a six and when he took the second new ball, I went for another and got out a few minutes after lunch to a skier to Godfrey.

It was Benaud's tenth Ashes game against England, and in 15 previous innings he had scraped 180 runs with a top score of 34. His overall Test record before he went in to bat was 572 runs in 30 innings, including a highest score of 121 which remains the third fastest in terms of minutes in Test history. He had passed 50 on only one other occasion, and topped 40 twice, while his 40 wickets from 23 Tests meant that his place in the Australian team had been far from automatic.

Benaud walked off to a terrific ovation from a generous crowd who knew that his innings had tilted the game Australia's way. The last three Australian wickets fell quickly, but the damage had been done to the England cause, and they now needed 372 to register their second win at Lord's against Australia in the 20th century - the only previous one being in 1934 on a rain-affected pitch on which Hedley Verity took 14 for 80 on the third day and 15 for 104 in the match.

If that was 'Verity's Match', the 1956 Lord's Test became known as 'Miller's Match', with the great all-rounder taking ten wickets in a Test for the only time. Without Benaud's innings, Australia might have lost a game which they finally won comfortably by 185 runs with over three hours to spare.

Benaud was not finished, winning a controversial LBW decision against Cowdrey in England's second innings. There was no argument about the decision - just about the events leading up to it. The England opener kept putting his bat and pad well down the wicket, and Benaud decided to do something about it.

I told the captain to put Peter Burge in Cowdrey's hip pocket at short-leg to make him think. Peter May immediately told the umpire that it was our responsibility if the fielder got injured, but we didn't budge, and it worked like a charm. I got him LBW two overs later because he could not afford just to play me with the bat and pad.

Miller repeated his first innings marathon with 36 overs out of 100, and his second bag of five wickets helped wicketkeeper Langley set up a world record with nine dismissals, including a stumping off Benaud and five catches off Miller. Considering Australia went into the game without the injured Lindwall and Davidson, and then lost Crawford, it was a wonderful achievement to beat such a powerful England side, and Benaud still enthuses about Miller's performance.

He also has one more vivid memory which could have forced him to choose another batting performance as 'the innings of my life'.

Before I scored on the Saturday evening, I got a faint touch to a lifting leg-cutter from Trueman which was deflected straight on to my right shoulder. I instinctively rubbed it because it stung, and when I looked around umpire Dai Davies had given me not out.

ENGLAND V AUSTRALIA (2ND TEST)

PLAYED AT LORD'S, LONDON, ON 21, 22, 23, 25, 26 JUNE 1956.
TOSS: AUSTRALIA. RESULT: AUSTRALIA WON BY 185 RUNS.

AUSTRALIA

	FIRST INNINGS		SECOND INNINGS	
C.C.McDonald	c Trueman, b Bailey	78	c Cowdrey, b Bailey	26
J.W.Burke	st Evans, b Laker	65	c Graveney, b Trueman	16
R.N.Harvey	c Evans, b Bailey	0	c Bailey, b Trueman	10
P.J.P.Burge	b Statham	21	b Trueman	14
K.R.Miller	b Trueman	28	(7) c Evans, b Trueman	30
K.D.Mackay	c Bailey, b Laker	38	(5) c Evans, b Statham	31
R.G.Archer	b Wardle	28	(6) c Evans, b Bailey	1
R.Benaud	b Statham	5	c Evans, b Trueman	97
I.W.Johnson*	c Evans, b Trueman	6	lbw, b Bailey	17
G.R.A.Langley†	c Bailey, b Laker	14	not out	7
W.P.A.Crawford	not out	0	lbw, b Bailey	0
Extras	lb 2	2	b 2, lb 2, nb 4	8
		285		257

	O	M	R	W	O	M	R	W
Statham	35	9	70	2	26	5	59	1
Trueman	28	6	54	2	28	2	90	5
Bailey	34	12	72	2	24.5	8	64	4
Laker	29.1	10	47	3	7	3	17	0
Wardle	20	7	40	1	7	2	19	0

FALL OF WICKETS
1-137, 2-137, 3-151, 4-185, 5-196, 6-249, 7-255, 8-265, 9-285, 10-285
1-36, 2-47, 3-69, 4-70, 5-79, 6-112, 7-229, 8-243, 9-257, 10-257

ENGLAND

	FIRST INNINGS		SECOND INNINGS	
P.E.Richardson	c Langley, b Miller	9	c Langley, b Archer	21
M.C.Cowdrey	c Benaud, b Mackay	23	lbw, b Benaud	27
T.W.Graveney	b Miller	5	c Langley, b Miller	18
P.B.H.May*	b Benaud	63	(5) c Langley, b Miller	53
W.Watson	c Benaud, b Miller	6	(4) b Miller	18
T.E.Bailey	b Miller	32	c Harvey, b Archer	18
T.G.Evans†	st Langley, b Benaud	0	c Langley, b Miller	20
J.C.Laker	b Archer	12	c Langley, b Archer	4
J.H.Wardle	c Langley, b Archer	0	b Miller	0
F.S.Trueman	c Langley, b Miller	7	b Archer	2
J.B.Statham	not out	0	not out	0
Extras	lb 14	14	lb 5	5
		171		186

	O	M	R	W	O	M	R	W
Miller	34.1	9	72	5	36	12	80	5
Crawford	4.5	2	4	0				
Archer	23	9	47	2	51.2	8	71	4
Mackay	11	3	15	1				
Benaud	9	2	19	2	28	14	27	1
Johnson					4	2	3	0

FALL OF WICKETS
1-22, 2-32, 3-60, 4-87, 5-128, 6-128, 7-161, 8-161, 9-170, 10-171
1-35, 2-59, 3-89, 4-91, 5-142, 6-175, 7-180, 8-184, 9-184, 10-186

Umpires: D.E.Davies and F.S.Lee

On such an incident is history built. Let Cowdrey have the last generous word: 'The strength of his batting lay in his driving. At the crease he always personified a sense of challenge and the will to attack. As a leg-break bowler he touched the heights. An advocate of practice, practice and yet more practice, he drove himself to the top. In his retirement, his involvement in the game has been maintained as a journalist and a highly respected television commentator.'

Having worked alongside him for over 50 televised Tests, I can add this to the Cowdrey tribute: it is as big a joy to watch and listen to his work with a microphone in his hand as ever it was to see him with either a bat or a ball. The man is an artist.

UMPIRE HAROLD 'DICKIE' BIRD ON JOHN EDRICH

John Edrich's 34 on the second day of the first Test between England and Australia at Edgbaston, 11 July 1975. Edrich's innings came out of an England total of 101 on a rain-affected pitch on which Dennis Lillee and Max Walker took five wickets each in conditions which were nearly unplayable. It was the Test match which cost Mike Denness the captaincy. He chose to field after winning the toss and, after Australia scored 359, a thunderstorm broke at 2.55pm on the second day, and England were doomed. The decision about the toss was supported by most of the England team, because the first morning was dull and grey. Local forecasts about the possibility of rain later in the match were ignored, and England paid the ultimate penalty by losing by an innings and 85 runs, with their 20 wickets going down in 120.5 overs. It was also the game in which Graham Gooch bagged a pair on debut, caught twice by Rodney Marsh, who took four other catches in the match. Edrich played a superb defensive innings under difficult conditions which Lillee, in particular, exploited to the full. The Surrey left-hander batted for 165 minutes, and dealt with the moving and lifting ball in a manner that impressed Bird more than any other innings he has seen from close quarters.

John Hugh Edrich, MBE, was born on 21 June 1937 in Blofield, Norfolk, and was the fifth of a famous family to play county cricket. Cousin Bill played for Middlesex and England, while other cousins Geoff and Eric played for Lancashire and Brian for Glamorgan. He made his debut for Surrey in 1958 and, in his first game as opener the following year, he scored two separate hundreds - the first of four times he achieved this feat - a total which has been bettered only by Zaheer Abbas (eight times), Walter Hammond (seven), Jack Hobbs and Glenn Turner (six) and Charles Fry (five).

An unspectacular, but brave and solid, batsman who, more than most left-handers, worked out what to play and what to leave, sheer consistency brought him 39,790 first-class runs, including 103 hundreds. He was the 17th batsman to join the exclusive club, and only the third left-hander after Phil Mead and Frank

Woolley. In 77 Tests for England, he scored 5138 runs at an average of 43.54, and of his 12 hundreds, seven were scored against Australia. His career-best 310 not out was a remarkable innings at Headingley against New Zealand in 1965, in which his ability to punish every loose delivery, despite playing and missing a great deal, was never better illustrated than by his boundary count of five sixes and 52 fours - the most in any Test innings. He insists: 'I stopped playing and missing after I got to 200.'

Totally unflappable, Edrich never flinched against the fastest bowlers of his period, and broken fingers and ribs never deterred him. Only 5ft 7in tall, he always got right behind the line, and England and Surrey have had no grittier batsman nor a more loyal servant. Typical acts of courage came in England's roughest-ever tour of Australia in 1974-75 where, against Lillee and Thomson at their most lethal, he scored 48, 6, 49, 4, 50, 33* and 70. In Brisbane in the first Test he broke a hand, followed by two ribs in the fourth Test in Sydney. He retired to hospital when England were 70 for two in their second innings but insisted on batting again when he returned to the ground, when his side was in deep trouble at 156 for six. This was the only game in which he captained his country, Denness having dropped himself, but his gutsy unbeaten 33 failed to stave off a crushing defeat by 171 runs.

SWEET AND SOUR. UMPIRE BIRD ENDS THE BEST DEFENSIVE INNINGS HE EVER SAW. LILLEE IS FINALLY SATISFIED.
(PATRICK EAGAR)

If the Dexters of his era were the officers, Edrich, like his colleague and great friend Ken Barrington, were the foot-soldiers. They might grumble, but never let it affect their approach to batting, which is why the departure of Edrich from Test cricket was a sad comment on one of the game's uglier faces. In 1976 at Old Trafford, he and Brian Close, aged 39 and 45 respectively, were subjected to an unchecked physical battering from Holding, Roberts and Daniel for the last hour of play on the third day. They survived, but Edrich later announced he had had enough. 'I wasn't scared, just frustrated that blatant intimidation was not curbed by the umpires. I couldn't see the point in standing out there for hours, waiting to get my head knocked off and wondering if I'd ever get a chance to score. I calculated that the amount of short-pitched bowling allowed me about six deliveries an hour to have a chance of runs. I was fed up with being a target man, with no hope of taking the fight to the bowlers. It was the last straw, coming after the way Lillee and Thomson had been allowed to bowl.'

Middlesex opening bowler Mike Selvey, whose Test debut it was, has a memory of that Saturday evening which shows that Edrich's dry and sometimes wry sense of humour never deserted him. Selvey says: 'I remember watching that last hour on Saturday evening. It was like a horror film, and it scared me although I was 100 yards away in the dressing-room. How "Edie" and "Closie" got through it I don't know but they did. When they came in, they reacted in different ways. "Edie" just sat in a corner, sipping a drink and staring into space, while "Closie" wandered around with a bottle of beer in one hand and a fag in the other.

'Suddenly, "Edie" started to cackle, and my first thought was that he'd cracked. No, he hadn't - he had just taken another look at the scoreboard, and he giggled at Brian: "Do you realise, you've stood up to that lot out there for an hour and you are one not out."'

At the end of that game, the phlegmatic Edrich walked away from an England dressing-room for the final time and an era was over, 11 months after a display of technical perfection on a rain-affected pitch which umpire Bird has never seen bettered. The views of fellow cricketers are always valued, but when an umpire picks one innings as the best he has ever seen, it adds another dimension. It is an ultimate judgement which is both definitive and objective, with no interest other than that of professional admiration.

It is only logical that, if an umpire is to be featured, it should be a man who has stood in more Tests than anyone else - 56 at the start of the 1993 English season. As with his on-field decisions, Bird did not take long to make up his mind.

I can't really split Graham Gooch and John Edrich. Gooch's Headingley innings against the West Indies in 1991 was marvellous, and it won the match. It had everything - guts, technique and wonderful concentration. But because of the pitch on which Edrich had to face Lillee, Thomson and Walker, I go for his 34 at Edgbaston in 1975. The Headingley pitch was helpful to bowlers, but not dangerous, whereas once it rained at Edgbaston, the ball lifted and moved all over the place.

I can just imagine people saying 'Dickie' must be crackers picking an innings of 34 ahead of all the hundreds he has seen, but I will never forget how Edrich played that day in 1975. England lost the game in four days anyway, but without him it would have been over in three. The luck was completely with the Aussies - they batted on a good pitch and then it bucketed down after Edrich and Amiss faced one over. We were off the field for 100 minutes, but the extra hour had just come in so that meant England had 2¾ hours to try to survive and then hope the pitch would dry out overnight. They needed 160 to save the follow-on, but as soon as we went back on, I knew they were in trouble.

Lillee bowled from my end and he made the ball talk. It lifted and it moved off the wet surface, often taking a divot. 'Thommo' couldn't pitch it, but Lillee did and so did Walker when he came on. Amiss was caught off Lillee and then, just as Edrich and Fletcher looked as though they might drop anchor, Walker got Fletcher, Denness, Gooch and Greig for 17 between them, and England were 54 for five.

The pitch was a pig, because the bounce was uneven as well. I don't know whether I should say this, but I reckon I said something to Lillee which helped him. He was bowling from my end at the Pavilion End, and he was really quick. But when something happened, it would beat everything because he was bowling a touch too short. Particularly against Edrich, that was no good, because he was such a great judge of what to play and what to leave, and he was not in any real trouble. Masterly really, because he would always be behind the line, yet he turned the wrists if one moved, or he would drop them if it lifted, and it was just as though he was conducting a coaching clinic.

I know Dennis was getting frustrated, and he moaned to me that the luck was against him, and what should he do? I told him: 'Pitch it up, lad, and see what happens.' He did and immediately bowled Alan Knott and from then on he was unplayable. He was gloving people and moving it all over the place - it was just like a snake biting the batsmen all the time.

It was as good a piece of fast, legitimately dangerous, bowling as you could ever see, yet still there was Edrich, dropping the ball in front of him, or angling the bat to nudge what runs he could. I can't think of any other English batsman who could have played like that, and it was easily the best bit of defensive batting I have ever seen.

The shame was that, just before the close of play, I had to give him out to that so-and-so Lillee. Just five minutes to go and England were 78 for six, in desperate trouble. But as long as Edrich stayed there until next morning, they could still have saved the follow-on. It was probably Lillee's last over, and he

---

ENGLAND V AUSTRALIA (1ST TEST)

PLAYED AT EDGBASTON, BIRMINGHAM, ON 10, 11, 12, 14 JULY 1975.
TOSS: ENGLAND. RESULT: AUSTRALIA WON BY AN INNINGS AND 85 RUNS.

AUSTRALIA

	FIRST INNINGS	
R.B.McCosker	b Arnold	59
A.Turner	c Denness, b Snow	37
I.M.Chappell*	c Fletcher, b Snow	52
G.S.Chappell	lbw, b Old	0
R.Edwards	c Gooch, b Old	56
K.D.Walters	c Old, b Greig	14
R.W.Marsh†	c Fletcher, b Arnold	61
M.H.N.Walker	c Knott, b Snow	7
J.R.Thomson	c Arnold, b Underwood	49
D.K.Lillee	c Knott, b Arnold	3
A.A.Mallett	not out	3
Extras	b 1, lb 8, nb 9	18
		359

	O	M	R	W
Arnold	33	3	91	3
Snow	33	6	86	3
Old	33	7	111	2
Greig	15	2	43	1
Underwood	7	3	10	1

FALL OF WICKETS
1-80, 2-126, 3-135, 4-161, 5-186, 6-265, 7-286, 8-332, 9-343, 10-359

ENGLAND

	FIRST INNINGS		SECOND INNINGS	
J.H.Edrich	lbw, b Lillee	34	c Marsh, b Walker	5
D.L.Amiss	c Thomson, b Lillee	4	c sub (G.J.Gilmour), b Thomson	5
K.W.R.Fletcher	c Mallett, b Walker	6	c Walters, b Lillee	51
M.H.Denness*	c G.S.Chappell, b Walker	3	b Thomson	8
G.A.Gooch	c Marsh, b Walker	0	c Marsh, b Thomson	0
A.W.Greig	c Marsh, b Walker	8	c Marsh, b Walker	7
A.P.E.Knott†	b Lillee	14	c McCosker, b Thomson	38
D.L.Underwood	b Lillee	10	(10) b Mallett	3
C.M.Old	c G.S.Chappell, b Walker	13	(8) c Walters, b Lillee	7
J.A.Snow	lbw, b Lillee	0	(9) c Marsh, b Thomson	34
G.G.Arnold	not out	0	not out	6
Extras	lb 3, w 5, nb 1	9	lb 5, w 2, nb 2	9
		101		173

	O	M	R	W	O	M	R	W
Lillee	15	8	15	5	20	8	45	2
Thomson	10	3	21	0	18	8	38	5
Walker	17.3	5	48	5	24	9	47	2
Mallett	3	1	8	0	13.2	6	34	1

FALL OF WICKETS
1-9, 2-24, 3-46, 4-46, 5-54, 6-75, 7-78, 8-87, 9-97, 10-101
1-7, 1-18, 1-20, 4-52, 5-90, 6-100, 7-122, 8-151, 9-167, 10-173

Umpires: H.D.Bird and A.E.Fagg (A.S.M.Oakman and T.W.Spencer deputised)

---

nipped one back to catch Edrich in front. It was an easy decision to give, but how ironic that I had to end the innings I have come to admire most of all in the Tests I have stood in.

Wisden was not overly effusive about Edrich's innings, with the reporter confining himself to saying: 'Lillee, in great form, caused the ball to lift awkwardly, but while Edrich defended gallantly until five minutes before the close, his partners were helpless against two splendid bowlers whose analysis at the end of the day read: Lillee 12-6-13-3, Walker 15-5-35-4.'

It is fitting that a Yorkshireman should award the palm to a southerner who played like a northerner that day. Edrich represented all that was best in English professional cricket. He is one of a handful of cricketers who squeezed the last drop from his well of talent - a well that was deeper than many people gave him credit for. The word 'nice' is not always applicable to international sportsmen - but it sits as naturally on John Hugh Edrich nowadays as when he graced the first-class game for two decades.

ALLAN BORDER

98* on the first three days of the second Test between West Indies and Australia at Port-of-Spain, Trinidad, 16-18 March 1984.

Australia were put in to bat by Viv Richards, skippering the West Indies for the second time because of an injury to Clive Lloyd, and were in deep trouble at 16 for three when Border joined his captain Kim Hughes. The only other batsman to top 40 was Jones, making his debut, as Border played a magnificent innings on a lively pitch, often in poor light, to enable his side to total 255. The home attack was brilliantly spearheaded by Joel Garner, and with Malcolm Marshall, Wayne Daniel and Milton Small making the ball lift, as well as seam and swing, survival was an achievement, irrespective of runs scored.

A llan Robert Border was born on 27 July 1955 in Sydney, the second of four sons of a wool trader. He is the most-capped cricketer in Test cricket, and by the end of 1993 he will have played in 1000 days of international cricket. That staggering statistic illustrates to perfection the difference between first-class cricket of the 1980s and 1990s, and that of any previous period. Since his Test debut in December 1978 in Melbourne against England, he has spent 2¾ years out of 15 playing Test or one-day international cricket.

Now approaching 25,000 first-class runs, over 40 per cent of them have been scored in five-day Test cricket, an even larger percentage than Sunil Gavaskar and Dilip Vengsarkar, his nearest challengers. He played first-grade baseball for Mosman at the age of 15, a year before he played first-grade cricket for the same club while he was still at Northern Sydney Boys High School. Debuts for New South Wales and Australia (29 and run out nought against England) were quickly followed by a move to Queensland in 1980, by which time he had tasted English cricket with a spell for Gloucestershire Second XI in 1977 and for East Lancashire the following year.

A compact nugget of a batsman, he methodically mowed down every Test record, thanks to a durability of temperament and technique possessed by few other cricketers in the history of cricket. He now has the most Test appearances, most consecutive appearances, most runs and, despite a run of 37 Tests without a hundred, he came to England in 1993 with an average for his country in excess of 50.

Like other captains before him, notably Garry Sobers and Clive Lloyd, he dropped himself into the middle of the order in the second part of what is still an unfinished career. Few runs come easily from the team's engine room, and his ability to call on apparently bottomless wells of strength of mind means that no Australian cause is lost until the back has been seen of Border.

Only a man of iron will could have shouldered the captaincy responsibilities for so long. Already he has led his country more times than the captain of any other country, and he could well notch up the most meritorious century of all by the end of 1994. His figures are remarkable enough, but the man is worth more to cricket than the record books show. A no-nonsense character, he has soldiered through a time of media hype without making any concessionary cliché answers to cliché questions. He is not only a player's player, he is an Aussie's Aussie, which is why the choice of his best innings inevitably takes into account his qualities of defiance and courage under difficult conditions.

THE STROKE WHICH TOOK BORDER PAST GAVASKAR AS THE HEAVIEST RUN-SCORER IN TEST HISTORY, AT CHRISTCHURCH, NEW ZEALAND IN 1993.

(ALLSPORT/JOE MANN)

I have always reckoned my 98 in Trinidad was the best thing I have ever done, because of the quality of the attack, the drizzly, overcast conditions and a pitch which was lively enough to start with. We kept going off for light or drizzle, and that helped big Joel Garner and Malcolm Marshall to stay fresh, as well as meaning I had to keep starting my innings again.

Garner was at his lethal best, and shot out Kepler Wessels, Wayne Phillips and Greg Ritchie for 16. Kim Hughes hung around for a while, but got out just before the close of what was only a short first day for 24 out of 50 for four. Next day, conditions were the same and when Joel bowled David Hookes for 24, we'd got a real problem at 85 for five. It left Dean Jones as the last batsman and, remember, it was Deano's debut and he was only 22.

It was just a matter of hanging in and hoping that things would get easier, but somehow we managed to put on a hundred. All the time we were fending off, and there was plenty of ducking and weaving. Sometimes we'd get out of the way and sometimes we'd get hit, but if you defended properly, you'd get the odd ball you could hit.

No wonder that Border, with ten Test hundreds already to his credit, chose a performance at Port-of-Spain which has been described as 'extraordinary' and 'epic'. Former Somerset batsman Peter Roebuck has written about Australian cricket for several years, and said this of Border's courageous effort: 'Defying overwhelming odds and a ferocious assault upon his body, he scored 98 and 100 in the Trinidad Test of 1984, single-handedly turning the ashes of defeat into the glory of rescue. Everyone recognises this as one of cricket's greatest efforts, this in a game which never forgets its moments of inspiration.'

Roebuck, a shrewd man whether with bat or typewriter, recognises a different form of shrewdness in Border. 'His genius lies in judgement, in attention to detail, in his consistency and in his ability to handle any sort of bowling on any sort of pitch. He has been underestimated because we associate genius with volatility, even brittleness, we fail to see it in the relentlessness of Steve Davis, or the regularity of a Colin Meads.'

His important sixth-wicket partnership with Jones ended when the junior partner was caught and bowled by Viv Richards for 48, to leave Border with bowlers Lawson, Hogan, Hogg and Alderman. His ability to organise the strike and switch to attack meant that the last four wickets produced 70 invaluable

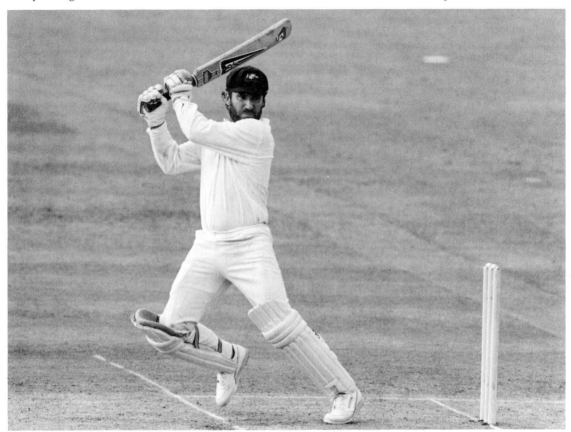

runs, of which his partners scored 26. If ever a man deserved a century, it was Border. But Alderman was quickly 'Garnered' to leave him stranded two short of what would have been an 11th hundred for his country. As evidence of his ability to organise and fight a rearguard action to the bitter end, it was the tenth time he remained not out in a completed innings. He batted for nearly six hours and, but for his finger in the dyke, the Garner-led demolition squad would have swept Australia out of the game.

HOW TO PLAY THE SQUARE CUT, WITH GOOD WEIGHT DISTRIBUTION AND A SOLID, STILL HEAD POSITION, WHICH IS THE HALLMARK OF TOP BATSMEN.
(PATRICK EAGAR)

Not only did Border overcome the high-quality pace attack in both innings - he was to score an unbeaten 100 in the second innings - he also had to cope with several interruptions for rain and bad light that reduced play on the first two days by six hours. Rarely has one batsman done so much to save an apparently lost cause. Without his unbeaten 98 in the first innings, Australia could have been bowled out for well under 200 and then, following the West Indies first innings of 468, Australia were again held together by a man who came in to bat at 41 for three, and whose final batting record in the match was 198 not out, out of 554 scored by his side, and he batted for over 10½ hours and faced 535 balls - 89 overs and one ball. When last man Terry Alderman joined him in the second innings, the score was 238 for nine - a lead of 25 - with 105 minutes left to play, yet still Border inspired his partner to stand foresquare with him on what was by now a much flatter pitch.

Garner dismissed Wessels, Phillips, Ritchie, Hughes and Hookes in the first innings, but Border denied him further success until, when he was 98, Alderman was caught by Richardson. This gave the giant bowler a return of 28.1-9-60-6 which, assuredly, would have been a match-winning one but for Border.

In the 1980s, there was no harder place than the West Indies for a batsman to score runs. Even on good pitches, the relentless rotation of four class fast bowlers posed problems seldom faced by cricketers of earlier times. An always stiff examination of technique and temperament became even more difficult - some would say impossible - under conditions like those in Trinidad, when Border played what he proudly calls 'the

WEST INDIES V AUSTRALIA (2ND TEST)

PLAYED AT QUEEN'S PARK OVAL, PORT-OF-SPAIN, TRINIDAD, ON 16, 17, 18, 20, 21 MARCH 1984.
TOSS: WEST INDIES. RESULT: MATCH DRAWN.

AUSTRALIA

	FIRST INNINGS			SECOND INNINGS	
K.C.Wessels	c Gomes, b Garner	4	lbw, b Garner	4
W.B.Phillips†	c Dujon, b Garner	4	run out	0
G.M.Ritchie	b Garner	1	b Small	26
K.J.Hughes*	c Dujon, b Garner	24	lbw, b Marshall	33
A.R.Border	not out	98	(6) not out	100
D.W.Hookes	b Garner	23	(7) c Richardson, b Gomes	21
D.M.Jones	c and b Richards	48	(8) b Richards	5
G.F.Lawson	c and b Daniel	14	(9) b Marshall	20
T.G.Hogan	c Greenidge, b Daniel	0	(5) c Logie, b Daniel	38
R.M.Hogg	c Marshall, b Daniel	11	c Garner, b Richards	9
T.M.Alderman	c Richardson, b Garner	1	not out	21
Extras	b 6, lb 4, nb 17	27	b 6, lb 1, w 1, nb 14	22
		255	(9 wickets)	299

	O	M	R	W	O	M	R	W
Garner	28.1	9	60	6	15	4	35	1
Marshall	19	4	73	0	22	3	73	2
Daniel	15	2	40	3	9	3	11	1
Small	10	3	24	0	14	2	51	1
Gomes	10	0	33	0	27	5	53	1
Richards	10	4	15	1	25	5	65	2
Logie					0.1	0	4	0

FALL OF WICKETS
1-4, 2-7, 3-16, 4-50, 5-85, 6-185, 7-233, 8-233, 9-253, 10-255
1-1, 2-35, 3-41, 4-114, 5-115, 6-153, 7-162, 8-196, 9-238

WEST INDIES

	FIRST INNINGS	
C.G.Greenidge	c Phillips, b Hogg	24
D.L.Haynes	run out	53
R.B.Richardson	c Wessels, b Alderman	23
I.V.A.Richards*	c Phillips, b Alderman	76
H.A.Gomes	b Lawson	3
A.L.Logie	lbw, b Hogan	97
P.J.L.Dujon†	b Hogan	130
M.D.Marshall	lbw, b Lawson	10
J.Garner	not out	24
W.W.Daniel	not out	6
M.A.Small	did not bat	
Extras	b 7, lb 12, w 2, nb 1	22
	(8 wickets declared)	468

	O	M	R	W
Lawson	32	3	132	2
Hogg	31	2	103	1
Alderman	35	9	91	2
Hogan	28	3	123	2

FALL OF WICKETS
1-35, 2-93, 3-124, 4-129, 5-229, 6-387, 7-430, 8-462

Umpires: D.M.Archer and C.E.Cumberbatch

innings of my life'. It helped to save the match - one of only two draws Australia managed in a series in which they were hammered 3-0, yet Border scored 521 runs in seven completed innings, more than twice the aggregate of any other Australian.

When he walks off the field for the last time, cricket will lose its most durable man. Durable? Indestructible is a better word - like a sea wall which has survived countless batterings from the ocean. The waves might wash over him, but he still comes up for more.

Cricket occasionally throws up a man who stands head and shoulders above his contemporaries - not just for cricketing skills, but for qualities of character which command respect and admiration. Such a man is Border, a trench-warfare man who never avoids a challenge. Just imagine a platoon led by Border, and including Javed Miandad, Allan Lamb and Ian Botham. Would you rather fight with or against them?

Not a man to search for glory, Border will still be thrilled that his favourite Mosman Oval has been renamed the Allan Border Oval as a tribute to his massive contribution to Australian cricket.

IAN BOTHAM

96* in the semi-final of the NatWest
Trophy between Middlesex and
Somerset at Lord's, 17 August 1983.

In reply to Middlesex's 222 for nine, Somerset lost early wickets before Ian Botham scored an unbeaten 96 to bring off an improbable victory by virtue of losing fewer wicket with the scores level. At the start of the 60th and final over of the Somerset innings, Botham was 96 out of Somerset's 222 for eight and, rather than risk getting out trying for a single, he deliberately blocked the last over, bowled by John Emburey. His performance enabled Somerset to win the 60-over trophy for the second time, to add to two Benson and Hedges Cup wins, and complete a run of four wins in a Lord's final in five seasons from 1979-83.

Ian Terence Botham was born in Heswall, Cheshire, on 24 November 1955. He joined Somerset following two years on the Lord's Groundstaff in 1972 and 1973, and made his first headlines the following year when, on 12 June 1974, he overcame a blow in the face from an Andy Roberts bouncer which broke several teeth to play a Boys' Own innings of 45 not out to win a Benson and Hedges Cup match against all the odds. Needing 183, Somerset were 113 for eight with Roberts still to bowl seven overs. Not only did Botham refuse to leave the field when hit, he counter-attacked fearlessly to win a game which seemed lost, and he was still a teenager.

Often, an innings like that heralds a false dawn, but for Botham it was the start of a prodigious career in which the sun shone on all-round feats which prompted Trevor Bailey to write: 'In my career, I encountered very few hitters and nobody in the same class as Ian Botham. His straight back stroke, whether used for defence or offence, is mainly with the full face, while his feet are in the correct position and his downswing from the top of a full backswing is copybook. He is our most spectacular, dynamic and successful all-rounder in Test cricket this century. His only serious rival is the immortal W.G.Grace from the previous one.'

That appraisal, made in the mid-1980s, appealed to Botham: 'What a double billing that makes - "Grace and Botham" - or should I insist on alphabetical order?'

The archetypal cricketer of the people, Botham has given rich entertainment to the cricketing publics of Somerset, Worcestershire and Durham, as well as to spectators all over the world and, although figures can never tell the full story about such a man, his progress through the record books from his debut for England in 1978 to the present day is so remarkable, a repetition will never dull the glitter.

He became the first man to achieve a 'Test Triple Double' of 3000 runs and 300 wickets, with the first

200 wickets coming in his 41st Test in the record time of four years and 34 days at the then youngest age of 25 years and 280 days. Even his massive physique could not stand up to the strain of being the fulcrum of the England side for 94 of his 101 Tests in ten years from debut, including 65 consecutive appearances, which equalled Alan Knott's record. His 300th wicket came in his 72nd Test, but then began a natural decline in match-winning effectiveness as wear and tear led to a run of serious injuries, and his average of wickets per game fell from over four to under three.

ONE OF THE ATTACKING STROKES THAT MADE IT POSSIBLE FOR BOTHAM TO PLAY THE FINAL OVER AS A MAIDEN TO WIN THE NatWEST TROPHY SEMI-FINAL AT LORD'S AGAINST MIDDLESEX IN 1983.
(PATRICK EAGAR)
(FAR RIGHT) THE UNIQUE LOFTED BOTHAM DRIVE, MADE POSSIBLE BY UNUSUALLY GOOD EXTENSION OF THE LEADING LEFT ARM AT THE BEGINNING OF THE STROKE.
(PATRICK EAGAR)

A third of his career aggregate of wickets were taken for his country, and over a quarter of his run aggregate, which stood at 18,983 at the start of the 1993 English season. The man possessed an unequalled sense of theatrical timing, taking his 100th Ashes wicket to clinch England's narrowest-ever win against Australia - by three runs at Melbourne in 1982 - and he equalled Dennis Lillee's world record of 355 wickets with his first ball against New Zealand at The Oval after his suspension from Test cricket.

No modern cricketer has changed the course of so many Test matches, with his two hundreds against Australia in 1981 being the ones that people remember best. If the Headingley unbeaten 149 defied belief - and bookmakers' odds against an England win of 500-1 - his 118 at Old Trafford was an even better piece of batting. He still holds the record for the fastest Test double hundred - against India off 220 deliveries at The Oval in 1982 - and, at county level, his record of 80 sixes in first-class cricket for Somerset in 1985 is unlikely ever to be beaten. At his peak, he had a rare ability to swing the ball at pace, and he has been England's best attacking bowler in the last three decades.

He would have played for England as a batsman had he never bowled, and vice-versa and, in addition, his brilliant slip fielding took him past 100 Test catches in Perth in his 87th Test to join Hammond and Cowdrey as the only Englishmen to do this. Some cricketers become legendary after their retirement - Botham is one of a few who did so while still playing.

He has strewn big-hitting performances along the way, so which would he choose as 'the innings of my life'? As so many of his 14 Test hundreds were against the odds, and turned matches upside down, which blitz on which hapless bowlers would he select? Ever unpredictable, Botham considered his choice for several days before committing himself:

I have ignored Headingley in 1981, because that was hilarious but nothing more. When Dilley and I were in we laughed and joked, and still it seems make-believe as we tried to see who could play the most idiotic stroke. There was no pressure, because we felt like men in a play, following a script someone else had written. Everything happened so quickly, it was like a mad interlude in a serious drama. The ball was moving a lot and we'd either miss it by a foot or edge it over the slips. The only difference between us and the other batsmen was that we had the luck. Mine was not a great innings, it wasn't really an innings at all - just an almighty heave.

Old Trafford was better, because I went out with the intention of winning the game, but in the end I go for my innings for Somerset in the NatWest Trophy semi-final at Lord's in 1983. Not only did I score 96 not out, but the pitch, the bowlers and, above all, the situation of the match when I went in make it definitely my best-ever knock. I went in at 43 for four, with Viv already out, and then Peter Roebuck was fifth out at 53. I was acting captain, because Brian Rose did not play, and perhaps that is why I suddenly realised it was all down to me. When you really bat, time has no meaning. Concentration is draining, and that day I lost myself in batting to a degree I have rarely done before or since. At tea, I can remember just sitting there already exhausted. You can't bat like that every day, especially if you are a bowler and captain as well.

Botham had already played his full part in preventing Middlesex running away with the match. At 117 for two, they looked likely to top 250, but his figures of 12-2-33-1 prevented the expected charge from materialising, and the last 20 overs of the home innings produced only 110 runs for the loss of seven wickets.

A relatively moderate target of 223 suddenly looked out of reach when Norman Cowans took the first two wickets in two balls, and when Neil Williams dismissed Slocombe and Richards, the result seemed a formality - unless some Botham heroics could recover the West Country chestnuts from what was now quite a blazing fire.

The drama of that Wednesday in August mounted as, first Nigel Popplewell and then Vic Marks played their full part in partnerships for the sixth and seventh wickets of 104 and 62 respectively. Botham's career is full of instances when his personal runs have dominated partnerships, but not this time. Popplewell, a vastly under-rated cricketer, scored 46 before he was caught at the wicket off Wayne Daniel, the spearhead of a strong Middlesex attack which had a helpful pitch to bowl on.

The only calculated risk Botham took was when Mike Gatting brought on John Emburey for the first time in the 19th over. The off-spinner's first over cost one run, but a six into the Mound Stand convinced the home captain that it was too risky to feed Botham, and the decision seemed justified when the late Wilf Slack came on to bowl nine overs for 26, taking the wicket of Marks. When he was caught by Emburey for 21, Somerset were nearly home at 218 for seven. Only five runs were needed in two overs with the captain still on the bridge in the 90s. What a vigil it had been!

A crowd of 20,000 grew increasingly appreciative of Botham's performance which eschewed the gung-ho approach that had swung so many games for country and county. Marks said: 'It was a tremendous innings. Botham at his very best, and showing what a naturally correct player he is. The temptation to hit or get out, particularly in the early part of his innings, must have been great, but he knuckled down magnificently.'

Botham recalls: 'Once Roebuck got out, I was the last senior player, and I decided they would have to get me out, rather than me take any risks.'

The innings, as it developed, became an election address to the Somerset Committee. Consciously or not, Botham convinced doubters that the club captaincy for 1984 would be in the hands of a man who could play for his side, and success in the NatWest Trophy undoubtedly tipped the vote his way.

But for the run-out of Joel Garner in the penultimate over, it is likely that Botham would have finished off the match in style by completing his hundred, but the arrival of Trevor Gard at the wicket changed his thinking. A single took him to the non-striker's end before, with eight balls of the match to go, the Somerset wicketkeeper was called down the pitch for a rare tactical talk with his captain.

Gard remembers: 'He told me not to get out. Great instruction that! But he said that if I blocked the next two balls, he would take the last over and do the same. Before Emburey started it, you've never seen so many people involved in a mid-wicket conference. Ian was there with the umpires, Jackie Birkenshaw and Don Oslear, and so were "Gatt" and the Middlesex senior players. "Both" wanted to make sure that Somerset would win if the scores stayed level, and then told me not to bother about thinking about a run, because he was going to play a maiden.'

The crowd only tumbled to the strategy halfway through the over. Everyone was round the bat, which meant a free hit over the top for glory, but Botham was not going to allow the subjugation of his natural instincts to relax, now that he knew that six defensive strokes would bring the victory for which he had battled for over three hours.

Deliveries number four and five were safely blocked, which left one ball. This one was straight and kicked away to provoke a frenzied appeal. Umpire Birkenshaw shook his head and grabbed the stumps prior to sprinting to the pavilion - to which a wildly excited Botham was also running.

> I've never felt so nervous in all my life in that last over. There were people all round me. It isn't natural for me to block and I'm not used to people staring at me from a yard away. They were safe too. I dreaded every ball, which is why I suppose as I charged off the field, there was such a feeling of release. It's not very English is it to charge about, waving your bat in the air, but you can't stop yourself, even though when you see it later on video, you realise you look an idiot.

Gard, a journeyman county cricketer, without whom cricketers like Botham and Richards could not play with such freedom, rates the Botham innings above any other he played for Somerset. 'It was a magnificent knock technically, but his concentration and the way he took over completely in the last part of the innings showed what a great cricketer he was. I never saw him play a better innings.'

The perfect thinking innings? It turned out that way, although even his two colleagues, Marks and

Gard, are not convinced it was thought through to the ultimate; i.e. was their hero aware of the outcome had he got out off the last ball of the match to square up the two totals and the number of wickets lost?

Gard says: 'To the best of my knowledge, the matter was never raised with the umpires, and when I went out to bat in the penultimate over, I am sure it had never been thought of in the dressing-room.'

Gard is probably right because, as the ingoing batsman, he would have been given a message for Botham, if anyone had thought of checking. Marks makes an even shrewder point: 'It seems that calculations about who was in front on run-rate after 30 overs were not done at the time. As it happened, Somerset were fractionally ahead, even though we had then lost five wickets and Middlesex only two.

'But if "Both" had known that, he would have realised that, after five balls, it did not matter if he got out, and he could have had a slog for his hundred. He didn't, which suggests to me that he thought he had to survive the last ball. That also means that his policy of blocking the maiden could have meant, as far as he was concerned that, if he got out, he was committing our number eleven, Colin Dredge, to come in and score a run. In a funny way, that makes it an even braver decision to block.'

Umpire Birkenshaw says that the last-ball appeal was irrelevant to the result because, in or out, Somerset would have won the match.

And what about the one man who could settle the arguments about his dangerous-looking strategy? The reader is advised to pose the question himself, because the author refuses on the grounds that it might spoil both a good friendship and a quirky tailpiece to an Ian Botham fairy tale. Fairy tale? What else, if the highlight of Botham's 'innings of my life' is a maiden over?

MIDDLESEX V SOMERSET (NatWest Trophy Semi-Final)

PLAYED AT LORD'S, LONDON, ON 17 AUGUST 1983.
TOSS: SOMERSET. RESULT: SOMERSET WON BY LOSING FEWER WICKETS.

MIDDLESEX

G.D.Barlow	c Botham, b Garner	8
W.N.Slack	c Slocombe, b Popplewell	57
C.T.Radley	b Marks	12
M.W.Gatting*	c Marks, b Popplewell	49
K.P.Tomlins	c Botham, b Garner	58
J.E.Emburey	c Marks, b Popplewell	1
P.R.Downton†	b Garner	12
N.F.Williams	lbw, b Botham	2
P.H.Edmonds	not out	7
W.W.Daniel	run out	0
N.G.Cowans	not out	0
Extras	lb 11, w 5	16
	(60 overs, 9 wickets)	222

	O	M	R	W
Garner	11	3	23	3
Botham	12	2	33	1
Dredge	9	0	48	0
Richards	12	3	23	0
Marks	8	0	45	1
Popplewell	8	0	34	3

FALL OF WICKETS
1-16, 2-55, 3-117, 4-148, 5-162, 6-204, 7-211, 8-213, 9-215

Umpires: J.Birkenshaw and D.O.Oslear

SOMERSET

J.W.Lloyds	c Downton, b Cowans	7
P.M.Roebuck	c Gatting, b Cowans	7
P.W.Denning	b Cowans	0
I.V.A.Richards	c Daniel, b Williams	23
P.A.Slocombe	c Downton, b Williams	2
I.T.Botham*	not out	96
N.F.M.Popplewell	c Downton, b Daniel	46
V.J.Marks	c Emburey, b Slack	21
J.Garner	run out	0
T.Gard†	run out	0
C.H.Dredge	did not bat	
Extras	lb 6, w 4, nb 10	20
	(60 overs, 8 wickets)	222

	O	M	R	W
Daniel	12	2	32	1
Cowans	12	2	48	3
Williams	12	0	54	2
Emburey	3	1	9	0
Edmonds	12	4	33	0
Slack	9	1	26	1

FALL OF WICKETS
1-13, 2-13, 3-41, 4-43, 5-52, 6-156, 7-218, 8-221

GEOFFREY BOYCOTT

146 in the final of the Gillette Cup between Yorkshire and Surrey at Lord's, 4 September 1965.

Surrey won the toss and put Yorkshire in on a drying pitch with a sodden outfield, and the game started 90 minutes late. Boycott's innings is still the record score for a Lord's final, and he was largely responsible for Yorkshire's total of 317, and their victory by 175 runs. From a man who, according to John Arlott's radio commentary that day, was 'a legendary stonewaller', it was an astonishing innings which settled the match well before the halfway stage.

G eoffrey Boycott, OBE, was born in Fitzwilliam, Yorkshire, on 21 October 1940, and became one of the heaviest run-scorers in history for England and Yorkshire. Possessed of a fiercely independent outlook on life, he never compromised beliefs which often brought him into direct conflict with colleagues, opponents and administrators alike. Boycott lives by his own principles, and will abrasively defend them to limits which few people understand or tolerate. With astute awareness of his own reputation, he has made a success in recent years of television commentary by developing a natural ability to communicate knowledge, combined with a slightly more forced extrovert sense of humour, which is markedly more in evidence when he is working for commercial television than for the BBC.

As with every other part of his life, he has his critics, but I find him the easiest of summarisers to work with. His delivery is a touch heavy for some viewers, but his content is flawless, and he and other ex-players are employed for their expertise first, and smooth broadcasting abilities second. He is a perfectionist, and will attempt little that affords him only limited success.

His career figures bear testimony to an unyielding determination to maximise his talent, and I doubt whether the number of acts of carelessness which cost him his wicket can be counted on the fingers of two hands. There are better-looking batsmen who review their careers and reflect that, given a second chance, they could have added a few thousand runs to their final aggregate.

Not so Boycott - his 48,426 first-class runs make him the eighth highest run-scorer of all time, and the most prolific of post-war batsmen. His total of 151 hundreds has been exceeded only by Hobbs, Hendren, Hammond and Mead, but he reached his 100th hundred in 176, 95, 34 and 247 fewer innings respectively. Unrelenting consistency brought him a three-figure score every 6.45 innings, the fourth best ratio among those with 100 centuries, and his career average of 56.83 is the highest in history of the 58 batsmen who have scored more than 30,000 first-class runs. Of an additional 48 batsmen who have topped 25,000 runs, only Bradman has a better average.

He became the first Englishman to score 8000 Test runs, and his 22 hundreds for England have been equalled - by Hammond and Cowdrey - but not exceeded.

Figures maketh man, or should it be, in Boycott's case, man maketh figures? He asked nothing more than to be judged on his record of what he put into the good book. Nothing else mattered to him, which is why he was England's most singular cricketer in living memory.

So which of his 1014 first-class visits to the crease would he pick as 'the innings of my life'? He could choose from Test hundreds scored on 14 different grounds around the world. Would it be one of four he scored at Headingley including, uniquely then, his 100th hundred in the Test against Australia in 1977, when he also became the fourth Englishman to be on the field for an entire Test match?

No, like Ian Botham, Martin Crowe, Neil Fairbrother and Javed Miandad in this book, Boycott has settled for a one-day innings, and this from a Yorkshireman whose county was professedly contemptuous of limited-overs cricket for at least the first decade of its existence.

A RARE AIRBORNE BOYCOTT STROKE. THIS WAS ONE OF THOSE AGAINST SYDENHAM WHICH BOYCOTT CITES AS LAUNCHING HIS MATCH-WINNING INNINGS IN THE 1965 GILLETTE CUP FINAL.
(SPORT AND GENERAL)

I have chosen my 146 against Surrey in the Gillette Cup final of 1965 for all sorts of reasons, including my own indifferent form that year, the conditions at Lord's on the day, and the background to the Yorkshire selection for the game. My criteria include the difficulty of batting on the day, and how well I performed to overcome the problems, some of which started much earlier in the season.

I had been in poor form. I lost my Test place after scoring 232 in eight innings, and I did not get a first-class hundred in the season, the only time that happened to me in my career. Pitches were uncovered then, so if you had a bad trot, you weren't helped by playing on wet pitches, but that was a vital part of a batting education. I missed two Tests that summer, one against New Zealand because I injured a shoulder in Yorkshire's game against South Africa, and was then dropped for The Oval Test against South Africa which finished four days before the Gillette final.

It summed up my year, and I remember going to The Oval earlier in the season to play in the three-day game against Surrey, and trying to ask advice from Len Hutton, who came to the game. I didn't get very far, in fact the one man who tried to help me most that year - and remember it was only my third full season - was the Yorkshire chairman Brian Sellers.

In the middle of August, he called all the players in one by one to remind us of a few things, and to us he was like Judge Jeffreys. I was last, and I was dreading what he would say as I was in such poor nick. Richard Hutton had been in and was told, 'There are three things you need as a seam bowler - line, length and pace - and you've got none of them.' It was like going into the condemned cell. There he was, looking at me over his pince-nez glasses, and I couldn't believe it when he started off: 'Now, what's the matter? Come and sit down and let's talk it out.'

He was magnificent to me. He said: 'You are trying too hard - you're too tense. Go and enjoy it.' Maybe out of sheer relief I hadn't got the firing squad, I went out next day and scored 84. He was magic to me. A crusty old so-and-so who could put fear into you. Sometimes, when he came into the dressing-room it was like a tidal wave, but he helped me more than anyone else.

I remember travelling down to Lord's on the Friday evening. We had a long journey and towards the end of it we drove through a lot of rain. Next morning, the ground was like a swamp. The sun was out, but there was a real chance we wouldn't play at all that day. The winners of the final were going to play the South Africans, which meant there was something extra in the game for John Edrich and me. We had both been invited to play in the Scarborough Festival, so only the loser could go.

The toss looked crucial, because rain had got on the pitch and it would be awkward to bat on as it dried out. Also, the outfield was desperately slow, and would be quicker later in the day. We lost the toss, and naturally Micky Stewart put us in. As I walked to the middle with Ken Taylor, I remember passing 'Edie' and he said: 'Good luck at Scarborough, Fiery.' I couldn't disagree because it looked a case of win the toss, win the match.

It had been a lively dressing-room beforehand because of the decision about who would be 12th man, and I remember saying to Brian Close 'I'll stand down.' I said this because it was getting heated and I'd had so many problems, but he refused the offer.

The first 12 overs of the game proved the theorists right. David Sydenham moved the ball about, and the Yorkshire openers could only battle for survival, and 20 runs came from those overs. Boycott continues the story:

I thought I'd got to do something, so after Ken Taylor got out, caught by Ken Barrington off Sydenham, I flipped Sydenham off my legs. It wasn't my sort of shot and, with a man down there, it was a risk. I got away with it, and again when I hit one in the air through mid-wicket. Brian Close had come in with Surrey well on top and when he came straight to me to have a chat everyone assumed he told me to get on with it.

They couldn't be more wrong. He said: 'Just keep going, and play it as you see it.' Once I got away with those two shots, everything changed. We thought 170 would be enough for our attack [Trueman, Hutton, Wilson, Illingworth and Close], but suddenly I found myself in total command. I played out of my skin - there was no error and it was as though I was in a dream. From being too tense for most of the year, I felt relaxed as the runs flowed all over the place. I went down the pitch twice to Geoff Arnold and hit him into the pavilion for two sixes - that took care of the slow outfield.

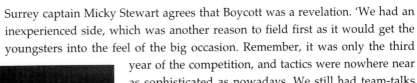

Surrey captain Micky Stewart agrees that Boycott was a revelation. 'We had an inexperienced side, which was another reason to field first as it would get the youngsters into the feel of the big occasion. Remember, it was only the third year of the competition, and tactics were nowhere near as sophisticated as nowadays. We still had team-talks and, because Geoff was such a strong square-cutter, I told the bowlers to make sure he got nothing short. They probably went the other way too much and pitched it up, but his driving was terrific.

'When an attack falls apart, it is usually because someone plays well, and that is what happened that day. He timed it so well, and only Stuart Storey bowled his overs for a reasonable amount of runs. Our other problem was that we had to fiddle a ration between Ken Barrington and Ron Tindall, and Geoff climbed into them so well that their eight overs cost 90. It was a superb innings, and showed what a good all-round batsman he was.'

Arlott's radio commentary was equally full of praise. 'Boycott has enjoyed himself, surprised himself and, at times, nearly rocked himself off his feet with the power of his shots. And this from a man who has already become a legendary stonewaller.'

From 22 for one in the 13th over, Yorkshire rocketed to 187 in the 43rd, with Boycott then 94 and Close on 76. The second-wicket partnership was then worth 165 and already a competition record, and it was to add 22 more before Close was caught by Edrich off Gibson. If Surrey thought things could not get worse, a re-jigged Yorkshire batting order soon disabused them. Trueman was promoted to number four, and hit 24 out of 34 for the third wicket with Boycott who, by now, was unstoppable.

His hundred came with a square-cut boundary off Barrington, and although the score was then 195 in the 44th over, the most optimistic Yorkshire supporters could not have expected the onslaught to become even more ferocious. It did, with 117 coming from the last 16 overs, at which point Arlott said: 'Surrey are now out of sight.'

Boycott was out in the 55th over, caught on the mid-wicket boundary by Storey off Barrington, who he had just pulled for six into a crowd of Yorkshire members in the Tavern. They rose to him, as did the entire crowd as he walked off. For once, he had unleashed a side of his talent which many people would have liked to have seen more often. He showed a mastery of difficult conditions which few other batsmen could have emulated and, typical of the man, it was that triumph over adversity which still pleases him most - even, for once, more than the actual runs scored.

'I used to bat with a light bat, 2¼ pounds at the most, so you couldn't slog it about, you had to time it.'

If and when the record goes, the odds are that it will not be broken by a bespectacled batsman, as was Boycott for the first seven seasons of his first-class career. It was another example of his attention to detail, even as a youngster, that he wrote to Mike Smith about the problems of batting with glasses, and gained some helpful tips.

Among a growing number of personal reminiscences about Boycott, I have three which reflect facets of his character which might surprise some people. Not the first one, maybe, that concerns a conversation between him and Tom Cartwright early in his career. An intense discussion was under way about discipline, and Tom advanced the theory that Geoff did not know the meaning of the word because he had missed National Service.

'What difference does that make?'

'Because true discipline is obeying an order you disagree with.'

'I'd never have done that.'

'If you were in the army and you were told to water the CO's garden, you'd do it, even if it was raining.'

'No I would not.'

'In that case you'd spend most of your time behind bars.'

The final remark was made in such a fiercely, earnest manner, with eyes blazing behind spectacles, that Cartwright believed him.

'In that case, I would have been put inside. I just will not do something that doesn't make sense.'

When Dennis Amiss retired in 1987, I rang Boycott to help me with a tribute for the *Birmingham Post*. He was not only generous in his praise, but he showed remarkable recall of their early games in opposition in second XI cricket nearly 30 years previously.

And, more recently, he organised a get-together for Amiss, Tony Lewis and me down to the last detail and he entertained us almost royally in his favourite restaurant in Barnsley. Royally? Apt, I suppose, because he is king to some people and clown to others. Me? Never mind 'the innings of HIS life', if ever I wanted someone to play one for mine, it would be Geoffrey Boycott.

YORKSHIRE v SURREY (GILLETTE CUP FINAL)

PLAYED AT LORD'S, LONDON, ON 4 SEPTEMBER 1965.
TOSS: SURREY. RESULT: YORKSHIRE WON BY 175 RUNS.

YORKSHIRE

G.Boycott	c Storey, b Barrington	146
K.Taylor	c Barrington, b Sydenham	9
D.B.Close*	c Edrich, b Gibson	79
F.S.Trueman	b Arnold	24
J.H.Hampshire	not out	38
D.Wilson	not out	11
D.E.V.Padgett		
P.J.Sharpe		
R.Illingworth	did not bat	
R.A.Hutton		
J.G.Binks†		
Extras		10
	(60 overs, 4 wickets)	317

	O	M	R	W
Arnold	13	3	51	1
Sydenham	13	1	67	1
Gibson	13	1	66	1
Storey	13	2	33	0
Tindall	3	0	36	0
Barrington	5	0	54	1

FALL OF WICKETS
1–22, 2–214, 3–248, 4–292

SURREY

M.J.Stewart*	st Binks, b Wilson	33
J.H.Edrich	c Illingworth, b Trueman	15
W.A.Smith	lbw, b Trueman	0
K.F.Barrington	c Binks, b Trueman	0
R.A.E.Tindall	c Wilson, b Close	57
S.J.Storey	lbw, b Illingworth	1
M.J.Edwards	b Illingworth	0
D.Gibson	lbw, b Illingworth	0
A.Long†	b Illingworth	17
G.G.Arnold	not out	3
D.A.Sydenham	b Illingworth	8
Extras		8
	(40.4 overs)	142

	O	M	R	W
Trueman	9	0	31	3
Hutton	8	3	17	0
Wilson	9	0	45	1
Illingworth	11.4	1	29	5
Close	3	0	12	1

FALL OF WICKETS
1–27, 2–27, 3–27, 4–75, 5–76, 6–76, 7–76, 8–130, 9–132, 10–142

DON BRADMAN

254 on the second and third days of the second Test between England and Australia at Lord's, 28 and 30 June 1930.

In his sixth Test, and aged only 21, his 254 was the first of seven scores of over 200 he was to make from 15 three-figure scores in Ashes Tests before he reached the age of 30. The innings was to remain the highest Test score at Lord's until Graham Gooch's 333 60 years later. It was then the highest Test score made in England - a record he expunged 11 days later at Headingley - and was also the highest score to date for Australia in a Test match. He scored his runs out of 423 while he was at the crease, and, despite England winning the toss and scoring 425 in just over a day, it proved to be a match-winning innings.

Sir Donald George Bradman, AC, was born on 27 August 1908 in Cootamundra. He was one of five children, all of whom, including three sisters, were taller than his height of 5ft 6¾in. He made his first-class debut in 1927 to launch the most prolific batting career in history in which he scored 28,067 runs at a freakish average of 95.14. He became the first overseas cricketer to enter batting's most exclusive club, batsmen who have scored 100 hundreds - Graham Gooch became its 23rd member in 1993 - but, as with all other batting records, he outstripped the greatest names to grace cricket by miles.

His 117 hundreds from 338 innings give him a ratio of a century in every 2.89 innings, whereas no other 'club member' achieved a ratio of one in six. Furthermore, of all the players who have ever scored over 10,000 first-class runs, only India's Merchant averaged over 70, and compatriots Ponsford and Woodfull are the only two batsmen to average in excess of 60.

Of those hundreds, 37 were doubles, five were triples and there was one quadruple - an unbeaten 452 scored in 400 minutes against Queensland a few months before his first tour of England. It was not just the volume of runs which put Bradman light years ahead of other batsmen, it was the rate at which they were scored. He always considered that important: 'The quicker I scored runs, the more time I gave my bowlers to take wickets.'

Figures do not always tell the whole story, but they do with Bradman. He still warrants an entry of 32 lines in the index of the *Wisden Cricketers' Almanack*, with only Hammond of pre-war cricketers having one of 20 lines. In modern cricket, Graham Gooch has 26 lines, so yet again Bradman is a long way ahead of cricketers past and present.

I hesitated to ask 'The Don' to choose one jewel out of such a cluster of glittering gems, and wondered what criteria he would invoke to mark out one performance as 'the innings of my life'. The reasons for his choice of such an early innings are simple:

> In my opinion, the best innings I ever played was my 254 at Lord's in 1930. I was on my first tour of England and we had already lost the first Test at Nottingham to give Percy Chapman a streak of nine successive wins as England captain.
>
> It was my first innings in a Test at Lord's, recognised as the home of cricket, and there was understandably a great deal of pressure on me. I have picked this innings because, although I played more valuable and important innings, I never played one so technically perfect. There was only one delivery I didn't hit where I wanted [coming when he was on 191], and even that went along the ground to second slip. The match was crucial to Australia, being one down in the series, and it was important to me because it was the first time I had batted for Australia at number three.
>
> First drop is the pivotal position in the batting order. Sometimes you go in in the first over when you are virtually an opener, and sometimes you wait, padded up, for hours, and that taxes concentration in a different way. The game itself had every facet of cricket, and that is why I consider my 254 to be so special.
>
> The weather was good and the pitch looked hard and fast. We were unchanged from Trent Bridge, but England brought in Duleepsinhji, White and Allen, making his debut, instead of the injured Sutcliffe and Larwood, and Dick Tyldesley.
>
> We were disappointed that England won the toss again, but their batting was surprisingly uneven. Only a really splendid 173 from Duleepsinhji saved them but, although he went after Grimmett successfully, I cannot profess to understand why he should deliberately appear to throw his wicket away before the end of the first day. At the close they were 405 for nine and there were many who thought this was good enough to win the match. I understand that one expert was doubtful if we would save the game, but that sort of total is not a safe score in four-day cricket.

Those last dozen or so words encapsulate perfectly the different approach of cricketers of Bradman's era compared with that of the modern player. The biggest difference is in the over-rates, as illustrated by the game's position at the end of the first day: England's 405 for nine came off 120 overs - a rate of progress which was maintained throughout the four-day game in which 1601 runs came from 505.4 overs bowled. The modern Test match calls for 450 overs to be bowled in five days, which means that spectators are robbed of at least 25 percent of what they used to enjoy. Put another way, they see more than 10 percent less cricket in five days than crowds used to enjoy in four.

Bradman explains further about his doubts of England's safety after scoring over 400:

> Cricket is a funny game, and anything may happen. In a Test match played at Sydney in 1887, England scored 45 in their first innings, but won the game by 13 and, seven years later on the same ground, Australia scored 586 in their first innings, but also lost by 13. [This game was the first instance in Test cricket of a side winning a game after following on - a feat which was not repeated until 'Botham's Test' at Headingley in 1981.]
>
> Our tour of England had started well, despite criticism that we would not do well, because we had only four players who had toured England before - Woodfull, Ponsford, Grimmett and Oldfield - and also because I had several critics, including England's Percy Fender, who believed that my method would let me down overseas. He also said that Archie Jackson would do better than me. The main criticism was about my grip, which had a fairly strong right-hand position because, having learned my early cricket on concrete pitches, it gave me a closed face of the bat and helped me to keep short deliveries down. Mind you, I could adjust the top hand an inch or so if I wanted to play towards the

off-side, but I reckon it offended a few people to see me pull short deliveries across the line between mid-on and mid-wicket. The pull shot became my best stroke, but my grip seemed to bother some people. All I can say is that Viv Richards has a similar grip, and I have not noticed too much criticism of him.

I was primarily a back-foot player from preference, so the slightly slower English pitches suited me perfectly. At Worcester I got 236, but I got even more pleasure from my unbeaten 252, later in May, against Surrey, captained by Fender, at The Oval. I had one of those days when everything seemed to go right, and there were plenty of gaps in the field. The innings doubly pleased me because it showed Fender and other people that I could play in England, and it also set me up for my first 1000 runs by the end of May. I was able to complete these against Hampshire, although rain nearly ruined my last chance.

Bradman's two double hundreds against Worcestershire and Surrey were scored at his usual rapid, almost rapacious, pace. At New Road he batted for 280 minutes and, although he took 145 minutes to play himself in for his first hundred at The Oval, he reached 200 in a further 80 minutes. There is no better way to rebut criticism than by performance.

Back to Lord's and the historic second and third days of the Test. Bradman says:

A total of over 400 does not mean you are out of the reckoning. I rate our reply in that Lord's Test as one of Australia's best-ever touring performances, with Woodfull and Ponsford giving us a magnificent start with a stand of 162. They took the sting out of the bowling, and undoubtedly paved the way for what was to follow.

(ABOVE RIGHT) BRADMAN ACKNOWLEDGES ANOTHER TEST CENTURY IN 1930. (TOPHAM PICTURE SOURCE)
(RIGHT) BRADMAN HITTING OFF-SIDE DURING HIS 254 AT LORD'S IN 1930. (HULTON-DEUTSCH COLLECTION)

What did follow was a display of attacking batting that was clinically destructive, and took the art of Test match batting to a level seldom, if ever, witnessed before in England. Wittingly or not, Bradman's entry was brought about by the visit to the ground of King George V.

'Play stopped while both teams were presented, and immediately on the resumption of play, Ponsford was out to a slip catch by Hammond off White. Someone said that made the King the best bowler in England, and I walked in to bat at 3.30pm.'

Bradman's first ball set the tone for an innings which took the game away from England in under half a day and finally gave the Australian bowlers sufficient time to win the game and square the series. The Australian 'Cardus' B.J.Wakeley's report of the game says: 'To his first ball, Bradman went yards down the pitch and drove a single to launch an innings which took him to 50 out of 66 in 45 minutes, and 100 out of 152 in 105 minutes. His brilliant footwork enabled him to score, more or less, as he pleased, and he not only gave no chance, he never even made a false stroke or lifted the ball off the ground. When Woodfull was dismissed, stumped by Duckworth, just before the close of play for 155, the pair had added 231 for the second wicket in 160 minutes. At the close, Bradman was 155 after 165 minutes, and he had caught up Woodfull after giving him 78 runs and 170 minutes start.'

Bradman reflected: 'We were now in an exceptionally strong position after two days at 404 for two, and with ordinary luck we were bound to finish with a big enough lead to make the English side fight hard to save the game.'

If ever the word 'circumspect' could be justifiably used about part of Bradman's epic innings, it would apply to the 45 runs he needed to reach 200. They took him 80 minutes on Monday morning, but his double hundred was still the fastest ever scored in a Test match played in England. At lunch he was 231, and one record was in his sights.

I had hopes of beating R.E.Foster's 287 at Sydney in 1903. As a Sydney player, I felt it was only fitting that I should take the record back to Sydney, and I believe I would have succeeded but for a wonderful catch by Chapman in the covers. During my long innings I had been careful not to lift a single ball, but on this occasion I slashed a loose ball from White well wide of the English captain, as I thought. I saw him make several amazing catches, but to this day I cannot think how he got his hand to the ball. It was to his wrong side as a left-hander, and the ball was only ever inches off the ground.

So ended a magnificent innings which produced 254 from 376 deliveries in 320 minutes, and took his side from 162 for one when he entered centre stage to 585 for three when he departed. Small wonder that Bradman insists that 'no other innings I ever played approached this one in regard to technical excellence'.

His point about the importance of scoring runs quickly is proved by the fact that had his innings lasted just one hour longer, Australia would not have won the game, would not have squared the series, and cricket history would be different. As it was, determined resistance from England in their second innings meant that chief wicket-taker Grimmett - six for 167 - had to bowl 53 of the 116.4 overs it took Australia to bowl the home side out a second time. Chapman scored a brilliant 121, including three sixes off Grimmett into the Mound Stand, before he was dismissed in a bizarre fashion - immediately after he swallowed a bluebottle.

Australia needed 72 to win in 90 minutes, and achieved this despite losing their first three wickets for 22, including Bradman, who suffered another fine Chapman catch - this time in the gully.

So ended a Test match which owed much to the presence and performance of Bradman, and the innings of his life. It was the first of a long sequence of great performances in England which were to bring him 9837 first-class runs in four tours from 120 innings, including 41 hundreds. Only once - in his debut season of 1927-28 - did he average under 50 in either a home season or a tour abroad.

For such a perfectionist and a man of consistent physical and mental neatness, it seems almost careless that he was dismissed for a duck in his final Test at The Oval in 1948. Just four more runs, and he would have retired with perfect symmetry - 7000 Test runs at an average of 100 - but a second-ball dismissal by an Eric Hollies googly thwarted him. The incident is on film in the BBC archives, even though an awful piece of editing and splicing means that future generations will see only the Warwickshire leg-spinner deliver the most celebrated coup de grâce of all time from around the wicket, although he took his famous wicket from the more orthodox side of the stumps.

Many men seek perfection, few achieve it. Bradman was one such person who dominated his sport both during and after his career to an extent never equalled in living memory. The equivalent of his achievement is a three-minute mile, a long jump of 33 feet, or a four-round Open aggregate of 256 in a howling gale at Royal St George's.

ENGLAND V AUSTRALIA (2ND TEST)

PLAYED AT LORD'S, LONDON, ON 27, 28, 30 JUNE, 1 JULY 1930.
TOSS: ENGLAND. RESULT: AUSTRALIA WON BY SEVEN WICKETS.

ENGLAND

	FIRST INNINGS		SECOND INNINGS	
J.B.Hobbs	c Oldfield, b Fairfax	1	b Grimmett	19
F.E.Woolley	c Wall, b Fairfax	41	hit wkt, b Grimmett	28
W.R.Hammond	b Grimmett	38	c Fairfax, b Grimmett	32
K.S.Duleepsinhji	c Bradman, b Grimmett	173	c Oldfield, b Hornibrook	48
E.H.Hendren	c McCabe, b Fairfax	48	c Richardson, b Grimmett	9
A.P.F.Chapman*	c Oldfield, b Wall	11	c Oldfield, b Fairfax	121
G.O.B.Allen	b Fairfax	3	lbw, b Grimmett	57
M.W.Tate	c McCabe, b Wall	54	c Ponsford, b Grimmett	10
R.W.V.Robins	c Oldfield, b Hornibrook	5	not out	11
J.C.White	not out	23	run out	10
G.Duckworth†	c Oldfield, b Wall	18	lbw, b Fairfax	0
Extras	b 2, lb 7, nb 1	10	b 16, lb 13, w 1	30
		425		375

	O	M	R	W	O	M	R	W
Wall	29.4	2	118	3	25	2	80	0
Fairfax	31	6	101	4	12.4	2	37	2
Grimmett	33	4	105	2	53	13	167	6
Hornibrook	26	6	62	1	22	6	49	1
McCabe	9	1	29	0	3	1	11	0
Bradman					1	0	1	0

FALL OF WICKETS
1-13, 2-53, 3-105, 4-209, 5-236, 6-239, 7-337, 8-363, 9-387, 10-425
1-45, 2-58, 3-129, 4-141, 5-147, 6-272, 7-329, 8-354, 9-372, 10-375

AUSTRALIA

	FIRST INNINGS		SECOND INNINGS	
W.M.Woodfull*	st Duckworth, b Robins	155	not out	26
W.H.Ponsford	c Hammond, b White	81	b Robins	14
D.G.Bradman	c Chapman, b White	254	c Chapman, b Tate	1
A.F.Kippax	b White	83	c Duckworth, b Robins	3
S.J.McCabe	c Woolley, b Hammond	44	not out	25
V.Y.Richardson	c Hobbs, b Tate	30		
W.A.S.Oldfield†	not out	43		
A.G.Fairfax	not out	20		
C.V.Grimmett	} did not bat			
P.M.Hornibrook				
T.W.Wall				
Extras	b 6, lb 8, w 5	19	b 1, lb 2	3
	(6 wickets declared)	729	(3 wickets)	72

	O	M	R	W	O	M	R	W
Allen	34	7	115	0				
Tate	64	16	148	1	13	6	21	1
White	51	7	158	1	2	0	8	0
Robins	42	1	172	1	9	1	34	2
Hammond	35	8	82	1	4.2	1	6	0
Woolley	6	0	35	0				

FALL OF WICKETS
1-162, 2-393, 3-585, 4-588, 5-643, 6-672
1-16, 2-17, 3-22

Umpires: F.Chester and T.W.Oates

Of all the 'innings of my life' included in this book, his must be the most special - if only because he had the widest choice of all. For him to select one innings as being 'one which no other approached for technical excellence' means it should be enshrined as the peak of a mountain which has overshadowed all else in cricket for 60 years, and will continue to do so for much longer than that.

CHRIS BROAD

116 on the first and second days of the second Test between Pakistan and England at Faisalabad, 7 and 8 December 1987.

Broad had been severely reprimanded ten days earlier in the Lahore Test for refusing to walk when given out but, despite this and a reputation for being more comfortable against pace than spin, he scored a century in England's first innings total of 292. The game became infamous for the incident between Mike Gatting and Shakoor Rana which resulted in the match being reduced to four days. It was Broad's fourth hundred of the six he scored for his country - all of them abroad - and it was also the third time he batted all day in a Test match.

Brian Christopher Broad was born on 29 September 1957 in Knowle, Bristol, and played for five seasons for Gloucestershire before he moved to Nottinghamshire in 1984 in the belief that he would have a better chance of Test cricket. He played the first of his 25 Tests within two months of the start of that season, scoring 55 against the West Indies at Lord's. At the end of the 1992 season, after nine successful seasons at Trent Bridge, he was surprisingly released, and rejoined Gloucestershire. At the start of the 1993 English season, he had scored 20,147 first-class runs at an average of 38.81 and he had hit 47 hundreds. In his 25 Tests, his 1661 runs came at a slightly higher average - 39.54 - a sure sign of a big-match temperament.

Broad's choice of his best innings was not automatic:

I thought hard about my highest score, 227 not out against Kent at Tunbridge Wells in 1990. I had had a rough patch and decided to wear a full visor, and I started pulling properly again. Everything clicked for me and I got to 100 before lunch out of 129 off only 123 deliveries. After that I slowed down, getting 127 in the other two sessions, but I was happy to take the supporting role to Derek Randall, who played an amazing innings. He scored 178 out of 285 we put on for the third wicket in 51 overs and he actually scored 130 in one session. He faced only 162 balls. At times like that, I make sure I don't get carried away, and am more than happy to rotate the strike.

Anyway, my first double hundred was a starter, but in the end the circumstances surrounding the Faisalabad Test made me choose that innings. Incidentally, it was the first hundred I had scored in any class of cricket since my century in the Melbourne Test, nearly 11 months earlier.

In that time, Broad played 33 first-class innings with a highest score of 80, but it never worried him unduly. 'Until I was told after my Faisalabad hundred that I had gone so long without one, I honestly did not know. I always have faith in my ability and my method, which is based on occupation of the crease, so I never lose faith if I have a bad trot.'

What about his refusal to walk in Lahore - an incident which further soured relations which were never sweet? It happened in England's second innings, just before tea on the third day. In the first innings, Broad held the England innings together with an innings of 41 in 192 minutes, without which Abdul Qadir would have been even more devastating than indicated by career-best figures of 37-13-56-9.

It was easily the best display of back-of-the-hand bowling I have ever seen and, even without the assistance of several controversial decisions from umpire Shakeel Khan, the leg-spinner's performance

deserved to win the match. From the time he came on in the first innings until he left the field in the second innings with a side strain on the fourth day, he took 13 of the first 16 wickets to fall, and bowled 73 overs, broken only by one over by Mudassar Nazar at the start of England's second innings.

GOOD FOOTWORK AND
HEAD POSITION.
(PATRICK EAGAR)

Although the end to which Qadir bowled turned more than the other in the first innings, he switched ends together with umpire Khan in the second innings when Broad and Graham Gooch opened the innings, facing a deficit of 217. Just before tea, Broad was given out to a catch behind the stumps off slow left-arm bowler Iqbal Qasim. He crossed his legs and refused to go, until persuaded otherwise, half a minute later, by Gooch. The peacemaker, for his pains, perished to the same bowler-keeper-umpire combination shortly after tea, and England were rushed to defeat by an innings and 87 runs inside four days. Broad recalls the atmosphere of those days:

The captain and manager spent most of the time between the first and second Tests trying to clear our minds of what went on in Lahore. We had a long team meeting on the eve of the Faisalabad match to put us at our ease and to try to get everyone to concentrate on the game. We were amazed to find what looked to be a result pitch - under-prepared with little grass, and it had a mosaic, cracked appearance. We were well aware that Pakistan is just about the hardest country in cricket to come back from a 1-0 deficit, and we knew England had never won a Test match there other than the very first one in Lahore in 1961, when Ted Dexter captained England to a win by five wickets.

The pitch looked as though it would turn straightaway, and we picked three spinners, Emburey, Cook and Hemmings, just as they did with Qadir, Tauseef and Qasim. Wasim Akram was unfit, so it was a big toss to win.

PAKISTAN V ENGLAND (2ND TEST)

PLAYED AT IQBAL STADIUM, FAISALABAD, ON 7, 8, 9 (NO PLAY), 11, 12 DECEMBER 1987.
TOSS: ENGLAND. RESULT: MATCH DRAWN.

ENGLAND

	FIRST INNINGS		SECOND INNINGS	
G.A.Gooch	c Aamer, b Qasim	28	lbw, b Qadir	65
B.C.Broad	b Tauseef	116	st Ashraf, b Qadir	14
C.W.J.Athey	c Aamer, b Qadir	27	b Mudassar	20
M.W.Gatting*	b Qadir	79	c Qadir, b Qasim	8
R.T.Robinson	c Ashraf, b Qadir	2	(8) not out	7
N.G.B.Cook	c Ashraf, b Qasim	2		
D.J.Capel	c Aamer, b Qadir	1	lbw, b Qasim	2
J.E.Emburey	st Ashraf, b Qasim	15	(5) not out	10
N.A.Foster	c Aamer, b Qasim	0	(6) c Miandad, b Qadir	0
B.N.French†	st Ashraf, b Qasim	2		
E.E.Hemmings	not out	1		
Extras	b 10, lb 5, w 1, nb 3	19	b 1, lb 9, nb 1	11
		292	(6 wickets declared)	137

	O	M	R	W	O	M	R	W
Aamer	5	0	19	0	3	0	20	0
Mudassar	3	0	8	0	12	1	33	1
Qadir	42	7	105	4	15	3	45	3
Tauseef	28	9	62	1				
Qasim	35.2	7	83	5	10	2	29	2
Shoaib	1	1	0	0				

FALL OF WICKETS
1-73, 2-124, 3-241, 4-249, 5-258, 6-259, 7-288, 8-288, 9-288, 10-292
1-47, 2-102, 3-107, 4-115, 5-115, 6-120

PAKISTAN

	FIRST INNINGS		SECOND INNINGS	
Mudassar Nazar	c French, b Foster	1	b Cook	4
Ramiz Raja	c Gooch, b Foster	12	not out	13
Salim Malik	b Cook	60	not out	28
Javed Miandad*	b Emburey	19		
Ijaz Ahmed	c Robinson, b Emburey	11		
Shoaib Mohammad	b Emburey	0		
Aamer Malik	c French, b Foster	5		
Ashraf Ali†	c French, b Foster	4		
Abdul Qadir	c Gooch, b Cook	38		
Iqbal Qasim	lbw, b Hemmings	24		
Tauseef Ahmed	not out	5		
Extras	lb 5, nb 7	12	b 4, lb 1, nb 1	6
		191	(1 wicket)	51

	O	M	R	W	O	M	R	W
Foster	18	4	42	4	3	0	4	0
Capel	7	1	23	0				
Hemmings	18	5	35	1	7	3	16	0
Emburey	21	8	49	3	2	0	3	0
Cook	20.3	10	37	2	9	3	15	1
Gooch					2	1	4	0
Broad					1	0	4	0

FALL OF WICKETS
1-11, 2-22, 3-58, 4-77, 5-77, 6-115, 7-122, 8-123, 9-175, 10-191
1-15

Umpires: Khizer Hayat and Shakoor Rana

When 'Gatt' won it, we set out to make as many runs as we could. Graham Gooch and I put on 73 before he got a doubtful decision to a bat-pad catch by Aamir Sohail, making his debut, off Qadir. I felt quite comfortable, despite the usual pressure of close fielders and appeals for everything that did not hit the bat.

I covered the game for BBC Radio and the *Birmingham Post*, and I remember wondering how the England side would react if any more controversial decisions went against them. If Gooch appeared unfortunate, Bill Athey was desperately unlucky to go the same way when bat and ball appeared to be some way apart, and it was into this smouldering atmosphere that skipper Gatting walked in to play one of the most devastating Test innings in living memory. Broad comments:

It was an amazing display. He danced down the pitch to the spinners and whacked them everywhere. When he plays like that he is great to bat with, because all you need to do is to give him the strike and watch. I've been in when other players have taken over - it happened several times with Zaheer Abbas when I was with Gloucestershire, and I soon learned not to join in. 'Both' did the same in Melbourne in the first leg of the World Series final in 1987, when I scored 12 out of our opening stand of 91, but I never let it bother me.

Of the contrasting innings of Broad and Gatting, which combined to produce a stand for the third wicket of 117, I wrote at the time: 'Broad's unbeaten 101 was a twin triumph of temperament and technique, which spoke volumes for his own resilience, following his traumas in Lahore. And without it, it is doubtful if Gatting could have played one of the most inspired, brilliant innings produced by an England captain for many years. After spending the previous week in trying to clear the minds of his players of everything but the job in hand, he walked in to bat yesterday after the second of two more awful decisions had chopped off Bill Athey.'

Broad continues the story:

I just kept on going, pleased that I was coping and even more pleased with the position we were building. When the captain got out, I just concentrated on being there at the close, even if I had to wait for my hundred. I never read Qadir from his hand, although he held the ball in such a way that you could see which way it was spinning in the air.

It helped me that there was not much rough outside my off stump because the seamers bowled only eight overs in the innings. Their spinners turned it a lot, but there was no real zip in the pitch, only a bit of bounce. It was a bit of a bonus for me, because whenever it did turn, it turned a lot and I would miss it by miles.

Tim Robinson got out cheaply and Nick Cook did nightwatchman as I just concentrated on seeing the day out. I was 97 at the start of the last over of the day, and I remember deciding to block the last six balls from Qadir. Then he bowled a full toss and I hit it to mid-wicket and I was there. It was a marvellous feeling, because it showed I could play spin, and it also proved I could put Lahore behind me.

The England management had been criticised for not fining Broad for his cross-legged strike, and the point was underlined when, three months later, he was fined £500 for stump abuse when out in the Bicentennial Test in Sydney. Broad is often accused of crossing the thin line between dissent and disappointment. He replies: 'I know I developed that sort of reputation, and I have tried to change. People must realise that my game is based on staying at the crease, although I admit that I have shown too much disappointment at times when I am out.'

Broad's hundred was one of the more pleasant memories of a game which was to deteriorate into an on-field free-for-all which made history. That should not detract from his innings, about which I wrote: 'For a man who struggles to score as fluently against spin as against pace, it was a great effort on the part of Broad to endure 5½ hours of Chinese torture. Particularly as, like a war veteran, he twice had to endure the nightmare recollections at close quarters of his own ordeal under fire in Lahore, re-enacted with the "dismissals" of Gooch and Athey.'

Broad sums up his innings thus: 'The beauty of it was the real pleasure it gave me not to give a chance, despite having fielders around me all day. I just had to keep the ball down, and my only false stroke was a nick through slips which didn't go to hand.'

Broad's consistency in Test matches is shown by the fact that, only once in 44 visits to the crease, did he ever play seven innings without a fifty, and after his first hundred for England at Perth in 1986 in his 12th Test innings, he scored five more in his next 32.

For a man whose stance looks like that of a man about to sit on a shooting stick, his technique is orthodox and pleasant - like the man himself, who, now that he has returned to his native Gloucestershire, could make the autumn of his career a golden one.

GREG AND IAN CHAPPELL

Greg scored 131 on the second and third days of the second Test between England and Australia at Lord's, while brother Ian made 56 on the second day of the same Test, 23 and 24 June 1972.

This game became known as 'Massie's Match', after the medium-fast bowler, making the first of only six appearances for his country, returned record-breaking figures of 60.1-16-137-16. The two brothers - men of contrasting character - independently picked the same Test as the one in which they played their best-ever innings. After dismissing England for 272 in ideal conditions for swing bowling, Australia were in deep trouble at seven for two when the Chappell brothers came together. Ian instinctively reacted to the pressure by blazing his way to 56 before he was well caught by the tumbling Mike Smith at fine-leg. The score was then 82 for three, and Greg was the ideal man to use the platform, established by Ian, to build one of his longest and best innings. He batted for 6¼ hours for 131 and hit 14 fours before he was seventh out at 250, with Australia now back in the match.

Ian Michael Chappell was born on 26 September 1943 in Adelaide, the eldest of three sons to Martin, a senior-grade cricketer and a baseball player who used the skills of both games to launch his eldest son on the road to hooking fame. Ian remembers the occasion well:

From when I was five, for about 12 years, I used to go to a friend of the family, Lynn Fuller, every Sunday for coaching and net practice. He had laid a pitch in his back garden, and he taught me all the basics about batting. He started me off with defensive strokes, off front and back foot, because he reckoned that attacking shots were just an extension. I would spend hour after hour with him, but never got fed up.

Martin [Ian always refers to his father in this way] never interfered, but occasionally when I had finished he would take me for extra practice with more emphasis on hitting the ball. He always impressed on me the need for the right sort of aggression, but he struck the right balance between encouragement and pushing too hard. Anyway, when I was about ten or eleven, he got hold of me one day after practice on Lynn's pitch. There was a bit of a hump in the middle because of all the top-dressing and the way he used to roll it, and Martin said to me: 'Now, let's see if you can look after yourself.'

He then, baseball fashion, threw on to the hump and I got a barrage of bouncers of different trajectories. I can laugh now, but it was pretty fearsome stuff. I guess that was when I learned about hooking. I'm often asked if such regular coaching and practice were too much for a kid, but I remember asking Greg recently if ever he was pushed too much, because he went through the same thing when he was a lad. He told me: 'No, in fact I couldn't wait for the next session to begin.'

I also remember one day when it was stinking hot and I didn't feel too well. I could have quit, but once I had been sick, I felt a bit better and carried on. It never occurred to me to do anything else.

Ian, Greg and Trevor all went to Prince Alfred College, where yet another great influence on their cricket education supplemented the regular coaching and practice from Lynn and Martin. The headmaster was John Dunning, who played four Tests for New Zealand against England between 1932 and 1937 as a seamer. Ian says:

I was 12 and my first coach there was Bill Leak. Later, I was coached by Chester Bennett, who captained Western Australia and South Australia. The college catered for all sports, but John Dunning naturally favoured cricket and a lot of guys who went on to play first-class cricket learned the game at the college.

He always kept an eye on our progress, and was tickled pink about a victory for South Australia against Queensland when we scored 240 to win, because all the runs were scored by Prince Alfred boys - two Chappells, John Causby and Ashley Woodcock. He was rightly proud of the college's great tradition - four captains of Australia is a marvellous record: Joe Darling, Clem Hill and Greg and myself.

For a man who was to have many brushes with the establishment, Ian has a surprising, but welcome, affection for the past, and remembers well some advice from his grandfather, Vic Richardson, who played in 19 Tests and captained his country five times in South Africa in 1935-36.

Vic once told me never to forget three things:
'1. Look like a cricketer, even if you're not, which means dressing neatly on the field.
'2. Remember, there's nothing new in cricket - it's a bit like an old suit. Every now and again it comes back into fashion.
'3. If ever you get the chance to captain Australia, don't captain like a Victorian.'

Ian would not elaborate, but his aggressive leadership of his country was certainly of a different style from that of Bill Woodfull, Lindsay Hassett, Jack Ryder and Bill Lawry, to name four Test captains from Victoria, for which state Vic apparently had no great admiration.

Ian made his first-class debut for South Australia in 1962, replacing Garry Sobers who flew home to play against India, and played the first of his 75 Tests (71 of which were consecutive) against Pakistan at Melbourne in December 1964. He was not selected for the tour of West Indies, and next played in the fourth and fifth Tests against Mike Smith's England side the following year.

A full series against South Africa in 1966-67 followed, despite a modest start to his international career. He did not pass 50 in his first 15 innings in nine Tests, but finally announced himself with 151 at Melbourne against India - the first of 14 hundreds in 136 Test innings which brought him 5345 runs at an average of 42.42. He succeeded Lawry as captain under controversial circumstances towards the end of the home series against England in 1971.

Richie Benaud has this to say of Lawry's sacking after the first five Tests. 'They gave him the selectorial axe right at the base of the skull in one of the most unfeeling acts I have ever seen from any group of selectors.'

It was not an easy start to a captaincy reign that was to bring 15 wins and only five losses in 30 games, and Ian's decision to join Percy McDonnell, George Giffen and Bobby Simpson as the only Australians to put the opposition in in their first games as captain was a recipe for early disaster. Only Simpson finished on the winning side, with Australia losing the final Test at Sydney in February 1971, and with it the Ashes, to Ray Illingworth.

Ian Chappell led his country as he batted for it. He called his approach one of aggression. Opponents and critics labelled him abrasive, even truculent, and there can be no denying that not only did he upset authority on occasions, he also gave every appearance of setting out to do just that. He neither expected nor asked for favours, and certainly gave none.

The eldest brother played a full part in World Series cricket and, after the rapprochement, ended a

(ABOVE) A TYPICALLY PUNCHY LEG-
SIDE STROKE BY ONE OF AUSTRALIA'S
MOST FORCEFUL BATSMEN AND
CAPTAINS.
(PATRICK EAGAR)
(RIGHT) NOT EVEN BROTHERLY LOVE
CAN TEMPT NON-STRIKER IAN INTO
GIVING GREG A 'HIGH FIVE'
TO CELEBRATE HIS HUNDRED AT THE
OVAL IN 1972.
(PATRICK EAGAR)
(FAR RIGHT) THE END OF THE GREG
CHAPPELL INNINGS WHICH SET THE
GAME UP FOR MASSIE'S RECORD-
BREAKING TEST AT LORD'S IN 1972.
(PATRICK EAGAR)

four-year absence from Test cricket with his final three appearances for Australia under the captaincy of brother Greg, against West Indies and England. He stepped down in some style from a stage on which he occupied centre position too prominently and too long for the comfort of many by scoring 75 and an unbeaten 26 in a win by eight wickets which completed a 3-0 clean sweep against Mike Brearley's side.

Ian ended his first-class career with 19,680 runs at an average of 48.35, and his total of 59 hundreds has been exceeded by only five Australians - Bradman, Harvey, Border, Simpson and brother Greg.

Gregory Stephen Chappell, MBE, was born on 7 August 1948 at Unley, South Australia, and followed Ian, the elder by five years, into the Prince Alfred College team, and those of the Glenelg club (for whom he played at the age of 12), South Australia six years later and, finally, in 1970 at the age of 22, Australia for whom he scored a glorious debut hundred to become only the sixth Australian to do this in his first innings.

Greg had to overcome the problem of being tugged along in the wash of Ian at all levels from school to Test, but among the many qualities passed on by father Martin to his three cricketing sons was a strong sense of individuality - particularly so with the elder two. The degree of outward aggression in each of the three Chappells is in proportion with seniority. However, while Ian usually wore his heart on his sleeve, it would be unwise to assume that the same streak of steel was not possessed by Greg, just because he was not such an extrovert on the field.

Both were hard men and, although Ian had a bigger reputation as a 'sledger', Greg could speak his corner - as Eddie Hemmings, for one, has said elsewhere in this book. As a batsman, Greg was more in the classical mould. Taller by a couple of inches than Ian, his ramrod-straight back gave him a strutting walk to the crease, where an equally straight bat was the cornerstone of one of the best methods among post-war batsmen.

Not all good-looking batsmen convert attractive techniques into runs, but Greg's magnificent record places him in the top bracket. His first-class debut for South Australia against Victoria brought him 53 and an unbeaten 62, and his two years with Somerset in 1968 and 1969 tightened some important nuts and bolts in a technique that was occasionally loose.

A successful Test career was inevitable after a wonderful debut in Perth in the second Test against England in December 1970. He went in to bat at 107 for five and had scored 108 when he was out at 326 for six, Australia were back in a game they eventually drew. Without Chappell, they would have lost, and his performance rewarded a typical piece of Australian selectorial bravery, as his previous four completed first-class innings were worth 72.

That was the first of 24 Test hundreds - only Gavaskar, Bradman, Sobers and Border had scored more at the beginning of the 1993 Ashes series in England - with his centuries coming in 151 Test innings, a high-class ratio. He scored 7110 runs for his country, with an average of 53.86 which has been bettered by only one Australian, Bradman. He became the first Australian to score 1000 first-class runs in the West Indies, which he did on his first tour there in 1973. It was inevitable that one Chappell would follow the other as captain of

Australia, and when Ian stepped down after the 1975 tour of England, Greg marked his first game in charge in historic fashion.

At Brisbane in November 1975, in the first Test against West Indies, he became the first cricketer to score hundreds in both innings of his debut Test as captain, and also the first Australian to score centuries in each innings twice, having previously achieved this against New Zealand in 1974. His 123 and unbeaten 109 enabled his side to beat the West Indies by eight wickets, and set up an unexpectedly crushing win in the series by 5-1.

He captained his country 48 times and was in charge either side of the gap created by World Series cricket. In first-class cricket, his 24,535 runs included 74 hundreds, and he averaged 52.20.

The vividly contrasting natures of Ian and Greg are reflected by the choice of their best innings. Greg played many great attacking innings, and Ian could defend with the best, but the brothers settled for performances which both, independent of the other, considered to be the most influential they ever produced. The fact that they chose the same Test is remarkable, and that it was Massie's historic Test at Lord's makes their choice, arguably, the most fascinating of the 43 innings featured in this book. Ian first:

The game was the turnaround in Australia's fortunes, because we had lost the first Test at Old Trafford and I was out for nought and seven, hooking both times. I middled the first one off Tony Greig and got a top edge second knock against John Snow.

England's Mike Smith remembers the first innings duck: 'I was down at fine-leg at the Warwick Road End, and Ian got hold of one which I thought was going for six. I managed to pull it down from overhead, and that started a collapse.' It certainly did, making Australia 69 for two after an opening stand of 68 between

ENGLAND V AUSTRALIA (2ND TEST)

PLAYED AT LORD'S, LONDON, ON 22, 23, 24, 26 JUNE 1972.
TOSS: ENGLAND. RESULT: AUSTRALIA WON BY EIGHT WICKETS.

ENGLAND

	FIRST INNINGS		SECOND INNINGS	
G.Boycott	b Massie	11	b Lillee	6
J.H.Edrich	lbw, b Lillee	10	c Marsh, b Massie	6
B.W.Luckhurst	b Lillee	1	c Marsh, b Lillee	4
M.J.K.Smith	b Massie	34	c Edwards, b Massie	30
B.L.D'Oliveira	lbw, b Massie	32	c G.S.Chappell, b Massie	3
A.W.Greig	c Marsh, b Massie	54	c I.M.Chappell, b Massie	3
A.P.E.Knott†	c Colley, b Massie	43	c G.S.Chappell, b Massie	12
R.Illingworth*	lbw, b Massie	30	c Stackpole, b Massie	12
J.A.Snow	b Massie	37	c Marsh, b Massie	0
N.Gifford	c Marsh, b Massie	3	not out	16
J.S.E.Price	not out	4	c G.S.Chappell, b Massie	19
Extras	lb 6, w 1, nb 6	13	w 1, nb 4	5
		272		**116**

	O	M	R	W	O	M	R	W
Lillee	28	3	90	2	21	6	50	2
Massie	32.5	7	84	8	27.2	9	53	8
Colley	16	2	42	0	7	1	8	0
G.S.Chappell	6	1	18	0				
Gleeson	9	1	25	0				

FALL OF WICKETS
1-22, 2-23, 3-28, 4-84, 5-97, 6-193, 7-200, 8-260, 9-265, 10-272
1-12, 2-16, 3-18, 4-25, 5-31, 6-52, 7-74, 8-74, 9-81, 10-116

AUSTRALIA

	FIRST INNINGS		SECOND INNINGS	
K.R.Stackpole	c Gifford, b Price	5	not out	57
B.C.Francis	b Snow	0	c Knott, b Price	9
I.M.Chappell*	c Smith, b Snow	56	c Luckhurst, b D'Oliveira	6
G.S.Chappell	b D'Oliveira	131	not out	7
K.D.Walters	c Illingworth, b Snow	1		
R.Edwards	c Smith, b Illingworth	28		
J.W.Gleeson	c Knott, b Greig	1		
R.W.Marsh†	c Greig, b Snow	50		
D.J.Colley	c Greig, b Price	25		
R.A.L.Massie	c Knott, b Snow	0		
D.K.Lillee	not out	2		
Extras	lb 7, nb 2	9	lb 2	2
		308	(2 wickets)	**81**

	O	M	R	W	O	M	R	W
Snow	32	13	57	5	8	2	15	0
Price	26.1	5	87	2	7	0	28	1
Greig	29	6	74	1	3	0	17	0
D'Oliveira	17	5	48	1	8	3	14	1
Gifford	11	4	20	0				
Illingworth	7	2	13	1				
Luckhurst					0.5	0	5	0

FALL OF WICKETS
1-1, 2-7, 3-82, 4-84, 5-190, 6-212, 7-250, 8-290, 9-290, 10-308
1-20, 2-51

Umpires: D.J.Constant and A.E.Fagg

Stackpole and Francis, and they were bowled out by Snow and Arnold for 142. Greig, making his debut, top-scored in both innings with 57 and 62 and England won by 89 runs. Ian remembers:

> I had a stack of letters telling me to stop hooking, including one from my grandmother - and she wasn't the greatest expert on the game. The day before the start of the second Test, I had a net and got Jeff Hammond to bowl short to help me decide what to do. I remember a guy behind the net saying to me: 'Even your mates are trying to bounce you out.' I still hadn't made my mind up when I was padded up and waiting to go in after we'd bowled England out for 272.
>
> In came Kenny Barrington and, bugger me, even he told me to stop hooking. He told me to wait until I'd got fifty before I even thought about it. I thought: 'I know he's trying to help, but the day I take advice from an Englishman will be the first - so I'll hook. But will I?' John Snow wanted a go from the Nursery End and he bowled Francis for a duck. Then Price got Stackpole caught by Gifford and we were seven for two - the crowd were wild and the game was on when Greg came in to bat.
>
> I knew I was going to get a few and, sure enough, the first one hit me as I was caught in two minds. Then John Snow hit me and that decided me. I went for everything and I reckon around 40 of my 56 came from hooks. Looking back, it was important for me to re-assert myself, and just as important for the other batsmen - especially Greg and Graeme Watson, who had also got out hooking at Old Trafford. The more short stuff I got, the more I hooked, because I was now sure it was the best way to establish a domination we badly needed after the way 'Snowie' got after us in 1971.
>
> My innings took the momentum away from England, which is why I rate it as such an important knock. Naturally, I would rather I'd scored 156 instead of 56, but I tried to drag one from Snow instead of hitting it square. I'd already hit one six over Mike Smith at long-leg, but top-edged this one and that was that. I've always tried to undermine the opposing captain and, having got out hooking twice at Old Trafford, I really had to show 'Illy' I was still going to hook.

Smith, recalled to Test cricket at the age of 38 and the only batsman in the match to reach 30 twice, made a fine, tumbling catch in front of the Mound Stand to end Ian's blazing counter-attack. *Wisden* said of Ian that 'he set a noble example as captain, leading the recovery with an aggressive display. He used his favourite hook to some purpose while his brother remained strictly defensive.'

When he walked back to the pavilion, Australia were 82 for three, which quickly became 84 for four when Walters was caught by Illingworth off Snow. The recovery was all but nipped in the bud, and probably would have been snuffed out but for the younger Chappell. Now it was his turn to play the best innings of his life.

> I can't recall having concentrated harder, nor being forced to concentrate harder. We were in deep trouble and somehow had to get somewhere near England's 272. I was so determined not to give my wicket away that I went what must have been my longest time in Test cricket without hitting a boundary. I reckon my first one came after three hours at the crease.

Despite this, Greg still dominated a crucial fifth-wicket partnership of 106 with Ross Edwards, who contributed 28. Two more dogged stands of 22 and 38 with nightwatchman John Gleeson and Rod Marsh followed, with Greg reaching his hundred just before the close of the second day's play. He has Illingworth to thank for not spending a sleepless night in the nervous 90s because, in fading light, the England captain took off his pace bowlers and shared the attack with Norman Gifford.

Greg's hundred was his second against England in seven Tests, and was an exceptionally mature performance for a man still only 23. The next morning, a Saturday, the gates were closed 20 minutes before the start of play with 31,000 in the ground. They saw Greg bat for another 90 minutes to score a further 26

THE INNINGS OF MY LIFE

before he was bowled by D'Oliveira with the score then 250 for seven, and Australia poised to take a narrow, but conclusive, lead of 36. Back to Ian:

> I said to the team that I wanted one or two wickets before they took the lead, but Lillee was terrific and we got five down for 31. I know Massie got the wickets and he swung it a mile, but people forget how well Lillee and Dave Colley bowled. I reckon Lillee also deserved eight wickets, and Colley put in one of the best spells I can remember for no wickets. At the start of the tour he told me he could bowl really quick if I needed it, and I filed it away but really thought he was having a lend of himself.
>
> When Dennis was done, I remembered what he'd said and went to him and told him now was the time. Marsh came up a metre from where he'd stood for Dennis, but within a few balls he was two metres further back. His great bowling kept the pressure on when Mike Smith must have thought things might get easier. Psychologically, it did a great deal for the team, and Massie cleaned them up.

The capacity crowd saw 193 runs scored on an historic day in which 14 wickets fell - half of them to Massie's swing, which was so prodigious that he went round the wicket to make his inswinger even more dangerous. The England innings was in ruins at 86 for nine on Saturday evening, and Australia completed a win on Monday by eight wickets to end their longest-ever run without a victory against England - 11 games since Manchester in 1968.

Having lost at Old Trafford, Australia could easily have gone 2-0 down, instead of which they were back in it and eventually squared one of the most exciting Ashes series ever played in England. To accomplish this, Australia needed to win the final Test at The Oval, which they did by five wickets, with Ian and Greg becoming the first brothers to score Test hundreds in the same innings. So it is perhaps surprising that if they were both to choose the same game it was not this one that they picked out.

'Massie's Match' now became memorable, certainly in the minds of the Chappell brothers, for two other performances. Ian first: 'After "Snowie" pinned me in the ribs early on, it was satisfying to inflict some pain of my own, and I know what my innings meant to the team.' While Greg remembers with pride that 'we were only the second side to beat England in 28 Tests, and it was great that my innings was a part of such a team victory.'

Grandfather Vic had died three years earlier at the age of 75 but, although his direct influence was minimal on his two celebrated grandsons, each of them inherited qualities which marked his wonderful sporting career between the two wars. Greg had a similar straight-backed physique to that of Vic, although he was taller. Grandfather Vic was described by Australian historian Jack Pollard as having 'the carriage of a great general'. Ian seems to have inherited his liking for the hook, and a case-hardened attitude towards his players that brooked no frailties.

When Vic captained in South Africa, his only complaint if a player was a party-goer was if he grumbled next morning. 'Got a headache? I've got one every morning, now get over there and field.' In the final Test at Durban, he was not satisfied with Bill O'Reilly's bowling, so he put him on the boundary and instructed Stan McCabe and Len Darling to keep baiting 'Tiger' by asking: 'Aren't you playing in this match?' When Richardson finally let his bowler out of the cage, he took four wickets in no time.

The two brothers bestrode the Test scene between 1965 and 1983, and Australian cricket benefited by 12,465 runs, most of which were scored with style, panache and character. They presented different faces of cricket, and occupy a unique niche in the history of sport. Their considerable contrast in style and approach can be likened to leading figures in other sports: Connors and Borg in tennis; Campese and Farr-Jones in rugby; Trevino and Nicklaus in golf; and Marciano and Ali in the ring.

Each of them was capable of turning a game with brilliance or, if necessary, a fighting performance only possible from men of rare ability and courage. Which one would I pick to play an innings for my life? Either but, if pushed, I would take Ian - just, but only if he was convinced my life was worth saving.

COLIN COWDREY

102 on the first day of the third Test between Australia and England at Melbourne, 31 December 1954.

Cowdrey's century, out of 191, in what was his third Test and fifth innings for England came after he went in at 21 for two, and had to cope with Keith Miller's best-ever Test spell of 9-8-5-3. His chanceless innings kept England in the game, after Hutton, Edrich, May and Compton scored 20 between them. Without his astonishingly mature performance for a 22-year-old, England could not have established a position from which Frank Tyson was able to win the match with a ferocious display of fast bowling.

Sir Michael Colin Cowdrey, CBE, was born on 24 December 1932 in Putumala, Ootacamund, India. His father bestowed on his only son the names of Michael Colin in order to complete a trio of initials which, not even such a parental cricket fanatic could have envisaged, would eventually grace the most prestigious offices in cricket, the presidency of the Marylebone Cricket Club, and the chair of the International Cricket Council. Educated at Homefield, Tonbridge and Oxford, Cowdrey broke many school records before he made his debut for Kent at the age of 17, scoring a modest 104 in seven innings in four games towards the end of the 1950 season.

It was the beginning of a magnificent career which lasted until 1976, and brought him 114 England caps - the first-ever cricketer to reach 100 or more. When he played his final Test in Melbourne in 1975 at the age of 42, he had then established world records of matches played, runs (7624), catches (120), and his 22 hundreds have yet to be exceeded by an Englishman. That last Test was his 43rd appearance against Australia on his sixth tour Down Under - two more records. His aggregate of 42,719 first-class runs is the 12th highest in history and only Boycott, Graveney and Amiss scored more runs among post-war batsmen. He was the 16th man to complete 100 hundreds, in 1973, although the fact that only three were converted into doubles is illustrative of the criticism sometimes levelled at him that he was too introspective about his own rare talents.

A great theorist, he often confounded colleagues by experimenting with minor adjustments of grip and stance. His apparent diffidence probably accounts for the fact that, while he captained his country 27 times, it was more often than not as deputy for someone else. It is one of the game's biggest mysteries why the selectors rarely gave him an extended run, yet turned to him so frequently.

He led twice against India at home in 1959, twice in the West Indies in 1960, followed by a run of seven consecutive Tests against South Africa and Australia in 1960 and 1961, once against Pakistan in 1962, three times against the West Indies in 1966, five times in the West Indies in 1968, four times against Australia the same year, and three times in Pakistan in 1969. Occasionally, injury to him or the appointed captain was the reason for change, but it says more about the selectors' indecision than his own alleged lack of positive leadership that he led the side in nine different series. He was thought only good enough to do a caretaker job, but nothing more, despite a record of eight wins, four defeats and 15 draws.

A touch player, he seldom destroyed an attack, but was also rarely overwhelmed by even the fastest bowling, or the best quality spin, as he showed with his 154-run share of England's record fourth-wicket partnership with Peter May at Edgbaston against the West Indies in 1957. Would he choose that performance as 'the inning of my life'? Or his unbeaten 100 on a wearing pitch in Sydney to secure England's only draw in a series they lost 4-0 in 1959?

> I thought long and hard, but I have to pick my first hundred for England in the second Test in Melbourne, after we had lost the first one in Brisbane by an innings and 154 runs, and then squared the series in Sydney, where Frank Tyson got ten wickets in the match.
>
> We had arrived in Australia on 5 October, and I couldn't see how I could play, because I was the 18th man of the party. However, I put the cat among the pigeons with two hundreds at Sydney in the state game against New South Wales. I remember being handed a cable on the way to the ground when I was 38 not out in the second innings. It was unsigned and said: 'See 2 Kings, 3, 14.' I stuffed it into my pocket without another thought. I was only a few days later when I was preparing my laundry when I found it again.
>
> I looked up the quotation in the Bible and there it was: 'The Lord said to Elija, do it a second time.' I never discovered who sent it, but the fact I did do it a second time helped my selection, especially as there were a couple of injuries.

Denis Compton's knee kept him out of the second Test, and Tom Graveney was hit in the ribs by Frank Tyson in the nets before the Melbourne game. The match was played nearly 40 years ago, but Cowdrey's memories of his favourite innings are vivid and detailed:

> In the first Test I managed 40 and 10, but we were thrashed after we put them in and they scored 601. In Sydney I scored 23 and 59, so I thought I might stay in at Melbourne. There was a drama on the morning of the game when Len Hutton said he was unwell and could not play. The senior players, Godfrey Evans and Bill Edrich, persuaded him otherwise, and Compton for Graveney was our only change, with Bill Edrich changing places as opener with Trevor Bailey.
>
> It was cloudy and humid, but Len dare not put them in - not after Brisbane. There was a bit of a breeze, but Ray Lindwall somehow could not get it quite right. What a morning of drama it was. Firstly, there was Len refusing to leave his bedroom. Then there was a dressing-room atmosphere because Alec Bedser was left out again - just as he was in Sydney. Len hated doing it, and Alec was obviously bitter. The dressing-room was a morgue of worry and stress, and was really in disarray.
>
> We prayed to lose the toss, but won it and so we had to bat. Bill Edrich was soon caught by Lindwall off Miller, and poor Peter May - it was his 25th birthday - was caught by Benaud, also off Miller for a duck, and I went in at 21 for two to join Len in front of 62,000 Australians. All I could do was to fight for my life, but things seemed to get even tougher when I watched Keith bowl to Len two of the greatest maiden overs I ever saw.
>
> It was a privilege to be at the non-striker's end and watch two great cricketers in opposition. Keith bowled out of his skin, but Len somehow coped. Those two gave me an insight into Heaven - one bowling like God, and the other one calling on every bit of his skill and experience. And there was me, an undergraduate, wondering what on earth I was doing there. Then Len was caught by Graeme Hole - off Keith of course, and I can hear the noise now as the scoreboard changed to 29 for three, and in came Keith's great friend, Denis Compton.

He got an amazing welcome, and I remember thinking what a fascinating prospect it was to see two such great cricketers, who were close friends, go flat out against each other in what was now a crisis point of the match. Miller roared in and the first ball nipped back and hit Denis. 'Morning, Mr Compton' from Keith, who then ran in and bowled the equivalent of a lightning leg-break which lifted as well. Not too surprisingly, Denis never got within several inches of what was a brute of a delivery.

I swallowed hard, and watched and listened. Nothing was said but, as Keith came back past me he winked and smiled and said: 'I don't know, Col - I've played against Compo since 1946, and still he doesn't get any better.'

And so it went on - the best bowling I had ever seen, or ever did see. He got Denis caught by Neil Harvey in the slips and, despite some leg trouble which made him doubtful for the game, he bowled unchanged to lunch in as near an unplayable spell as I have ever seen. Just think of it, nine overs, eight maidens and three wickets for five runs. Remember they were eight-ball overs, so in 72 balls, Miller dismissed Hutton, Edrich and Compton, and only one of the two scoring strokes off him had then been played. Denis hit him for three past cover, and I managed a two off the back foot, also past cover.

Trevor Bailey came in at 41 for four, and we held on until lunch. The moisture in the pitch started to dry, and things seemed easier. I got to 17 quite quickly, and was never in much trouble.

COWDREY DRIVES LINDWALL DURING HIS MASTERLY MAIDEN TEST HUNDRED IN MELBOURNE. HEAD AND POSITION OF FEET SHOW HOW HE STAYED SIDEWAYS THROUGH THE HITTING AREA OF THE STROKE.
(HULTON-DEUTSCH COLLECTION)

Wisden is more expansive about Cowdrey's modest comment: 'For four hours, Cowdrey batted without mistake, getting his body behind short rising balls which Lindwall and Miller were able to bowl almost at will. Cowdrey specialised in perfectly timed drives, both straight and to cover, and he forced the ball skilfully off his legs.'

Cowdrey and Bailey added 74 for the fifth wicket, helped by the fact that Miller bowled only three more overs, and those much later in the day. Cowdrey says:

Perhaps it was his injury, but there was still a bit in the pitch after lunch, and Bill Johnston was an easier proposition, although he got Trevor caught behind by Len Maddocks.

The ball was never far from the middle of my bat, and with Godfrey encouraging me all the time, we shared another useful stand of 54. Johnston switched to his slower style, rather like Derek Underwood with slow-medium cutters. My only problem, however, came against their captain, Ian Johnson, with his flighted off-spinners. There was a stiff breeze, and he used it to float the ball from leg to off, and I got stuck on 64 for 35 minutes.

The crowd got on to me and I have never been barracked like it, before or since. It was daft really, but it got to me and I thought I had to do something about it, so I had a go at one which went hard, but oh so close to mid-on. I can imagine what Len was saying in the dressing-room, and I reckon if I'd have got out then I would not have played again. Fortunately, the narrow escape put me back on track, and I got everything in the middle as I got into the 90s. Godfrey was LBW to a shooter from Ron Archer and I was then 90 out of 169 for six, with Johnny Wardle the new man in.

I hit Archer through the covers to go from 93 to 97, and I was so close to making a dream come true. Sometimes, players get stuck in that sort of position through no fault of their own. The bowling stays tight and the fielding becomes keener, with the opposing captain understandably trying to play on nerves, but this time I had no problem. Archer dug one in short and I played the Peter May trademark shot - wide of mid-on. I knew I'd got a chance of three, and so did the crowd. They had given me the treatment earlier when I got stuck in the 60s, but now the cheering rose to a crescendo. It was generous and I found it touching, because they knew what it meant to me, over and above the match situation.

My father had died a few weeks earlier, just before we arrived by boat in Australia, and the hundred was a fulfilment of all his hopes and dreams for me. I tried to settle myself and go on, but I got out to a combination of Johnston and Johnson. The left-handed Johnston had created quite a bit of rough outside my off stump, and Ian Johnson dropped one right in the middle of the patch. What made it more difficult was that, before pitching outside off stump, it floated from leg to off and drew my front leg so far over that I was bowled in a freakish manner. It turned past my left pad and actually went between my legs to hit the stumps.

What was so satisfying was that I did not give a chance, and I hardly played a loose stroke. I got a bit bamboozled with the field placings, when the fielders went back a bit deeper after I managed a few boundaries. It was inexperience that I did not then look for the singles, but that was the only mistake I made. It was a day that had everything for me. Miller's marvellous spell - the interplay between him and Denis, and then the two vital partnerships with Trevor and Godfrey. And all in my third Test in front of the biggest crowd I had ever seen.

The dramas were to continue, with charges of pitch doctoring between the end of the third day and the beginning of the fourth, when large cracks had mysteriously closed. The Victorian Cricket Association and the Melbourne Cricket Club held an inquiry and issued this statement. 'After a searching inquiry, it is emphatically denied that the pitch or any part of the cricket ground has been watered since the commencement of the third Test match on Friday, 31 December.'

That innings kept England in a game that was to go most of the way towards settling the result of the series, and ensure the retention of the Ashes. Peter May scored 91 in the second innings - the only other score over 50 in a low-scoring game which produced 812 runs from the equivalent of 350 six-ball overs.

Cowdrey scored 21 more hundreds for England, including one in his 100th Test, and maintained his appetite for batting right up to his retirement. Only a man deeply in love with cricket would have responded to the bugle call when it sounded for him just before his 42nd birthday in 1975. The England captain, Mike Denness, had canvassed his shell-shocked, injury-ravaged party to ask them which player they would most like to join them from England.

Cowdrey has received many accolades in his distinguished career, but none was more prized than to be told he was the players' choice to take on Dennis Lillee and Jeff Thomson. There was a long list of reasons why he might have refused: he had had a good domestic season, but was not selected for the original party; he had not batted for three months, and could hardly be expected to cope with extreme pace after a complete absence of preparation.

Yet, within five days, he walked in at number three to face bowlers who had broken hand bones of Dennis Amiss and John Edrich, to which list was added Brian Luckhurst in that Test - the first one in which Cowdrey

AUSTRALIA V ENGLAND (3RD TEST)

PLAYED AT MELBOURNE CRICKET GROUND, ON 31 DECEMBER 1954, 1, 3, 4, 5 JANUARY 1955.
TOSS: ENGLAND. RESULT: ENGLAND WON BY 128 RUNS.

ENGLAND

	FIRST INNINGS		SECOND INNINGS	
L.Hutton*	c Hole, b Miller	12	lbw, b Archer	42
W.J.Edrich	c Lindwall, b Miller	4	b Johnston	13
P.B.H.May	c Benaud, b Lindwall	0	b Johnston	91
M.C.Cowdrey	b Johnson	102	b Benaud	7
D.C.S.Compton	c Harvey, b Miller	4	c Maddocks, b Archer	23
T.E.Bailey	c Maddocks, b Johnston	30	not out	24
T.G.Evans†	lbw, b Archer	20	c Maddocks, b Miller	22
J.H.Wardle	b Archer	0	b Johnson	38
F.H.Tyson	b Archer	6	c Harvey, b Johnston	6
J.B.Statham	b Archer	3	c Favell, b Johnston	0
R.Appleyard	not out	1	b Johnston	6
Extras	b 9	9	b 2, lb 4, w 1	7
		191		279

	O	M	R	W	O	M	R	W
Lindwall	13	0	59	1	18	3	52	0
Miller	11	8	14	3	18	6	35	1
Archer	13.6	4	33	4	24	7	50	2
Benaud	7	0	30	0	8	2	25	1
Johnston	12	6	26	1	24.5	2	85	5
Johnson	11	3	20	1	8	2	25	1

FALL OF WICKETS
1-14, 2-21, 3-29, 4-41, 5-115, 6-169, 7-181, 8-181, 9-190, 10-191
1-40, 2-96, 3-128, 4-173, 5-185, 6-211, 7-257, 8-273, 9-273, 10-279

AUSTRALIA

	FIRST INNINGS		SECOND INNINGS	
L.E.Favell	lbw, b Statham	25	b Appleyard	30
A.R.Morris	lbw, b Tyson	3	Cowdrey, b Tyson	4
K.R.Miller	c Evans, b Statham	7	(5) c Edrich, b Tyson	6
R.N.Harvey	b Appleyard	31	c Evans, b Tyson	11
G.B.Hole	b Tyson	11	(6) c Evans, b Statham	5
R.Benaud	c sub (J.V.Wilson), b Appleyard	15	(3) b Tyson	22
R.G.Archer	b Wardle	23	b Statham	15
L.V.Maddocks†	c Evans, b Statham	47	b Tyson	0
R.R.Lindwall	b Statham	13	lbw, b Tyson	0
I.W.Johnson*	not out	33	not out	4
W.A.Johnston	b Statham	11	c Evans, b Tyson	0
Extras	b 7, lb 3, nb 2	12	b 1, lb 13	14
		231		111

	O	M	R	W	O	M	R	W
Tyson	21	2	68	2	12.3	1	27	7
Statham	16.3	0	60	5	11	1	38	2
Bailey	9	1	33	0	3	0	14	0
Appleyard	11	3	38	2	4	1	17	1
Wardle	6	0	20	1	1	0	1	0

FALL OF WICKETS
1-15, 2-38, 3-43, 4-65, 5-92, 6-115, 7-134, 8-151, 9-205, 10-231
1-23, 2-57, 3-77, 4-86, 5-87, 6-97, 7-98, 8-98, 9-110, 10-111

Umpires: C.Hoy and M.J.McInnes

played since June 1971 at Edgbaston against Pakistan. Innings of 22 and 41 were almost miraculous, and a testament to a technique and temperament which coped with every card dealt to him by the cricketing fates.

Generous, kind, sensitive and many other similar epithets can be applied to a man whose influence in the first-class game, as a player and administrator, has invariably been used wisely. Of all the subjects in this book, Cowdrey's recall was the best. That 102 in the Melbourne Test truly was the innings of his life. Not many men leave cricket a better game than they found it. Cowdrey will be just such a man.

MARTIN CROWE

81* in the Benson and Hedges World Cup match between New Zealand and West Indies at Auckland, 8 March 1992.

The game was New Zealand's fifth in the World Cup qualifying stages and, although Crowe had captained his side to four straight wins, the fifth game was important because victory would guarantee his team a semi-final place and make it more difficult for West Indies to qualify. This match in the round-robin section of the fifth World Cup was thus a crucial and pivotal one. Crowe's innings made possible a home victory which was in doubt following the dismissals of Mark Greatbatch and Ken Rutherford soon after he came in to bat at 97 for two. The West Indies pace attack, spearheaded by Curtly Ambrose and Malcolm Marshall, threatened to turn the match until Crowe batted brilliantly for 81 off the same number of deliveries, with his 12th boundary winning the match for New Zealand by five wickets with nine balls to spare.

Martin David Crowe was born on 22 September 1962 in Henderson, Auckland. His father, David, played for Wellington and Canterbury, and elder brother Jeff captained New Zealand in six of his 39 Tests. Martin Crowe was educated at Auckland Grammar School, and made his first-class provincial debut at the age of 17, two years before his Test debut at Wellington against Australia, when he was run out for nine.

Scores of two, nought and nine in the next two Tests led to his omission the following year against Sri Lanka, but his immense promise earned selection for the tour of England which followed the 1983 World Cup. A series aggregate of 163 in eight innings tested the patience of the selectors, as did his next three series against England at home, and Sri Lanka and Pakistan away. In nine Tests he scored only 419 runs, despite a maiden century in Wellington.

By this time, Crowe had moved to Central Districts, and his undoubted talent began to blossom for his country in 1984-85. He scored 295 in five innings at home against Pakistan, and the breakthrough came on tour against the West Indies later that season. An otherwise poor tour for him was redeemed by 188 at Georgetown against Marshall, Holding and Garner, and he repeated the score seven months later at 'The Gabba' to set up New Zealand's first-ever win in Australia.

He played for Somerset at various times between 1984 and 1988, and was the overseas cricketing catalyst of the upheaval which led to the departures of Botham, Richards and Garner. His magnificent batting form earned him six Championship hundreds in 1984 and 1987, in which calendar year he scored 4045 first-class runs around the world. Occasionally beset by self-doubt, Crowe has still developed into one of the heaviest run-scorers in the modern game, and his ratio of innings per hundred is, with the exception of Graeme Hick, the best among current batsmen - he averages one every six visits to the crease, and a career average in excess of 55 is also only bettered by Hick among current cricketers.

At the end of the 1992-93 season, he was approaching 5000 Test runs - only John Wright had scored more for New Zealand - and with 15 Test hundreds to

A LOVELY SQUARE CUT BY CROWE, WITH THE RIGHT FOOT STAYING BEAUTIFULLY SQUARE AND NEARLY PARALLEL TO THE CREASE.

(PATRICK EAGAR)

choose from among his 112 Test innings, which one would he pick as his best? Perhaps his 299 against Sri Lanka at the Basin Reserve in Wellington? He said after getting out with three balls of the match remaining, 'It's a bit like climbing Everest and pulling a hamstring in the last stride.' But no:

> The Test innings which meant a lot to me was also against Sri Lanka. It was the 107 I scored in the second innings of the second Test in Colombo in December 1992, and although we lost the game, I was proud of my performance for several reasons. It was a difficult tour after the four deaths caused by a bomb strapped to a suicide motorcyclist, and six players went home. The team had been split right down the middle about going home or staying, and I was pretty down after scoring 19, 11 and a duck in the first Test and the first innings of the second one.
>
> When I went in to bat for the second time, we had followed-on early on the third day, 292 behind, and we were 30 for two. The pitch was a real turner, and their spinners were a handful. I got 107 and played as well as I could. My only problem came when I was 39. I was given out caught bat-pad on the off-side, but I asked Gurusinha if he had caught it. When he said no, I stood my ground, and I managed to hit a hundred which gave me a great deal of personal satisfaction.

Crowe hit ten fours and four sixes, with his runs coming out of 159 added with Wright but, because the innings did not prevent Sri Lanka from their third-ever Test victory and the first one against New Zealand, he discarded it as 'the innings of my life'.

> It was a fascinating exercise to pick my best, because there are so many factors to take into account. I decided it had to be a match in which I influenced the result, and it had to be against a top attack. That is the real satisfaction for me - to perform against the best when they are in top form, which is why I have gone for the World Cup innings against the West Indies in Auckland. We worked hard at the tactical side of the competition, and our home pitches helped our attack.

What Crowe did was to use an old-fashioned ploy which was deemed revolutionary, because it had never been used in top cricket in living memory. He gave the new ball to off-spinner Dipak Patel in the opening game against Australia, and it worked like a charm with the former Worcestershire all-rounder producing figures of 70-8-213-8 in the seven games in which he opened the bowling.

His most economical figures were in Crowe's chosen game, and the meagre 19 runs that Messrs Haynes, Lara, Richardson and Hooper could squeeze from him meant that New Zealand were set a not overly demanding target of 204. Undemanding, that is, if they could get off to a good start. The second part of the Crowe master-plan was to give Greatbatch his head, and the left-hander launched himself at the West Indies pace attack - admittedly handicapped by the no-bouncer rule - so effectively that his partner, Latham, scored only 12 in an opening partnership of 67 in 12 overs.

The large home crowd were in high spirits and, even when Latham and Jones went to catches by wicketkeeper Williams off Cummins and Benjamin, it all looked too easy when Crowe joined Greatbatch. It is rare in one-day cricket for the wheels to remain firmly bolted, and the first wobble came when Greatbatch gave Haynes a steepling catch off Benjamin to end an innings which drove the opposition to distraction. Not every day do their fast bowlers see a batsman giving them the charge, which Greatbatch did so successfully that he hit Marshall over extra-cover for six, and the Ambrose jaw dropped when he, too, went for the maximum over the head of deep third-man.

Another half an hour, and the game would have been won and lost, but the 77th delivery faced by the left-hander was his last, and it put New Zealand into the position their captain least wanted: 100 for three with two new batsmen on nought. It is then that a fielding side is lifted, and when the batting side usually decides to regroup for a few overs to avoid further disasters.

The innings was at a typical one-day crossroads, with one signpost pointing to 'caution and probable success' and the other to 'attack and possible failure'.

Crowe did not hesitate. He backed himself to take on the best and beat them and he succeeded gloriously: 'I didn't miss a ball and I was at my best against the best.'

He lost Rutherford for eight and Harris for seven, but his attacking approach never wavered, and he clinched victory by five wickets, with the crowd of 24,281 now on the verge of hysteria. They saw their hero score his 81 out of 109 added while he was at the crease. Had he gone cheaply, it is doubtful if New Zealand would have won, and Crowe's performance adds point to this assessment by Sir Richard Hadlee, made in 1989:

'He is an excellent technician, ruthless on himself about perfecting his technique, and he has hardened his attitude towards the game. Not unlike Viv Richards, he likes to use his physical presence as an added weapon. He has the talent to become one of the great batsmen, and I suspect he'll go on and do that.'

As he has, and as he proved once more on 8 March 1992.

New Zealand subsequently headed the table after the qualifying stages, and thus earned a home semi-final against Pakistan. His innings, together with shrewd captaincy, earned him his third Man of the Match award in five games, and confirmed his right to be considered the best batsman in the competition. His final record was 456 runs for four times out, including two run-outs, and his inspired batting and captaincy were the main reasons for New Zealand's successful march through the qualifying games.

NEW ZEALAND V WEST INDIES (World Cup)

PLAYED AT EDEN PARK, AUCKLAND, ON 8 MARCH 1992.
TOSS: NEW ZEALAND. RESULT: NEW ZEALAND WON BY FIVE WICKETS.

WEST INDIES

D.L.Haynes	c and b Harris	22
B.C.Lara	c Rutherford, b Larsen	52
R.B.Richardson*	c Smith, b Watson	29
C.L.Hooper	c Greatbatch, b Patel	2
K.L.T.Arthurton	b Morrison	40
A.L.Logie	b Harris	3
M.D.Marshall	b Larsen	5
D.Williams†	not out	32
W.K.M.Benjamin	not out	2
C.E.L.Ambrose }	did not bat	
A.C.Cummins }		
Extras	lb 8, w 7, nb 1	16
	(50 overs, 7 wickets)	203

	O	M	R	W
Patel	10	2	19	1
Harris	10	2	32	2
Morrison	9	1	33	1
Watson	10	2	56	1
Larsen	10	0	41	2
Latham	1	0	14	0

FALL OF WICKETS
1-65, 2-95, 3-100, 4-136, 5-142, 6-156, 7-201

NEW ZEALAND

M.J.Greatbatch	c Haynes, b Benjamin	63
R.T.Latham	c Williams, b Cummins	14
A.H.Jones	c Williams, b Benjamin	10
M.D.Crowe*	not out	81
K.R.Rutherford	c Williams, b Ambrose	8
C.Z.Harris	c Williams, b Cummins	7
D.N.Patel	not out	10
I.D.S.Smith†		
G.R.Larsen }	did not bat	
D.K.Morrison		
W.Watson }		
Extras	lb 7, w 5, nb 1	13
	(48.3 overs, 5 wickets)	206

	O	M	R	W
Ambrose	10	1	41	1
Marshall	9	1	35	0
Cummins	10	0	53	2
Benjamin	9.3	3	34	2
Hooper	10	0	36	0

FALL OF WICKETS
1-67, 2-97, 3-100, 4-135, 5-174

Umpires: K.E.Liebenberg and P.J.McConnell

TED DEXTER

52 on the fourth and fifth days of the second Test between Australia and England at Melbourne, 2 and 3 January 1963.

England began their second innings needing 234 to win. They began the last day on nine for one, with Sussex and ex-Cambridge colleagues Dexter and David Sheppard together. Dexter's innings in a partnership of 124 added for the second wicket laid the foundations for an England win by seven wickets - only the second time Dexter had played on a winning side against Australia in nine games, and the first time in Australia.

E dward Ralph Dexter was born on 15 May 1935 in Milan, and played for Sussex, in his own words, 'as the nearest English county to Italy'. He played for Cambridge University for three years, beginning in 1956, made his debut for Sussex in 1957, and for England in July 1958 at Old Trafford against New Zealand. Despite scoring 52 in his only innings of the game, Dexter missed the final Test and was not originally chosen for Peter May's 1958-59 tour of Australia. However, he and John Mortimore, the Gloucestershire off-spinner, were summoned as reinforcements following injuries to Watson, Subba Row, Milton and Bailey.

He played in the drawn third Test at Sydney, and the final match in Melbourne, where England lost by nine wickets, but scores of one, eleven, nought and six did not suggest he would be appointed captain of his country 2½ years later. He led England in 30 Tests, winning nine and losing seven and, if for nothing else, is in the record books as the only England captain to win a Test in Pakistan.

Few post-war batsmen have been gifted with such authoritative ability to strike the ball cleanly, and there were many memorable performances among his 102 innings for England, including a blazing but unavailing 76 in 84 minutes at Old Trafford in 'Benaud's Test' in 1961, and a ferocious 70 at Lord's in 1963 against Wes Hall and Charlie Griffith at their peak. Would he choose one of these cameos, as 'the innings of my life'? Or perhaps he would pick one of his nine hundreds for England, five of which were over 170, including his career-best 205 in Karachi to secure a draw in the match and a win in the series?

The fact that he batted for 8¼ hours in that game gives the lie to critics who said his concentration was suspect, although his record for county and country suggests that his flair and natural talents were more consistently fulfilled in Test cricket, where he responded to the atmosphere and pressure in a manner given to few.

Not known as 'Lord Edward' because of an unimposing appearance, he was undoubtedly a man for the big occasion. Not only did he average more for England than in first-class cricket - 47.89 compared with 40.75

- but he is one of a handful of England cricketers who responded to captaincy positively enough to average more when he was captain than when he was an ordinary member of the side - Peter May, Douglas Jardine and Graham Gooch are three others. He has a higher Test batting average than any other regular England captain in history except Walter Hammond and Len Hutton and, even more impressive, is the fact that he averages more for England than, among many others, Boycott, Gower, Cowdrey, Graveney, Gooch, both Edriches, Amiss and May.

His choice of innings is as apparently baffling as were many of his ideas and theories about the game he graced for a dozen years. He bettered his final choice - 52 at Melbourne in 1963 - no fewer than 33 times for England, and also ignored his 42 first-class hundreds. It was not a fast innings, nor did it contain many boundaries, but the fascinating feature of of such choices of a personal best is the criteria applied.

Some batsmen take into account the pitch - Gavaskar, D'Oliveira, Boycott, and Kallicharran for instance - while others consider the quality of the bowlers. Perhaps significantly, captains like Dexter and Lewis have an extra factor to assess - the responsibility of leading England and the importance they attach to setting an inspiring example to their team.

Hence Dexter's choice of a relatively unimportant-looking innings in what was a comfortable win after Sheppard scored the third and last of his Test hundreds. Even the alternative to his final choice is one plucked out of the inner reaches of a mind that is rarely predictable - and all the more refreshing for that.

I toured the West Indies with the Cavaliers, and I played as well as I could at Sabina Park, where I got a hundred in 70 minutes, and I remember pinging one of their quicks with a shot that was like a well-struck one iron, out of the ground into an old banana plantation. Good stuff, because he had just taken the second new ball and it was a pre-meditated decision to whack him. Jim Laker said it was the best he had ever seen me play, but in the end I go for Melbourne.

It was the final day, and although it wasn't a bad pitch, it was cracking and slightly unreliable. The first innings was even - their 316 to our 331 - with Colin Cowdrey getting 113 and I managed 93.

In that first innings, England were 19 for two, with openers Sheppard and Pullar gone, and Dexter's third-wicket partnership with Cowdrey of 175 in 198 minutes was crucial against a rampant Alan Davidson - six for 75 - but still Dexter picks his second innings.

We bowled them out for 248 on the fourth day, just before the close, after they were going well at 161 for four with Brian Booth and Bill Lawry having added 92. Then I got my only wicket of the match: I bowled Lawry for 57 [he batted for 275 minutes, then the slowest recorded fifty for Australia]. Fred Trueman cleaned up the tail to leave us needing 234, with a few minutes to bat out that night.

Pullar was caught behind, and the big question was whether or not we should have a nightwatchman. I have mixed feelings about them, but this time I felt it important, as captain, to show an example and I refused to have one and went out myself. I suppose it would have been egg-on-my-face time if I'd got out, but you have to show confidence in yourself, even if it means a gamble.

The old pros in the side, like Barrington, Graveney, and Titmus, probably thought I was wrong, but it enabled me to be in a position to dictate first thing next morning, and that was what I wanted. The target was gettable, of course it was, but the pressure on a side to score runs to win a match is immense, and I didn't want that to spoil our chances by getting bogged down early in the innings.

Now Melbourne is a big playing area, and not the easiest ground to hit boundaries on, so David Sheppard and I decided that we would run as positively as we could. He might not have looked a quick or agile runner, but the secret is in the understanding and calling between two batsmen. I had always done well with him in the Sussex side, and we decided to take on the Aussies on the last morning.

It worked like a charm. We ran them ragged and, even though we both perished by the sword, we carried out the plan so successfully, that it showed everyone what could be done. We demoralised them so much that in the end we won with 75 minutes to spare.

After Dexter was run out, Cowdrey and Sheppard shared a third-wicket partnership of 104, until the Reverend was also run out with the scores level. Dexter's strategy was so successful that England's runs came off the equivalent of 86 six-ball overs, compared with the 128 needed by Australia in their second innings to score 11 runs more.

It is typical of Dexter's fiercely independent character that, after successive innings in the series of 70, 99 and 93, which followed 172 in the Test at The Oval against Pakistan 12 weeks before the start of the Ashes series, that he should choose one of the least spectacular innings of his career.

You asked me for 'the innings of my life', and I have no doubt that the game was the high point of my cricketing career. The setting was perfect - the historic Melbourne ground staging an Ashes game that was watched by 247,831 spectators. Also, we had been smashed 4-0 on the previous tour, and I knew I hadn't exactly impressed the Aussie crowds then. In the final Test on that tour, we were thrashed by nine wickets and I got nought and six, so it gave me extra satisfaction to carry out a plan for victory.

In terms of an innings which really counted, that is the one in which I felt completely in control, even though I did not smash the ball around. When I got out in the first innings for 93 to follow my 99 in Brisbane, I was Richie Benaud's only wicket of the game, but this time I was batting with the Church. In the end, I answered one too many of his calls, but by then we had the game by the throat.

Trying to anticipate the selections of the subjects of this book is difficult enough - with the chairman of the England selectors it was impossible. Not averse to a gamble himself, perhaps 'Lord Edward' took special delight in making a choice that, in bookmaking terms, would rate among the 33-1 outsiders in the eyes of most people. But that non-conformity is one of his many charms.

Past England captains have vacated their position for a variety of reasons - Close for time-wasting in a county game, Gatting because of a veto applied by Ossie Wheatley against the wishes of Dexter and Michael Stewart, and Botham who resigned minutes before he was pushed in 1981. Only Dexter would have ended a 30-game reign by deciding to fight the lost cause of a General Election in Cardiff South East against James Callaghan. And which other man would pilot his family to Australia in 1970 to report on the tour?

AUSTRALIA V ENGLAND (2ND TEST)

PLAYED AT MELBOURNE CRICKET GROUND, ON 29, 31 DECEMBER 1962, 1, 2, 3 JANUARY 1963.
TOSS: AUSTRALIA. RESULT: ENGLAND WON BY SEVEN WICKETS.

AUSTRALIA

	FIRST INNINGS		SECOND INNINGS	
W.M.Lawry	b Trueman	52	b Dexter	57
R.B.Simpson	c Smith, b Coldwell	38	b Trueman	14
N.C.O'Neill	c Graveney, b Statham	19	c Cowdrey, b Trueman	0
R.N.Harvey	b Coldwell	0	run out	10
P.J.P.Burge	lbw, b Titmus	23	b Statham	14
B.C.Booth	c Barrington, b Titmus	27	c Trueman, b Statham	103
A.K.Davidson	c Smith, b Trueman	40	c Smith, b Titmus	17
K.D.Mackay	lbw, b Titmus	49	lbw, b Trueman	9
R.Benaud*	c Barrington, b Titmus	36	c Cowdrey, b Trueman	4
G.D.McKenzie	b Trueman	16	b Trueman	0
B.N.Jarman†	not out	10	not out	11
Extras	b 2, lb 4	6	b 4, lb 5	9
		316		248

	O	M	R	W	O	M	R	W
Trueman	23	1	83	3	20	1	62	5
Statham	22	2	83	1	23	1	52	2
Coldwell	17	2	58	2	25	2	60	0
Barrington	6	0	23	0	5	0	22	0
Dexter	6	1	10	0	9	2	18	1
Titmus	15	2	43	4	14	4	25	1
Graveney	3	1	10	0				

FALL OF WICKETS
1-62, 2-111, 3-112, 4-112, 5-155, 6-164, 7-237, 8-289, 9-294, 10-316
1-30, 2-30, 3-46, 4-69, 5-161, 6-193, 7-212, 8-228, 9-228, 10-248

ENGLAND

	FIRST INNINGS		SECOND INNINGS	
Rev.D.S.Sheppard	lbw, b Davidson	0	run out	113
G.Pullar	b Davidson	11	c Jarman, b McKenzie	5
E.R.Dexter*	c Simpson, b Benaud	93	run out	52
M.C.Cowdrey	c Burge, b McKenzie	113	not out	58
K.F.Barrington	lbw, b McKenzie	35	not out	0
T.W.Graveney	run out	41		
F.J.Titmus	c Jarman, b Davidson	15		
A.C.Smith†	not out	6		
F.S.Trueman	c O'Neill, b Davidson	6		
J.B.Statham	b Davidson	1		
L.J.Coldwell	c Benaud, b Davidson	1		
Extras	b4, lb 4, nb 1	9	b 5, lb 3, nb 1	9
		331	(3 wickets)	237

	O	M	R	W	O	M	R	W
Davidson	23.1	4	75	6	19	2	53	0
McKenzie	29	3	95	2	20	3	58	1
Mackay	6	2	17	0	9	0	34	0
Benaud	18	3	82	1	14	1	69	0
Simpson	7	1	34	0	2	0	10	0
O'Neill	5	1	19	0				
Booth					0.2	0	4	0

FALL OF WICKETS
1-0, 2-19, 3-194, 4-254, 5-255, 6-292, 7-315, 8-324, 9-327, 10-331
1-5, 2-129, 3-233

Umpires: C.J.Egar and W.Smyth

An innovator, he was responsible for introducing the current World Ratings system of Test cricketers, which are based upon the value of a particular performance. I wonder how the computer would deal with the 52 he rates as 'the innings of my life'? Outstanding innings can lift a player several rungs in the top 30 ladder, but how would the computer take into account the same factors as did Dexter? Dexter was a source of joy, albeit, at times, a puzzling one. He has just proved it once again.

BASIL D'OLIVEIRA

114* on the second and third days of the second Test between Pakistan and England at Dacca, 1 and 2 March 1969.

In reply to Pakistan's 246, England were 139 for seven at the end of the second day, with D'Oliveira then on 16. On a pitch of baked mud which began to break up on the second and third days, the first Cape Coloured cricketer ever to play Test cricket hit an unbeaten century out of 274, with 98 coming on the third day out of 135 added for the last three wickets. D'Oliveira's innings not only saved the game, but completed his rehabilitation in the England side, which began two Tests earlier at The Oval the previous August, when his historic 158 led to the cancellation of England's proposed tour of South Africa that winter.

Basil Lewis D'Oliveira, OBE, was born on 4 October 1931 in the Signal Hill area in Cape Town, and came to England, with the assistance of the late John Arlott, following a series of prodigious batting feats achieved under the pitiful conditions allowed under the regime of apartheid. On primitive pitches he scored 80 hundreds, many of them in phenomenally fast times, and I was on the receiving end of one of them in Natalspruit, the main ground of the Coloured Cricketers' Association in Johannesburg.

The former England and Glamorgan cricketer Peter Walker, who was born in Bristol but brought up in South Africa, defied police pressure to organise a two-day game between his team of South African Test players and English coaches and a Coloured XI which would be supplemented by D'Oliveira and Cecil Abrahams from the Cape. Abrahams was the father of former Lancashire captain, John, and he, Basil and a massively built all-rounder named 'Tiny' Ahmed were the stars of the opposition.

The game began on Boxing Day, but the start was delayed because of the late arrival of the Cape representatives. Rumour - which has never been denied - has it that, having missed the train to Johannesburg, they hailed a taxi in Cape Town and hired him for the thousand-mile journey. A crowd of around 4,000 - nearly double the official capacity - watched Walker's stars completely outplayed on matting.

None of us had seen D'Oliveira, then officially 29 years old, although I know several of his Worcestershire colleagues of the 1960s who would not take out a second mortgage on the accuracy of that particular birth certificate. Doubts were expressed about the strength of bowling from which he had plundered the odd double century in under an hour and a half, but we were soon to be convinced, after I brought him to the crease by taking the first wicket of the match.

It was odd in that, for the one and only time in my career, the first player to congratulate me on my wicket was the non-striker, who was one of several of his team who thought the selectors should not have picked his opening partner. My first ball to D'Oliveira was straight and a good length and, when he raised his bat to leave it alone, I thought I was on a hat-trick. I was not familiar with the bounce of the mat, and saw the ball go over the top of middle by 18 inches. No problem, I thought, just pitch it up that bit further, and see what Wonderman does. What he did was to deposit it over extra-cover for six right in the middle of the one tin-roofed stand on the ground in which at least a quarter of the crowd had crammed. My other painful

memory of the game, which we lost by eight wickets, is of the 'Tiny' man hitting me over the sightscreen, over the fence and into the bottom of a gold mine dump at least 120 yards from the batting crease. All that glisters was not gold that day.

D'Oliveira landed in England a few months later and qualified to play for Worcestershire in 1965, and his subsequent performances must rank as remarkable, bearing in mind his lack of coaching and his age, whatever it was, when he made his first-class debut. He hit six of his 43 first-class hundreds in Worcestershire's Championship title win in 1965, and made what was, arguably, the most romantic Test debut in history the following year at Lord's against the West Indies. It was the first of his 44 games for England, out of a possible 48, with his final game coming against Australia at The Oval in 1972. Only four times did he bat higher than number five, with a third of his innings played from the pivotal positions of six and seven. His 2484 Test runs came at an average of 40.06, marginally higher than his first-class career average of 39.57, and underlined a steely temperament that matched a technique that was all his own. Strong forearms, a tiny back-lift and the patience of Job combined to make him a rescuer of lost causes, and capable of taking on the world's best under any conditions.

He played for Worcestershire until 1980, by which time his slightly more ample figure was part of the fixtures and fittings at

A TRADEMARK
D'OLIVEIRA SHORT-ARM
PULL FROM, AS IS
SHOWN BY THE POSITION
OF WICKETKEEPER
JARMAN, OUTSIDE OFF
STUMP. (HULTON-
DEUTSCH COLLECTION)

New Road. His choice of his best innings shows how much of cricket is played in the mind, not that the unbeaten 114 is undeserving of his accolade that it was 'the innings of my life'. It ranks with any single-handed performance in Test cricket in the last 40 years, but he had another reason for considering it extra-special.

Most cricketers, however much they deny it, are sensitive to media criticism, and it seems that D'Oliveira had in his sights the cricket correspondent of the *Evening Standard*, John Thicknesse. He had voiced doubts about the all-rounder's chances of being successful for England:

'Thickers' was one of a few press men who had doubts in their minds about me, so I was determined to prove him wrong. I had a poor tour of the West Indies in 1967-68 [137 in eight innings], and missed the middle three of the Ashes series before I got back at The Oval. I nearly picked that innings, but it was a good pitch and I never had to fight all the way as I did in Dacca. When the South African tour was called off, I felt as though I was to blame, although I knew I was not.

The substitute tour of Pakistan was therefore my big chance, and I got only 26 and five in the first Test in Lahore. When I walked in to bat at Dacca, we were 113 for five, and their four spinners were well on top. The finger spinners, Pervez Sajjad and Saeed Ahmed, were more dangerous than Intikhab and Mushtaq because, although the surface started to powder, it was slow in pace. Before the close of play it was turning square - and remember this was only the second day, and they had scored 246 - and both Alan Knott and David Brown had also fallen.

I could have gone as well, because the only chance I gave should have been taken. A bat-pad nick off Saeed shot about 12 feet in the air between Mushtaq and Hanif at short leg. They looked at it, looked at each other and neither went for it, otherwise I was gone. That evening, I told myself: 'You've had your bit of luck, now make it count.' What helped me was that I had taught myself to bat on worse pitches than that so, in a funny sort of way, I reckon I had an advantage over everybody else. The problem was that I had only John Snow, Derek Underwood and Bob Cottam to bat with, and if they got rolled over quickly on the third day, we would be around 100 runs behind with nearly half the game to go.

I know I got the runs, but I can't praise the three of them enough. They were surrounded by fielders, the appeals and general pressure were coming every other ball and, whether you could play or not, you had to be bloody-minded to put up with it and stay there.

Wisden reports that 'Snow stayed for an hour and three-quarters, Underwood nearly as long, and Cottam for more than an hour while D'Oliveira played his magnificently resourceful innings.'

Snow's nine runs came out of 40 added for the eighth wicket, Underwood's 22 out of 66 for the ninth, and Cottam's four out of 34 for the last wicket. D'Oliveira batted 4¾ hours in total and the difficulties were such that he hit only nine boundaries.

D'Oliveira's innings was, according to Snow, 'a masterly performance under such conditions. It probably made him feel as though he was back in the Cape, but he was such a great adjuster, who never missed a chance to put the loose ball away for four.'

Tom Graveney agrees: 'Basil was an amazing player, and I shared a lot of time at the crease with him for Worcestershire and England. That innings saved us from collapse, and was a typical mixture of wonderful defence against the turning ball with punchy pulls and cuts whenever they dropped short. The pitch was broken, variable and it turned a lot, yet he was hardly ever in serious trouble.'

Best of all, Thicknesse went out of his way to congratulate him. 'I thanked him and then said: "Make sure you write it."'

The four-day Test was drawn - nothing remarkable about such a result in Pakistan, but few games have been played against such a backdrop of political unrest, which continued throughout the tour, and bizarre arrangements for crowd control, which were exclusively in the hands of the rioting students. Neither the army nor the police was present following an astonishing agreement reached by all parties, except the vainly demurring England players.

Snow says: 'We went to the British High Commission the night before, and we were wished well and assured that we would be well protected by army and police. Up to a point, this was reassuring, but we were not overjoyed at the thought of another game being played in a rioting city. Much less so when, as the function ended, we were asked to leave the room but the ex-patriates were told to stay. A couple of us played snooker, and then found out that while we were expected to play cricket, plans had been made for evacuation of the ex-pats.

'I remember our manager, the late Les Ames, being approached by student leaders in our hotel foyer to ask him about crowd control for the Test. He told them it was all taken care of by the army and the police. They told him they would not be allowed near the stadium, and the students were going to do it.'

Graveney had already been at the receiving end of a salvo of bouncers from Snow at net practice, with the fast bowler anxious to show he should not have been omitted from the first Test, and he also shared the general feeling of unease about playing a Test match in such a dangerous environment.

Ironically, it was the only riot-free Test of the three, although Snow recalls: 'There were no interruptions in play, although every day there were a couple of running fights between the two student factions who sat in adjoining blocks. A whistle would blow and they would have a punch-up which lasted until the whistle blew again. In the next Test, a week later in Karachi, the mob came on and every player except one headed for the pavilion. "Knottie" was 96 not out and didn't see them advancing behind him, so he couldn't work out why David Brown was trying to drag him off. He was asked later why he did not stay for one more ball and said, "I'd rather be 96 not out and alive than 100 and dead."'

PAKISTAN V ENGLAND (2ND TEST)

PLAYED AT DACCA STADIUM, ON 28 FEBRUARY, 1, 2, 3 MARCH 1969.
TOSS: PAKISTAN. RESULT: MATCH DRAWN.

PAKISTAN

	FIRST INNINGS		SECOND INNINGS	
Mohammad Ilyas	c Knott, b Snow	20	c Snow, b Cottam	21
Salahuddin	c Brown, b Snow	6	lbw, b Underwood	5
Saeed Ahmed*	b Brown	19	(5) c Knott, b Underwood	33
Asif Iqbal	b Brown	44	(3) b Underwood	16
Mushtaq Mohammad	c Cottam, b Snow	52	(4) c D'Oliveira, b Underwood	31
Majid Khan	c Knott, b Brown	27	not out	49
Hanif Mohammad	lbw, b Snow	8	lbw, b Underwood	8
Intikhab Alam	lbw, b Underwood	25	not out	19
Wasim Bari†	c Knott, b Cottam	14		
Niaz Ahmed	not out	16		
Pervez Sajjad	b Cottam	2		
Extras	b 4, lb 4, nb 5	13	lb 5, nb 8	13
		246	(6 wickets declared)	195

	O	M	R	W	O	M	R	W
Snow	25	5	70	4	12	7	15	0
Brown	23	8	51	3	6	1	18	0
Underwood	27	13	45	1	44	15	94	5
Cottam	27.1	6	52	2	30	17	43	1
D'Oliveira	8	1	15	0	9	2	12	0

ENGLAND

	FIRST INNINGS		SECOND INNINGS	
J.H.Edrich	c Mushtaq, b Intikhab	24	not out	12
R.M.Prideaux	c Hanif, b Pervez	4	not out	18
T.W.Graveney	b Pervez	46		
K.W.R.Fletcher	c Hanif, b Saeed	16		
M.C.Cowdrey*	lbw, b Pervez	7		
B.L.D'Oliveira	not out	114		
A.P.E.Knott†	c and b Pervez	2		
D.J.Brown	c Hanif, b Saeed	4		
J.A.Snow	c Majid, b Niaz	9		
D.L.Underwood	c Ilyas, b Mushtaq	22		
R.M.H.Cottam	c Hanif, b Saeed	4		
Extras	b 14, lb 8	22	b 2, nb 1	3
		274	(0 wickets)	33

	O	M	R	W	O	M	R	W
Niaz	10	4	20	1	2	0	2	0
Majid	11	4	15	0				
Pervez	37	8	75	4	3	2	1	0
Saeed	37.4	15	59	3	3	2	4	0
Intikhab	26	7	65	1	4	0	19	0
Mushtaq	11	3	18	1				
Asif					4	2	2	0
Hanif					3	2	1	0
Ilyas					1	0	1	0

FALL OF WICKETS
1-16, 2-39, 3-55, 4-123, 5-168, 6-184, 7-186, 8-211, 9-237, 10-246
1-8, 2-48, 3-50, 4-97, 5-129, 6-147

FALL OF WICKETS
1-17, 2-61, 3-96, 4-100, 5-113, 6-117, 7-130, 8-170, 9-236, 10-274

Umpires: Gulzar and Shujauddin

D'Oliveira could look back on the Dacca game as one which re-established him in Test cricket, and he played in England's next 26 Tests, before he bowed out at The Oval against Australia in 1972 with 43.

I only once came close to exacting retribution for that six he hit off me in 1960. I introduced him to the '99' club at New Road in a three-day game in the mid-1960s, when I bowled him out one short of the prized three figures. Bowled him out? 'I dragged one on from a mile wide, you bastard.' As usual, D'Oliveira is right. His career stands as a monument to what natural ability and fierce determination can achieve in the face of the unspeakable deprivations of his youth. His six-year Test career stands as a cricketing miracle.

NEIL FAIRBROTHER

113 in the third Texaco Trophy one-day international between England and West Indies at Lord's, 27 May 1991.

Fairbrother, in an innings which he believes would have been his last chance for England had he failed, went in to bat with the score 48 for two in the 15th over, after West Indies scored 264 for nine in their 55 overs.

Against the strongest possible West Indies attack - Ambrose, Patterson, Walsh and Marshall - Fairbrother hit a dazzling 113 out of a third-wicket partnership with Hick (86 not out) of 213 in 31 overs to win the game by seven wickets with 8.5 overs to spare. It was a record partnership for any wicket in one-day international cricket in England, and the Lancashire left-hander hit two sixes, a five and ten fours from 109 balls faced. Fear of failure often leads to just that, which is why Fairbrother attaches so much importance to his innings at Lord's in May 1991.

Neil Harvey Fairbrother was born on 9 September 1963 in Warrington and joined Lancashire in 1982, a seemingly inevitable move once his parents named him after Australia's famous left-hander. He made his debut the same year but did not bat, and his first innings, at Edgbaston in 1983, was marked with controversy. An agreed declaration time between Bob Willis and John Abrahams resulted in the Warwickshire players walking off the field on the second day, with Fairbrother on the brink of a maiden hundred. With a philosophical approach that he would need later in his career, the teenage left-hander refused to criticise what appeared to most people to be unnecessary inflexibility, and soon established himself as one of the most promising attacking batsmen in county cricket.

He was awarded his county cap in 1985, and played his first Test for England on his home ground against Pakistan in 1987. For the next six years he suffered because of being labelled as a one-day batsman - a tag hotly denied by admirers, who believed that his Championship runs for Lancashire proved otherwise. At the start of the 1993 English season, he had scored 12,414 first-class runs at an average of 41.51, with 26 hundreds including a career-best 366 at The Oval in 1990, where he scored over a hundred in each of three sessions in a day in which he scored 311.

After scoring 64 runs in his first seven Tests at an average of 8.00, he did not play in a Test between July 1990 and January 1993 in Calcutta. Although he returned from that tour of India and Sri Lanka with a modest aggregate of 155 Test runs at an average of 25.83, he played one fine innings of 83, and showed that, nearing

30 years of age, he might still establish himself in five-day cricket.

Certainly at county level, there are few more destructive batsmen, and he thought seriously about an innings in a three-day game at Chesterfield as the best one he has ever played. It was in August 1989, and he had just gone through a bad patch.

Things had not gone well that season, starting with a duck for MCC against Australia in May, and I did not get into the Texaco squad. It was a green pitch and Ian Bishop hit me on the chin just after I went in, when we were 14 for two, but our physio sorted me out and told me to get on with it.

That blow seemed to change everything, and I hit everything in the middle. I remember clattering all their seamers except Bishop, and I reckon I played as well that day as I can.

Statistics support that view. Fairbrother hit 161 from 124 deliveries and shared in a remarkable third-wicket partnership with Graeme Fowler (83) of 256 in 39 overs. He hit six sixes and 21 fours, and all but 41 of his innings came in boundaries in one of the best innings seen on the ground. Messrs Newman, Base and Jean-Jacques have memories which are different and, probably, less pleasant. The hapless trio's combined figures were 49-2-269-6, and they illustrate what a handful Fairbrother is when he cuts loose.

However, he finally decided upon his century against West Indies in the third Texaco Trophy game in 1991. In the previous two Texaco matches, his scores were four and five not out and, after being omitted from England's tour of Australia the previous year and going instead with the 'A' party to Pakistan and Sri Lanka, he badly needed a score to remain in contention for Test selection. England had already won the Trophy after exciting, narrow wins at Edgbaston by one wicket and by nine runs at Old Trafford, but a capacity Bank Holiday crowd at Lord's watched a spectacular and competitive match, with England keen to make a clean sweep, and West Indies equally anxious to salvage something from the three-match series before the first Cornhill Test started at Headingley ten days later.

'SHALL WE GO OFF FOR THE LIGHT OR NOT?' THE CRUCIAL MOMENT IN NEIL FAIRBROTHER'S DAZZLING 113 AGAINST THE WEST INDIES IN THE TEXACO TROPHY GAME AT LORD'S IN 1991.

(PATRICK EAGAR)

I chose my 113 at Lord's mainly because of the occasion, the quality of the opposition attack and, above all, the pressure I was under because it was just about my last chance for England. After failing against New Zealand the year before, I missed the senior tour of Australia, but they had a terrible time and there were several changes for the Texaco squad against the West Indies. Graeme Hick had just qualified for England, and they brought in Mark Ramprakash and me for the three Texaco games.

It was really my last throw of the dice at Lord's, because I did nothing in the first two games. What helped was an injury to Allan Lamb, which meant I was put up to number four. That was important, because all you can ask for when you play is a chance to bat for a reasonable period. The game before, at Old Trafford, I got in with only a couple of overs to go, and while I waited to go in at Lord's, all I could think of was that I wanted to get out in the middle.

He may not have known his exact one-day record for England while he waited on the players' balcony, but 241 runs from ten completed innings could only be considered a moderate return. Waiting to go in to bat is more daunting on some grounds than others, with Lord's high on any list of nerve-stretchers. Does a batsman sit on the balcony, in which case he sees and hears every action and word of the biggest crowd that can be accommodated in any English ground, or does he prowl around in the cavernous dressing-room, peering at the action through a narrow doorway or perhaps following the television pictures?

I love the place, and the Bank Holiday crowd was one of two extra-special reasons for me that day. The other one was the opening of the Compton-Edrich Stands at the Nursery End during lunch. What a reception Denis got as he walked around the ground, and it made you realise what a player he was and what a great ground he played a lot of his cricket on.

Logie's 82 off 99 balls helped his side to 264 but, on what was a good pitch, England had a chance if they could make a sound start and keep wickets in hand. It was not to be, with Gooch brilliantly run out by Hooper and Atherton caught by Dujon off Marshall. So Fairbrother had got his wish - an ideal opportunity to fashion a big innings. A target of 214 in 40 overs is often routine in a 40-over Sunday League game, but it is not so easy against the West Indies.

It turned out to be my best day for England. Graeme and I got away with a bit at the start but, once we clicked, we seemed to inspire each other to play as we do for our counties. That is the hardest thing to do for England - and I should know, because I tried it in my first few Tests, but the extra quality in bowling meant I often got out to silly-looking strokes. The secret is to adapt your game to each step-up in class, and I can look back on that day at Lord's and say that was the turning point for me. I had passed 50 only twice in 13 innings in one-day internationals, so it really was a huge breakthrough.

We got into their support bowlers [Hooper and Simmons went for 57 from 37 balls], and in the end we ran away with the game. Another thing which pleased me a lot was when we refused an offer of bad light. We were going well anyway, but it would have been rough on the crowd if we had come off, so we took the gamble of staying on, even though at the time we were ahead of the run-rate. The only disappointment was that I holed out when we wanted only four to win, but I got the Man of the Match award, and I knew I was back in the thoughts of the selectors. I know I did not get into the Tests, but it was that knock which took me to the World Cup in Australia where I had several good innings. I am sure I would not have gone if I had failed at Lord's, but who knows?

Fairbrother's fifty came off 54 balls and, as he reached three figures off an additional 49 deliveries, the sun popped out to acknowledge his arrival on the lower reaches of the steep climb to the Test match summit.

I wrote at the time: 'Fairbrother hit Patterson for 2-6-2-4 before he was caught. His innings won the game, the Man of the Match award, and the hearts of the crowd, who gave him a rare standing ovation as he walked off. Only an innings of such brilliance could deflect media hype from Hick's 86 off 102 balls.' *Wisden Cricket Monthly* described the Lancastrian as 'a sunny, bright-eyed cricketer, and the majority must hope that the conviction in high places that he is essentially a limited-overs batsman will soon die the death.' It did not but, if Fairbrother does finally establish himself in official Test cricket, he will not be the first to arrive after several false starts.

As for the decision to refuse the offer of the light, Fairbrother explained to his first major press conference that when he looked to the dressing-room, he got 'the thumbs up', but was not certain what the gesture meant.

A no-nonsense, straightforward character, Fairbrother is a born crowd-pleaser, but has he been treated unfairly by those who insist on pigeon-holing him as a one-day cricketer? Durham captain David Graveney believes he has, although not without qualification. 'A first-class career average of 40 tells me that that player deserves a chance at Test level. It is the first cut-off point which separates an above average batsman from the rest. It does not mean that he will be successful for England, but it tells me that he has the ability to play better and longer innings than the ordinary county batsman.

'As for Neil, he is very difficult to contain, because he has now learned to play leg-side. When he started, he used to make a bit of room and smash away on the off-side, usually square of cover. He still does that, which means the face of his bat is open a bit more often than is ideal. He has shown he can make big hundreds, but I wish he would play a bit more towards mid-off and mid-on. All left-handers have problems around their off stump, but Neil seems to want to play everything, whereas someone like John Edrich would just play for his stumps, and if the ball was doing too much to hit the wicket, he would not be drawn into following it. It can look as though the batsman is playing and missing a lot - and sometimes by miles - but it makes the bowler alter his line.

'I think Neil deserves a run in the England side - after all, nine of his first ten Tests came in five different series, with the other game against Sri Lanka. At county level, he seems to want to score off every ball, and you cannot do that in five-day cricket - the quality of the bowling will not allow it.'

Fairbrother is now around the halfway stage of what, so far, has been a spectacular career at county level. Test cricket needs players like him as much as he wants to play for England. Would I want him to play an innings of fifty for my life? Only if I wanted to know my fate sooner rather than later, and it would be a toss-up who would be called into action first, the firing squad or the gaoler with the key to the door.

ENGLAND V WEST INDIES (TEXACO TROPHY)

PLAYED AT LORD'S, LONDON, ON 27 MAY 1991.
TOSS: ENGLAND. RESULT: ENGLAND WON BY SEVEN WICKETS.

WEST INDIES

P.V.Simmons	c Russell, b DeFreitas	5
P.J.L.Dujon†	b Lawrence	0
R.B.Richardson	c DeFreitas, b Illingworth	41
B.C.Lara	c and b Illingworth	23
I.V.A.Richards*	c Illingworth, b DeFreitas	37
A.L.Logie	c and b Gooch	82
C.L.Hooper	c Fairbrother, b Lawrence	26
M.D.Marshall	c DeFreitas, b Lawrence	13
C.E.L.Ambrose	not out	
C.A.Walsh	lbw, b Lawrence	0
B.P.Patterson	not out	2
Extras	b 1, lb 9, w 14, nb 5	29
	(55 overs, 9 wickets)	264

	O	M	R	W
Lawrence	11	1	67	4
DeFreitas	11	1	26	2
Reeve	11	1	43	0
Illingworth	11	1	53	2
Pringle	9	0	56	0
Gooch	2	0	9	1

FALL OF WICKETS
1-8, 2-8, 3-71, 4-91, 5-164, 6-227, 7-241, 8-258, 9-258

ENGLAND

G.A.Gooch*	run out	11
M.A.Atherton	c Dujon, b Marshall	25
G.A.Hick	not out	86
N.H.Fairbrother	c Richards, b Patterson	113
M.R.Ramprakash	not out	0
D.A.Reeve		
D.R.Pringle		
R.C.Russell†	did not bat	
P.A.J.DeFreitas		
R.K.Illingworth		
D.V.Lawrence		
Extras	b 4, lb 12, w 10, nb 4	30
	(46.1 overs, 3 wickets)	265

	O	M	R	W
Ambrose	8	0	31	0
Patterson	10	0	62	1
Marshall	11	1	9	1
Walsh	11	1	50	0
Hooper	4.1	0	36	0
Simmons	2	0	21	0

FALL OF WICKETS
1-28, 2-48, 3-261

Umpires: M.J.Kitchen and D.R.Shepherd

MIKE GATTING

207 on the second and third days of the fourth Test between India and England at Madras, 14 and 15 January 1985.

Gatting's double century, out of England's 652 for seven declared, finally launched a career for England that had stuttered for 31 Tests prior to the first Test of that series, in Bombay. In 52 innings, played in 12 different series, he scored 1144 runs at an average of 24.83, and he managed to pass fifty on nine occasions, with a highest score of 81. With so many opportunities before the age of 27, he was fortunate to be chosen to tour India, and has the captain, David Gower, to thank for pressing for his inclusion. His next 52 innings included the notorious Faisalabad Test in 1987, by the end of which stormy game he had increased his aggregate by 2529 runs, scored at an average of 58.81, including nine hundreds and nine other scores over fifty.

His 207 in Madras was the start of the most extraordinary metamorphosis of any post-war England batsman, and was an overdue justification of the England selectors' faith in him. The innings helped England to beat India by nine wickets and take a 2-1 lead in the series, which they won by drawing the fifth Test in Kanpur. He and Graeme Fowler became the first pair to score double hundreds for England in the same innings, and it was only the sixth time in all Test cricket. The tour provided England with what is still only their second victorious series in nine post-war tours of India.

Michael William Gatting, OBE, was born on 6 June 1957 in Kingsbury, Middlesex, and played club cricket with Brondesbury before joining Middlesex in 1975. He made his debut the same year, was capped in 1977 and appointed club captain in 1983, following a public trial, together with John Emburey and Phil Edmonds, in Mike Brearley's final match the previous year at New Road, Worcester. He succeeded Gower as England captain in 1986, and led his country 23 times before the captaincy was taken away from

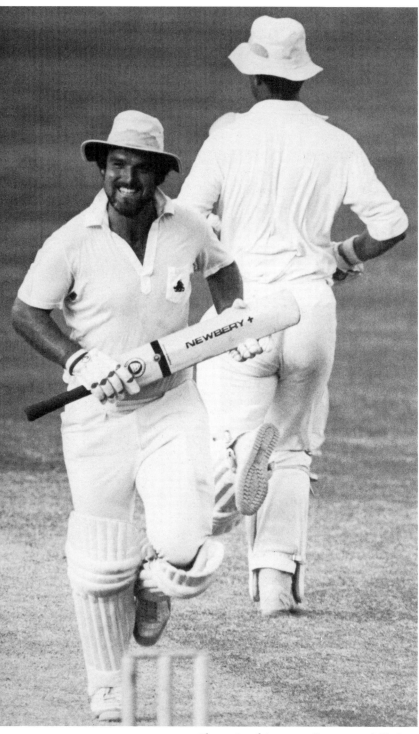

ONE OF 207 REASONS FOR
MIKE GATTING TO SMILE IN
MADRAS 1985.
(ALLSPORT/ADRIAN
MURRELL)

him three years later. One of only three England captains to retain the Ashes in Australia, his two wins in the 1986-87 tour were the only ones while he was in charge - a surprisingly poor record for such a positive cricketer.

Disillusioned with the English establishment after he lost the captaincy, he opted out of Test cricket for what he thought would be for five years by leading an English side to South Africa in 1990. When the ban was halved, he was one of three cricketers from that tour - John Emburey and Paul Jarvis were the other two - to be chosen for the trip to India and Sri Lanka in the first part of 1993, and a fourth, Neil Foster, played in the second Ashes Test of that summer. After scoring 81 in the first Test in Calcutta, he had a moderate tour, although his 266 runs from eight innings took him past 4000 Test runs. At the beginning of his 11th season in charge of Middlesex, his career record was a total of 28,982 runs at an average of 49.96 - the highest of any batsman qualified for England, except for Graeme Hick.

A bustling, aggressive cricketer, Gatting has long been one of the best players of slow bowling in county cricket, and has a splendid captaincy record for Middlesex, leading them to two Championships, two Benson and Hedges Cup wins, two NatWest Trophy successes and one Sunday League title. He is a good motivator and a man who possesses tremendous guts, both mental and physical. Brian Johnston captured the Gatting public image perfectly when he said: 'When he walks out to the wicket you can see his determination. He seems shorter than his 5ft 10in and, with his short, now greying beard, and his stocky, chunky figure, he looks every inch an Elizabethan sailor, out to repel an invader. You know, whatever happens, that he will fight and not be intimidated.' Broadcaster Don Mosey chooses a different military analogy. 'In military terms, Gatting would be the sergeant-major who had taken over the company when its officers had been wiped out.'

He will forever be tarred with the Shakoor Rana brush, as shown when the first recommendation from the newly appointed Ted Dexter, as chairman of the England selectors in 1989, that Gatting be re-appointed as England captain, was vetoed at Lord's, with the Faisalabad affair quoted as one of the reasons.

As Tom Graveney says, 'Lord's love a captain who speaks his mind, until he does so to them.' A comment which might well be echoed by Ray Illingworth, Ian Botham and Brian Close. It is a surprising paradox that such a patently honest cricketer should have his career so affected by controversy - perhaps because he cannot understand why unswerving loyalty is easier for him to give than for others to return.

If Gatting were to choose a hundred as 'the innings of my life', he had 72 from which to choose at the end of the ill-fated tour of India and Sri Lanka, and he thought long and hard before settling for his double hundred in Madras.

> If I had to pick my best innings for Middlesex, it would be my 119 not out at Derby in 1990. It was a dodgy pitch, and I got my runs out of our first innings total of 209. We lost by 171 after rain got under the covers over the weekend, and that was as good an innings I have ever played under such conditions.

Gatting might have said, but did not, that the home side were docked 25 points by the Test & County Cricket Board's pitch sub-committee for 'a pitch which was clearly unsuitable for first-class cricket'. After a match which relegated Derbyshire from eighth in the table to 12th, and extinguished all hopes of prize money, their chairman, Chris Middleton, wrote to Middlesex thanking Gatting for his attitude in an embarrassing situation for the home county.

So it was back to Madras for Gatting:

> It was one of those lovely matches in which everything went as planned, except that we didn't win the toss. After we'd bowled them out for 272, we had about 90 minutes' batting on the first day, and before we started our innings, we decided that we'd try to bat two days in the hope of winning by an innings.

Fowler and Tim Robinson prepared the way with an opening stand of 178, before Gatting strode to the middle to begin a second-wicket partnership with Fowler which was to add a record 241. He had the confidence created by his elusive first Test hundred in the first Test in Bombay - a curio there was that Pat Pocock became only the second man to play

NO NEED TO RUN. MURDER IN MADRAS.

(ALLSPORT/ADRIAN MURRELL)

for England with two generations of the same family. Pocock played with Colin and Christopher Cowdrey, while the other man to match this achievement was Wilfred Rhodes, who played with Fred and Maurice Tate.

The gregarious Cowdrey made his verbal mark on the first day in Gatting's chosen match at Madras. Having bowled Azharuddin and brought Kapil Dev to the crease for his comeback innings after being dropped for disciplinary reasons, Gower asked Cowdrey: 'Would you like "Gatt" wider at slip?' The reply is now a part of folklore: 'If he gets any wider, he'll burst.'

Gatting has a simple attitude towards spin bowlers - he does not think they should be allowed to bowl and, because he punishes them so heavily, he cannot understand why any other batsman has problems against the twirly stuff. Thanks to his dominant innings, the contrasting spin of Sivaramakrishnan (leg-breaks) and the finger spin of Yadav and Shastri had final combined figures of 109-17-364-3, and nothing gave Gatting more pleasure than the way he raced through the 190s.

Slow left-arm bowler Shastri switched to over the wicket in an attempt to stop the Gatting rush, and bowled a negative line by pitching the ball outside leg-stump to seven on-side fielders. This tactic is not the easiest to combat, particularly when a batsman is approaching such an important milestone as a Test double hundred.

What added to the challenge was that the chairman of the selectors, Peter May, was watching from the members' stand and, rightly or wrongly, the impression was that May was not one of Gatting's most ardent admirers, nor had he been wholly in favour of his selection for the tour.

What is also likely is that May is not a great fan of the reverse sweep, so his thoughts can be imagined when Gatting proceeded to score 12 runs in one over, with a six over fine-leg, followed by two successive back-hand sweeps for two and four to third man. The perfect ending to the interlude would have been for another such piece of improvisation to bring up the double hundred, but that came in more orthodox fashion with a back-foot cover drive for four off Armanath.

Even allowing for Fowler needing to be more circumspect as an opener, establishing the platform from which Gatting and the others could play freely, the statistics of the historic double hundreds reveal the plundering nature of the Gatting innings. Fowler hit 102 in boundaries and Gatting 98, but whereas the opener batted for 565 minutes and faced 409 deliveries, Gatting was at the crease for an hour less and faced 308 balls - 101 fewer.

My report in the *Birmingham Post* said: 'England positively squashed India's bowlers into the Chepauk dust and then, with Fowler and Gatting scoring double hundreds, they trampled all over them. If all the records broken, major and minor, were listed, the reader would soon become uninterested, as did Sunil Gavaskar, who did not appear after lunch because of "an allergy of palms". Perhaps some local clairvoyant had read them for him. The accelerator pressure was increased all day with 75 coming off 26 overs before lunch, 102 in 24 in mid-afternoon, and 141 off the last 30 overs.'

England ended the third day 339 in the lead, in a commanding position they were unlikely to match again until, as one local scribe said, 'the Ganges flows the other way.' Thanks to Neil Foster taking five for 59 in the second innings, to give him match figures of 11 for 163, England won during the last 20 overs on the final day, thus underlining the importance of the pace of Gatting's innings.

I also wrote of how well Gatting looked after the tiring Fowler when he went in to bat. 'Fowler had to bathe his eyes during every interval because of the accumulation of sweat and dirt, and he also paid tribute to both his partners for the way they helped him maintain concentration. Gatting, in particular, clucked over him between overs like a mother hen.'

Nobody watching could have failed to be impressed, but it turned out that one particular television viewer that day will never forget what he saw. It was an old-fashioned Test in that there was a rest day and, together with the then cricket correspondent of the *Guardian* and current editor of *Wisden*, Matthew Engel, I visited the magnificent Madras racecourse, where they were holding evening bloodstock sales.

We met an Anglo-Indian jockey who, every time we spoke about horses, wanted to talk about cricket. He was both knowledgeable and passionate about the game, and could hardly contain his admiration for the flair and sheer cheek of Gatting the day before, who he had watched as soon as he had finished riding work. 'Those reverse sweeps. Marvellous! To be able to do it is one thing. To have the nerve to do it in a Test is another, but fancy doing it when you are nearing a double hundred. It's the greatest thing I've ever seen in cricket.'

Messrs Engel and Bannister, in a vain attempt to get him talking about the horses, asked him what would be the equivalent of the reverse sweep in jockeyship. His reply is one of my favourite memories of the magical sub-continent. He took our sales card, and pointed out the names of one trainer and one owner.

INDIA V ENGLAND (4TH TEST)

PLAYED AT CHIDAMBARAM STADIUM, CHEPAUK, MADRAS, ON 13, 14, 15, 17, 18 JANUARY 1985.
TOSS: INDIA. RESULT: ENGLAND WON BY NINE WICKETS.

INDIA

	FIRST INNINGS		SECOND INNINGS	
S.M.Gavaskar*	b Foster	17	c Gatting, b Foster	3
K.Srikkanth	c Downton, b Cowans	0	c Cowdrey, b Foster	16
D.B.Vengsarkar	c Lamb, b Foster	17	c Downton, b Foster	2
M.Amarnath	c Downton, b Foster	78	c Cowans, b Foster	95
M.Azharuddin	b Cowdrey	48	c Gower, b Pocock	105
R.J.Shastri	c Downton, b Foster	2	c Cowdrey, b Edmonds	33
Kapil Dev	c Cowans, b Cowdrey	53	c Gatting, b Cowans	49
S.M.H.Kirmani†	not out	30	c Lamb, b Edmonds	75
N.S.Yadav	b Foster	2	(10) c Downton, b Cowans	5
L.Sivaramakrishnan	c Cowdrey, b Foster	13	(9) lbw, b Foster	5
C.Sharma	c Lamb, b Cowans	5	not out	17
Extras	lb 3, nb 4	7	b 1, lb 4, nb 2	7
		272		412

	O	M	R	W	O	M	R	W
Cowans	12.5	3	39	2	15	1	73	2
Foster	23	2	104	6	28	8	59	5
Edmonds	6	1	33	0	41.5	13	119	2
Cowdrey	19	1	65	2	5	0	26	0
Pocock	7	1	28	0	33	8	130	1

FALL OF WICKETS
1-17, 2-17, 3-45, 4-155, 5-167, 6-167, 7-241, 8-243, 9-263, 10-272
1-7, 2-19, 3-22, 4-212, 5-259, 6-259, 7-341, 8-350, 9-361, 10-412

Umpires: M.Y.Gupte and V.K.Ramaswamy

ENGLAND

	FIRST INNINGS		SECOND INNINGS	
G.Fowler	c Kirmani, b Kapil Dev	201	c Kirmani, b Sivaramakrishnan	2
R.T.Robinson	c Kirmani, b Sivaramakrishnan	74	not out	21
M.W.Gatting	c sub (G.Sharma), b Shastri	207	not out	10
A.J.Lamb	b Amarnath	62		
P.H.Edmonds	lbw, b Shastri	36		
N.A.Foster	b Amarnath	5		
D.I.Gower*	b Kapil Dev	18		
C.S.Cowdrey	not out	3		
P.R.Downton†	not out	3		
P.I.Pocock	} did not bat			
N.G.Cowans				
Extras	b 7, lb 19, nb 17	43	lb 1, w 1	2
	(7 wickets declared)	652	(1 wicket)	35

	O	M	R	W	O	M	R	W
Kapil Dev	36	5	131	2	3	0	21	0
Sharma	18	0	95	0				
Sivaramakrishnan	44	6	145	1	4	0	12	1
Yadav	23	4	76	0				
Shastri	42	7	143	2	1	0	2	0
Amarnath	12	1	36	2				

FALL OF WICKETS
1-178, 2-419, 3-563, 4-599, 5-604, 6-640, 7-646
1-7

'They are difficult men to ride for, because they never think a jockey should make a mistake. So imagine I am riding one of his horses [a flick of a pencil against the trainer] owned by him [another tick] in the Madras Derby. Then imagine I am in a wall of horses in the final furlong all riding a desperate finish and, suddenly, *I switch to side-saddle.*'

Marvellous and evocative imagery! As is this assessment of Gatting the man, as well as the cricketer, from Don Mosey. 'The respect he received from his players came from his own determination as an unflinching batsman, a fielder who would stand as close as he ever asked anyone else to do, and for appreciation that he was a professional's professional.' I suspect that, if he could choose a cricketing epitaph, it would be 'He was honest'. Nobody is ever in doubt where he stands with Michael William Gatting, particularly those three Indian spinners who suffered in Madras in 'the innings of my life'.

SUNIL GAVASKAR

57 on the second and third days of the second Test between England and India at Old Trafford, 6 and 7 August 1971.

In the tourists' first innings, Sunil Gavaskar made 57 before he was fifth out with the score then 104. It was his ninth half-century in 11 Test innings, beginning with his sensational series in the West Indies a few months earlier in which he scored 774 runs in five completed innings. The Old Trafford pitch was green, with overhead conditions helping swing and, without Gavaskar's masterly resistance on the third day when batting conditions were at their most difficult, it is unlikely that India would have saved the follow-on, which they eventually managed with their eight-wicket pair together.

Sunil Manohar Gavaskar was born in Bombay on 10 July 1949. He was educated at St Xavier's High School and Bombay University, where the appetite for batting, which was to take him to the then record aggregate of 10,122 Test runs soon surfaced. In 1970, the year before his debut for India, he scored 327 for his university - a signpost towards a first-class career that was to bring him more runs (25,834) than any other Indian batsman.

He played for his country a record 125 times, and captained them on 47 occasions - also a record. Technically a delight to watch, Gavaskar charmed his way into history with 34 Test hundreds and 81 in all. The true test of an international record is the ratio of innings per hundred, and Gavaskar's one in 6.26 brackets him with Greg Chappell, Neil Harvey and Garry Sobers among the most successful post-war batsmen - a distinguished quartet whose record is bettered only by Everton Weekes (one in 5.4).

Known as 'The Little Master' - except to opposing bowlers, perhaps - he is the only batsman ever to score over 1000 Test runs in a calendar year four times, three times in the four years between 1976 and 1979. His 221 at The Oval in 1979 is his best-remembered innings in England. It took India close to a record victory - needing 438 to win in a minimum of 498 minutes, he was fourth out at 389, half an hour before the end of a game which saw India nine runs short with two wickets in hand.

Surely this was the innings of his life? And, if not, what about one from his first series in the West Indies, a few months earlier, when his scores were 65, 67*, 116, 64*, 1, 117*, 124 and 220? His performances helped India to win a series in the Caribbean for the first time - an astonishing performance from a 21-year-old.

I approached him for his choice in December 1992 in South Africa, where we worked together for the television coverage of his country's historic first tour of the Republic. He asked for a few days to consider his options, and our commentary team, including Allan Lamb and Robin Jackman, had a 'fun' sweep on the final choice. We were all wrong - and by miles.

Almost apologetically he took me to one side between microphone stints at Newlands and said:

I have thought about all my big innings, and some of them were special. But you asked me to name one which, now that I have retired, I can look back on and say 'that is the one I remember with the most satisfaction'. I have therefore picked my 11th Test innings - it was 57 at Old Trafford in the second Test in 1971.

The hundreds against the West Indies beforehand were on good pitches against a reasonable attack, but with no outright pace. I have always felt that batting against genuinely quick bowling is the supreme examination of a batsman.

So was it John Snow, England's best fast bowler at the time? 'No, he was not playing. Remember, he was suspended for charging me to the ground when I was batting in the first Test at Lord's, two weeks earlier.'

Then who and what was the reason for what must rank as the most astounding choice in this book?

John Price of Middlesex bowled me the fastest couple of spells I ever faced in Test cricket. The pitch was so green that, looking at it from the players' balcony before the start of play, you couldn't pick it out from the rest of the square. A bowler with a strong body action like Price was always going to be a handful, particularly as the pitch was livened up on several occasions on the first two days by rain. We had them in trouble on the first day, after Abid Ali got John Jameson, John Edrich, Keith Fletcher and Basil D'Oliveira for 28 between them, and they were 41 for four and 116 for five.

GAVASKAR'S FOOTWORK MAKES THIS OFF-DRIVE. LIKE MANY OVERSEAS PLAYERS, HIS INITIAL MOVEMENT WAS BACK, BUT HE WAS STILL ABLE TO THROW THE WEIGHT FORWARD INTO THE SHOT. (HULTON-DEUTSCH COLLECTION)

Then Ray Illingworth, Peter Lever and Alan Knott took advantage of a wet ball and, from 219 for seven at the end of the first day, they got to 386. Ashok Mankad and I were both four not out at the end of the second day, but before I talk about my 57 on the third day, let me give you the background about a superstition of mine which certainly did not help.

When I made my debut in Trinidad, I scored 65 and 67 not out, and I did not wear a sweater in either innings. Nor did I for the rest of that series so, by the time we got to Lord's in the third week in July for the first Test, I decided that I would not risk changing my luck until I failed. I am not unduly superstitious but, like many cricketers, when I am in a good run of form, I try to repeat everything in my preparation for an innings.

I got four and 53 at Lord's, so not only had I not failed in my first six Tests, but India had not lost one of them, so whatever the weather at Old Trafford, I was certainly not going to risk changing the luck by batting in a sweater.

In the field was different, and it was so cold and gloomy on the first two days in the second Test that I wore two sweaters while we fielded. I hoped that the Saturday morning would be brighter and warmer, but as Ashok and I walked to the middle, I knew differently. I had a short-sleeved silk shirt on, and my arms were a mass of goose-pimples, and I was frozen. It was typical Manchester weather - a biting wind and just a hint of drizzle in the air, but neither that nor the light were bad enough to halt play.

I thought long and hard about sending for a sweater as John Price and Peter Lever marked out their run-ups, but decided to stick to my game-plan.

Gavaskar then proceeded to fight for his batting life against Price in particular, although Lever was sharp enough at the other end. Think of it: he was just 22 years old, 5ft 4¾ in tall, he wore no helmet and was batting in a temperature at least 25 degrees cooler than his home city of Bombay. Problems enough there without Price suddenly clicking into a top gear which generated the fastest bowling Gavaskar had ever faced, before or since.

'I faced all the quicks in my career, but the only one who came close to Price that day was Jeff Thomson in Perth in December 1977. That pitch was quicker anyway, but Thomson bowled faster at me than he ever did before.'

The Test Gavaskar refers to was the second of a magnificent high-scoring series in which there was not a drawn game, and Australia finally edged home 3-2 in Adelaide when, set 493 to win, India scored 445 - the second highest fourth-innings total in Test cricket.

Judgement of raw pace can only be subjective, but as Gavaskar says:

I was only 22 and my reflexes were therefore at their sharpest. I know that Price was not considered an out-and-out fast bowler, but that day everything clicked into place. Real speed comes from rhythm and, to bowlers with strong actions like Price, that does not always come easily. But that day, he found it, and I was at full stretch against him. As often happens, he did not take any of the early wickets to go - Lever took three and Richard Hutton one, but Price helped them by unsettling everyone.

Price's figures were relatively unspectacular, 22-7-44-2, but *Wisden* had this to say of his bowling: 'Although Lever gained the best bowling figures, Price had one superbly hostile spell which brought him Gavaskar's wicket. He showed remarkable pace which belied his age of 34.' Gavaskar says:

In the end I was caught by Knott off him, but before that I reckon I played and missed only a couple of times and got away with one top edge over slips for four. It was an innings I look back on with more pride than any other, simply because of the quality and speed of Price's bowling, and the conditions. While I was batting, I remember what an exhilarating experience I found it to have to move my feet so quickly into line. All my hard work in practice paid off, and I actually began to feel good about batting, although I was keen for Price to be rested.

Old Trafford has one more sartorial memory, which also had superstitious connotations for Gavaskar.

I got a hundred on the next tour in 1974, and split my trousers about halfway through the innings. I remember coming off at tea and was changing into another pair when my skipper, Ajit Wadekar, asked me what I was doing. When I showed him the split pair, he told me: 'I don't care about that. Put them back on and you don't change them until you are out.'

I did as he said, and will always remember Tony Greig's remark from short leg as I took guard after the interval. 'Nice bit of air-conditioning Sunil.'

Developing the theme of superstition, Gavaskar recalls two incidents in his first series in the West Indies.

My first runs in Test cricket were actually two leg-byes off Vanburn Holder but, when there was no signal, my first thought was of relief that I could not now bag a pair. Garry Sobers smiled at my luck, and when he scored 29 and a duck, followed by four in the first innings of the next Test in Georgetown, he decided to treat me as a lucky mascot. I had got my first hundred at the Bourda, so before he batted in the second innings, he touched me for luck.

He scored 108 not out, and he touched me before every other innings in the series. Something worked for him - he scored 178 and nine in Barbados and 132 in Trinidad.

How long did his own sweaterless superstition last? 'Believe it or not, it was four years before I wore one when I batted - and it was my second tour of England that convinced me that warmth was more important.'

Gavaskar's aggregate of Test runs was overtaken by Allan Border in early 1993, but his place in the roll-call of great batsmen is safe. Whatever he does, he does to the best of his considerable ability, so it is no surprise that he has established himself in the media world, both in journalism and television commentary.

I worked with him for the BBC during India's tour of England in 1990, and his slight accent confused one letter-writer who asked for the name of 'your new commentator, who I like very much. His accent sounds Irish to me. Am I right?' For the rest of the summer, he was known as Sean O'Gavaskar. The luck of the Irish? Of all batsmen in history, he needed it least, but if ever the leprechauns had smiled on him, Border would never have caught him.

ENGLAND V INDIA (2ND TEST)

PLAYED AT OLD TRAFFORD, MANCHESTER, ON 5, 6, 7, 9, 10 (NO PLAY) AUGUST 1971.
TOSS: ENGLAND. RESULT: MATCH DRAWN.

ENGLAND

	FIRST INNINGS		SECOND INNINGS	
B.W.Luckhurst	c Viswanath, b Bedi	78	st Engineer, b Solkar	101
J.A.Jameson	c Gavaskar, b Abid Ali	15	run out	28
J.H.Edrich	c Engineer, b Abid Ali	0	b Bedi	59
K.W.R.Fletcher	lbw, b Abid Ali	1	not out	28
B.L.D'Oliveira	c Gavaskar, b Abid Ali	12	not out	23
A.P.E.Knott†	b Venkataraghavan	41		
R.Illingworth*	c Gavaskar, b Venkataraghavan	107		
R.A.Hutton	c and b Venkataraghavan	15		
P.Lever	not out	88		
N.Gifford	c Engineer, b Solkar	8		
J.S.E.Price	run out	0		
Extras	b 6, lb 12, w 1, nb 2	21	lb 5, nb 1	6
		386	(3 wickets declared)	245

	O	M	R	W	O	M	R	W
Abid Ali	32.4	5	64	4	26	2	95	0
Solkar	21	5	46	1	5	0	23	1
Chandrasekhar	30	6	90	0	2	0	5	0
Bedi	40	10	72	1	5	0	21	1
Venkataraghavan	35	9	89	3	16	3	58	0
Gavaskar	2	0	4	0	12	3	37	0

FALL OF WICKETS
1-21, 2-21, 3-25, 4-41, 5-116, 6-168, 7-187, 8-355, 9-384, 10-386
1-44, 2-167, 3-212

INDIA

	FIRST INNINGS		SECOND INNINGS	
A.V.Mankad	c Knott, b Lever	8	b Price	7
S.M.Gavaskar	c Knott, b Price	57	c Knott, b Hutton	24
A.L.Wadekar*	c Knott, b Hutton	12	b Price	9
D.N.Sardesai	b Lever	14	not out	13
G.R.Viswanath	b Lever	10	not out	8
F.M.Engineer†	c Edrich, b Lever	22		
E.D.Solkar	c Hutton, b D'Oliveira	50		
S.Abid Ali	b D'Oliveira	0		
S.Venkataraghavan	c Knott, b Lever	20		
B.S.Bedi	b Price	8		
B.S.Chandrasekhar	not out	4		
Extras	b 1, lb 4, nb 2	7	lb 2, nb 2	4
		212	(3 wickets)	65

	O	M	R	W	O	M	R	W
Price	22	7	44	2	10	3	30	2
Lever	26	4	70	5	7	3	14	0
D'Oliveira	24	11	40	2	3	2	1	0
Hutton	14	3	35	1	7	1	16	1
Illingworth	7	2	16	0				

FALL OF WICKETS
1-19, 2-52, 3-90, 4-103, 5-104, 6-163, 7-164, 8-194, 9-200, 10-212
1-9, 2-22, 3-50

Umpires: A.E.Fagg and T.W.Spencer

GRAHAM GOOCH

154* on the third and fourth days of the first Test between England and West Indies at Headingley, 8 and 9 June 1991.

Graham Gooch carried his bat for a magnificent unbeaten 154 under conditions in which only three other batsmen in the match passed fifty. The hazards of a typically variable Headingley pitch, off which the ball seamed throughout the game, were complicated still further by overhead conditions. The heavy cloud cover and damp atmosphere helped the ball to swing. Gooch's performance, over 7½ hours of unblinking concentration, is generally acknowledged as being one of the finest innings ever played against an attack of the quality of Ambrose, Patterson, Walsh and Marshall. He scored nearly two-thirds of England's second innings total of 252 and, as well as making him only the second England batsman after Hutton to carry his bat in a Test match in England, his innings also completed a full set of hundreds on each of England's six international grounds.

Rarely can an innings be said to have won a Test match, but, without it, England would probably have lost a game in which they finally triumphed by 115 runs. Not only did the performance enhance an already growing reputation as a Test captain who thrived on responsibility, it inspired his players to halve a series against the West Indies for the first time for 17 years in eight attempts. It must be acknowledged as the best single-handed batting performance by an England captain since the Second World War.

Graham Alan Gooch was born on 23 July 1953 in Leytonstone. After a secondary school education at Norlington School in Leyton, he joined his home county Essex in 1974, following an apprenticeship as a toolmaker, and his first-class career is a typical example of a slow development by a young English professional. He bagged a pair on debut for Essex and England and, even when he became a regular member of the Essex side, he averaged over 40 only once in his first four seasons. A three-year gap between his second and third England caps ended at Lord's in 1978 against Pakistan, but three fifties in his first 21 Test innings gave no hint of a career that would bring his 100th Test appearance in Calcutta in January 1993.

Never a keen tourist, Gooch opted out of official Test cricket to lead the first 'rebel' England tour of South Africa in 1982. But for the subsequent three-year ban, which cost him the chance of 32 more caps, his Test aggregate of 7620 by the start of the 1993 English season would probably have been much higher.

Some men slip easily into captaincy. Others, like Bob Willis before Gooch, are more reluctant because of fears about the effect it might have on their performances. Such a reason was advanced by Gooch when he resigned after his first two years of captaincy with Essex. However, there were no such reservations when the England selectors turned to him as fourth choice to lead England against the West Indies in 1988. Although the advent of Ted Dexter as chairman of the England selectors meant he was deposed against Australia the following year, he was given a second chance and responded in a manner no other England batsman has ever done when saddled with the extra responsibility.

From the age of 35 onwards, the output of most batsmen declines, but Gooch is a notable exception. His career average has improved from 43 to 48, and a third of his 100 hundreds (whatever the International Cricket Council said in January and July 1993 about the validity of a century he scored in South Africa in 1982) have come between the end of the 1988 English season and the beginning of the 1993 summer.

For England, the improvement is even more startling. When he returned from India in March 1993, his overall Test record revealed that, as captain in 30 Tests, he had scored 3100 at an average of 60.78, compared with 4520 scored before he became captain at an average of 35.87. An even more telling statistic is that, as captain, he passed fifty 24 times in 53 innings, and converted nine innings into hundreds. Before, he passed fifty 34 times in 130 innings, and converted eight into three figures.

No other man has shouldered the burdens of international captaincy so successfully, and it reflects a dedication to the ethos of hard work and physical effort perhaps never known before in an England captain. Critics will say that this quality is occasionally a weakness as well as a strength but, not having sought the captaincy, it came to him twice by default, with English Test cricket in disarray. The Indian tour was a self-confessed disaster, but that should not detract from his achievements as batsman and captain in the previous 3½ years.

For a man with such pride in performance, and such a patriot, it seemed inevitable that he would choose as 'the innings of my life' one of several great efforts against the West Indies, perhaps even his first hundred for England at Lord's against Clive Lloyd's side in his 36th innings in his 22nd Test match. Not so.

The most enjoyable innings I ever played was for Essex at Derby in September 1992. It was our 21st Championship game in our 22-match programme and, although we really clinched the title the previous game at Chelmsford against Hampshire, the game against Derbyshire provided one of the most amazing turnarounds I have ever known. Ian Bishop bowled us out for 96, and we were finally left to score 440 to win in two days. Not on was it?

Certainly they did not think so when we were 85 for three before lunch on the third day. John Stephenson and Nadeem Shahid started a recovery, and I took over at number six. We lost only one wicket on the last day, and they bowled 183 overs at us in total, so we didn't fluke it by slogging. That counts as my favourite innings, but the innings of my life - that is different. I have to choose one for England because the quality of the bowling is better and the match situation concerned was just about the most important I have known.

Every Test match is important, but Headingley in 1991 was extra-special. We got so close to beating them the previous year in the West Indies when we looked like going 2-0 up in Trinidad but ended up losing 2-1. I broke my hand and missed the last two games in Barbados and Antigua, and this was my first chance to have another go at them. I would rather have had the first Test anywhere but Headingley, because you know that it is going to be one of the most difficult pitches of the series.

Gooch lost the toss and, predictably, England were put in by Viv Richards and bowled out for 198 - the seventh time in nine innings they had failed to reach 200 against the West Indies. Bad light and rain reduced play on the first day by 104 minutes, and by only marginally less on a tense second day. Richards scored 73 but, crucially, accepted the offer of bad light when he was on top of the England bowlers. Shortly after the

players went off, it rained, but the touring captain's decision was an untypically defensive one which revealed an unusual anxiety in the West Indies camp.

Richards was out to the third ball of the third day to give England an unexpected lead of 25, but Ambrose restored the balance by taking the first three England wickets to fall for 38. Three more wickets fell before the close of another truncated day to leave England on 143 for six, and leading by 168.

Ambrose put himself on a hat-trick twice, first with the wickets of Hick and Lamb, and later when he dismissed Ramprakash and Smith, but all the time at one end was Gooch, playing an innings which was already being talked about as the performance of a lifetime.

A CONTROLLED PULL WITH
THE WRISTS, SHOWING
GRAHAM GOOCH'S QUALITY
OF BEING ABLE TO MIX
STERN DEFENCE WITH THE
ABILITY TO PUNISH A LOOSE
DELIVERY.
(PATRICK EAGAR)

I have always considered the ultimate challenge is to score runs against the best bowlers in the world, and there is no doubt in my mind that the West Indies attack in my time has been one of the best there has ever been. It isn't just that each of their bowlers is fast, but there are always four of them, and they are different in method. In that match at Headingley, for instance, Curtly Ambrose whacked it in from a great height and he had a good yorker; Malcolm Marshall skidded it through with a fast arm action; while Courtney Walsh slanted the ball in from wide, but still held the odd one up. Add in the pace of Patrick Patterson and it was a terrific attack. Let it loose under conditions as they were at Headingley, and any batsman was bound to struggle. All I could do was to fight every ball and hope that runs would come from somewhere. It's funny, but even on a pitch like that, if you can stay there for a session, things don't seem quite so bad. The ball gets a bit older, and often the bowlers get frustrated because they think they should be bowling a side out.

All I could concentrate on was trying to give us something to bowl at in the fourth innings but, just when we seemed to be making a bit of progress, another wicket would go and the battle was on again.

Gooch needed allies, and he found two of a contrasting nature in Mark Ramprakash and his own county colleague Derek Pringle - the young blood and the old sweat. Both contributed 27 which were the only other double-figure scores of the innings, sharing in priceless partnerships with Gooch of 78 and 98 for the fourth and seventh wickets respectively.

ANOTHER LANDMARK HIGHLIGHT DURING ONE OF THE GREATEST INNINGS EVER PLAYED BY AN ENGLAND CAPTAIN: HEADINGLEY, AGAINST THE WEST INDIES IN 1991. (PATRICK EAGAR)

Few England captains have had to deal with such difficulties. Survival was beyond most batsmen in the match - in addition to Gooch, only Richie Richardson and Pringle reached double figures twice. Another problem on the fourth day was the three further interruptions for rain. Not only did this enable Richards to keep his bowlers fresher, but the breaks in play were no help towards maintaining concentration.

At the end of a day which was mentally, as well as physically exhausting, Gooch had already served his country well with 82 out of 143, with Pringle then on 10. Gooch continued on the fourth morning as though he had spent the entire night at the crease. Comfortable with his partner, he set about squeezing every run from the mean West Indies attack, who were to bowl 106 overs before they chipped out the last of Gooch's ten partners.

The England captain scored 72 of the 109 runs added before Devon Malcolm was bowled by Marshall, with only 24 of the remainder coming from the bat. Lengthy defensive innings are often played, but a batsman usually finds that, once he is locked into a defensive mode, he is unable to switch to attack when a loose delivery appears. Also, outstanding attacking innings often tread a dangerous tightrope between success and failure, with scant attention paid to defence.

But Gooch's innings avoided both pitfalls and that is why it was a masterpiece. He repelled 106 overs of hostile pace for well over seven hours, yet he missed little that could be scored off, as evidenced by a boundary count of 18 fours.

Wisden said this: 'Gooch gloriously confirmed his standing on the international stage... Unyielding concentration... and mental toughness enabled him to survive a series of disasters at the other end.'

What he also did was to put the game out of the reach of the West Indies, unless they could find a counterpart with the same combination of concentration and applied technique. They could not, although Richardson threatened briefly, and the West Indies were bowled out in the 57th over. Gooch faced 65 overs himself - and that comparison underlines a superiority over all other batsmen in the match which has seldom been equalled in Test cricket.

Against a much more modest-looking attack, West Indies lost 20 wickets in 110.5 overs, while England's 20 wickets fell in 182.2 overs, thanks to much stiffer resistance, especially from Gooch, whose 'innings of my life' was also the best played under such circumstances in living memory. Certainly as far as chairman Dexter was concerned: 'It was the most decisive innings to win a Test match that I have seen.'

ENGLAND V WEST INDIES (1ST TEST)

PLAYED AT HEADINGLEY, LEEDS, ON 6, 7, 8, 9, 10 JUNE 1991.
TOSS: WEST INDIES. RESULT: ENGLAND WON BY 115 RUNS.

ENGLAND

	FIRST INNINGS		SECOND INNINGS	
G.A.Gooch*	c Dujon, b Marshall	34	not out	154
M.A.Atherton	b Patterson	2	c Dujon, b Ambrose	6
G.A.Hick	c Dujon, b Walsh	6	b Ambrose	6
A.J.Lamb	c Hooper, b Marshall	11	c Hooper, b Ambrose	0
M.R.Ramprakash	c Hooper, b Marshall	27	c Dujon, b Ambrose	27
R.A.Smith	run out	54	lbw, b Ambrose	0
R.C.Russell†	lbw, b Patterson	5	c Dujon, b Ambrose	4
D.R.Pringle	c Logie, b Patterson	16	c Dujon, b Marshall	27
P.A.J.DeFreitas	c Simmons, b Ambrose	15	lbw, b Walsh	3
S.L.Watkin	b Ambrose	2	c Hooper, b Marshall	0
D.E.Malcolm	not out	5	b Marshall	4
Extras	lb 5, w 2, nb 14	21	b 4, lb 9, w 1, nb 7	21
		198		252

	O	M	R	W	O	M	R	W
Ambrose	26	8	49	2	28	6	52	6
Patterson	26.2	8	67	3	15	1	52	0
Walsh	14	7	31	1	30	5	61	1
Marshall	13	4	46	3	25	4	58	3
Hooper					4	1	11	0
Richards					4	1	5	0

FALL OF WICKETS
1-13, 2-45, 3-45, 4-64, 5-129, 6-149, 7-154, 8-177, 9-181, 10-198
1-22, 2-38, 3-38, 4-116, 5-116, 6-124, 7-222, 8-236, 9-238, 10-252

WEST INDIES

	FIRST INNINGS		SECOND INNINGS	
P.V.Simmons	c Ramprakash, b DeFreitas	38	b DeFreitas	0
D.L.Haynes	c Russell, b Watkin	7	c Smith, b Pringle	19
R.B.Richardson	run out	29	c Lamb, b DeFreitas	68
C.L.Hooper	run out	0	c Lamb, b Watkin	5
I.V.A.Richards*	c Lamb, b Pringle	73	c Gooch, b Watkin	3
A.L.Logie	c Lamb, b DeFreitas	6	c Gooch, b Watkin	3
P.J.L.Dujon†	c Ramprakash, b Watkin	6	lbw, b DeFreitas	33
M.D.Marshall	c Hick, b Pringle	0	lbw, b Pringle	1
C.E.L.Ambrose	c Hick, b Pringle	0	c Pringle, b DeFreitas	14
C.A.Walsh	c Gooch, b DeFreitas	3	c Atherton, b Malcolm	9
B.P.Patterson	not out	5	not out	0
Extras	lb 1, nb 5	6	lb 1, nb 6	7
		173		162

	O	M	R	W	O	M	R	W
Malcolm	14	0	69	0	6.4	0	26	1
DeFreitas	17.1	5	34	4	21	4	59	4
Watkin	14	2	55	2	7	0	38	3
Pringle	9	3	14	2	22	6	38	2

FALL OF WICKETS
1-36, 2-54, 3-58, 4-102, 5-139, 6-156, 7-160, 8-165, 9-167, 10-173
1-0, 2-61, 3-77, 4-85, 5-88, 6-136, 7-137, 8-139, 9-162, 10-162

Umpires: H.D.Bird and D.R.Shepherd

Umpire David Shepherd considers himself privileged to have watched every ball of the Gooch epic from close quarters. 'I always rated the unbeaten 189 by Viv Richards at Old Trafford in 1984 as the finest innings I ever saw - until Headingley in 1991. Gooch was magnificent. It was a superb exhibition against a top attack with conditions in their favour. His innings had everything - guts, technique and of course, as a captain's innings, it had to inspire his side.'

The cricket correspondent of *The Times*, John Woodcock, is not a man given to overstatement, nor to dealing in hyperbole. Having witnessed over 400 Test matches in the previous 40 years, his view carries considerable weight. 'Since the Second World War, no innings by an England captain has surpassed this. It stands out, not for artistic merit, but for skill and courage against a very formidable attack in awkward conditions at a crucial time.'

For a man who tries not to deal in peaks and troughs, Headingley 1991 stands as the summit of a wonderful career.

DAVID GOWER

157 on the first day of the sixth Test between England and Australia at The Oval, 29 August 1985.

Gower, having won the toss, scored 157 out of England's first innings total of 464 and shared a second-wicket partnership with Graham Gooch (196) of 351 which set his side on course for victory - and the Ashes. Gower batted for just over 5½ hours, and his hundred was his third of the series, his fifth against Australia and his 12th for England in what was then his 73rd Test match. It also took his aggregate for the series to 732 - then the fourth highest for England, behind Walter Hammond (905 in 1928-29), Denis Compton (753 in 1947) and Herbert Sutcliffe (734 in 1924-25). Graham Gooch has since scored 752 against India in 1990. The innings was the climax to a golden summer for Gower, who led Leicestershire to victory in the Benson and Hedges Cup by beating Essex at Lord's by five wickets.

David Ivon Gower, OBE, was born on 1 April 1957 in Tunbridge Wells and has been the most stylish, cultured batsman to play for England, certainly since the Second World War. He joined Leicestershire in 1975, moved to Hampshire in 1990, and started the 1993 English season with just over 25,000 first-class runs - virtually a third of which have charmed Test match spectators around the world. The possessor of natural dignity, he has somehow survived four blows to his pride, handed out by different sets of England selectors, whose common denominator has been, sadly, an insensitivity which is impossible to understand, considering the nature of the man they were dealing with.

He is one of only a few Test cricketers whose worth exceeds his runs in the book, because his impact on a game is immediate and, like Ian Botham and Viv Richards, he is one of a handful of modern Test cricketers whose appeal to spectators is immeasurable. A dictionary definition of 'charisma' is 'a power to inspire devotion and enthusiasm', to which the authorities seem to have added 'irritation and impatience'.

It is difficult to work out which of the four decisions was the most crass. In chronological order they were the sacking of Gower at the end of the Lord's Test against India in 1987, or rather the manner of it. Then came his omission from the England party to tour West Indies the next winter, followed by an almost unbelievable breakdown in communications between Gower and the England management in Antigua. This resulted in him knocking up before the Test in the belief he was playing, only to be informed in front of the crowd that he was not.

The third slight was when he was again omitted from the England side in 1991 against the West Indies, after scoring three hundreds in his previous six Test matches. Lack of application and his attitude on the tour of Australia were the reported reasons. Finally, his omission from the side to tour India and Sri Lanka in 1993 provoked more reaction from the public than the selection or omission of any other player in many years. This latest slight followed three Tests in England against Pakistan in which he averaged 50 and received public acknowledgement from Gooch for his part in the win at Headingley. Each instance has been franked by authority with the same stamp of insensitivity. The miracle is that, unlike other sportsmen of a similar stature who, when treated similarly, threaten to take their boots, racquet, or ball home and stay there, Gower bounces back with a smile and still reiterates his wish to play for his country. No, he cannot be squashed into a mould, and, yes, authority might have to make allowances for a freedom of spirit which is unquenchable, but the man is capable of scores that his replacements are not. In addition, he has the ability to add grace and charm to an England set-up that is patently short of both qualities.

DAVID GOWER HITTING GEOFF LAWSON OFF THE BACK FOOT DURING HIS INNINGS OF 157 WHICH CLINCHED THE ASHES AT THE OVAL IN 1985.

(ALLSPORT/ADRIAN MURRELL)

An example is the ready way he made himself available to provide material for this chapter. Every cricketer featured has co-operated to the best of his ability. The recall of some has been sharper than others, and trawling the best cricketers in the world was often a logistical problem, due to geography and time differences, but Gower's response was immediate and generous.

It didn't take me long to choose my 157 at The Oval in 1985, because the state of the series made it a vital match for England, and therefore for me as captain. I thought about two other innings which I look back on now with some personal pleasure - albeit for different reasons. The first was in Kingston in 1981 when I batted in the final Test for nearly eight hours to help save the game. I got 154 not out, but it was not so much the runs, as the fact I scored them against Holding, Marshall, Croft and Garner on a pitch which was cracked. I had scored only 222 in my previous seven innings in the series, although I played better than the scores might suggest, but it was nice to finish the series on a high note. I rate it a good innings and it is still my only hundred against the West Indies.

The other innings I considered was in the first Test in Perth in November 1982. I went in at 14 for one and had scored 72 when I was caught by John Dyson off Terry Alderman at 109 for two. I played as well as I could, and was pleased with my footwork against Alderman, Lillee and Lawson. Perhaps if I'd scored 172 I might have picked it.

This was the Test in which Alderman dislocated a shoulder on the second day tackling a pitch-invader, and it also brought Ian Botham his 3000th run and 250th wicket for England for a then unique double in his 55th Test match.

I asked Gower about his back-to-back hundreds in Faisalabad and Lahore when he took over the captaincy from Bob Willis in 1984. After all, he scored 152 in seven hours to save the first game, and his unbeaten 173 in three minutes less at Gaddafi Stadium set up a thrilling final day in which England survived an opening partnership of 173 between Mohsin Khan and Shoaib Mohammad before taking the first six wickets for an additional 26 runs. Briefly, they threatened a sensational win. Did either innings merit a mention - perhaps a bronze medal? 'If I could remember much about them, they might - but they are just a bit of a blur really.'

That answer reveals a great deal about an attitude towards life and cricket that infuriates people who cannot begin to understand the priorities of a man like Gower. His standards are always high, but a performance has to be hallmarked with a 22-carat stamp to lodge in his memory bank.

His ability to refuse to accept attempts to make him conform to other people's standards troubles critics and, seemingly, the England selectors. His well-documented 'laid-back' attitude hides a caring side of his nature he never wishes to reveal. Authority seems unable to change its mind about him, and he certainly will not change his mind about the men who run English cricket. The public must hope that they have not seen the last of him in an England team - that would be the ultimate condemnation of the depths into which English cricket has plummeted, ignoring one of the best batsmen ever to play for his country. So his choice is of special interest:

> I go back to the Ashes series in 1985, because we had done well to survive the usual defeat by the Aussies at Lord's, and win that astonishing game at Edgbaston when rain seemed to have done us. But a defeat at The Oval would have squared the series and left the Ashes with Allan Border, and I badly wanted to build an early advantage against them. It was a good toss to win, although the pitch was quick and bound to do something early on.
>
> McDermott bowled Tim Robinson and I joined Graham Gooch at 20 for one. There are two levels of satisfaction in sport in my opinion - one where you play well, and one where what you do sets up your side for a win, and a rare time when they happen together, as at The Oval, is the most satisfying of all.

Wisden's comments on Gower's innings are curiously muted - almost grudging. 'Australia's modest chance of salvaging the Ashes vanished on the opening morning when Gower won an exceptionally good toss and was then blessed with a good deal of luck in the first hour of what blossomed into a match-winning second-wicket stand of 351 with Gooch. The opener made a chanceless 196 but although Gower, too, went on to play brilliantly in scoring 157, he had started loosely, lobbing the slips at two while attempting to kill a rising ball from McDermott, and survived further narrow escapes at 31 and 35 from Lawson.'

There is also a mention - more of an afterthought - that 'the runs in partnership with Gooch came at 4.6 an over', so presumably the England captain played more than a few authentic strokes. He says: 'I remember the McDermott escape. It caught the shoulder and just cleared the slips, but apart from that I reckon I was pretty well in control.'

A lunch score of 100 for one from only 25 overs supports him, and it must be remembered that his innings was a calculated attempt to influence the course of the game. He had to contend with a woeful over-rate, and if further evidence is needed of the merit of a true captain's innings, it came on the second day after his dismissal at 371 for two, when the last eight wickets went in 2½ hours for the addition of only 93.

Despite lengthy interruptions because of rain, England made Australia follow on and won the match by an innings and 94 runs. The fact that the three seamers, Botham, Ellison and Taylor, took 16 of the 20 wickets which fell in 130.3 overs underlines the importance of the stand between Gooch and Gower. Paul Downton was third highest scorer with 16, and only Ritchie and Border passed fifty for the Australians.

That game was to be the highlight of Gower's captaincy of his country but, cricket being an avenging angel of a game at times, it swooped on him in 1989, when Border's next tour resulted in Australia winning 4-0 - the only other captain to achieve such a victory was Bradman in 1948. Such a margin is almost unheard of - only Warwick Armstrong's side in 1921 won three Tests, and both his and Bradman's sides toured England following a world war when English cricket was at its weakest.

ENGLAND V AUSTRALIA (6TH TEST)

PLAYED AT KENNINGTON OVAL, LONDON, ON 29, 30, 31 AUGUST, 2, 3 SEPTEMBER 1985.
TOSS: ENGLAND. RESULT: ENGLAND WON BY AN INNINGS AND 94 RUNS.

ENGLAND

FIRST INNINGS

G.A.Gooch	c and b McDermott	196
R.T.Robinson	b McDermott	3
D.I.Gower*	c Bennett, b McDermott	157
M.W.Gatting	c Border, b Bennett	4
J.E.Emburey	c Wellham, b Lawson	9
A.J.Lamb	c McDermott, b Lawson	1
I.T.Botham	c Phillips, b Lawson	12
P.R.Downton†	b McDermott	16
R.M.Ellison	c Phillips, b Gilbert	3
P.H.Edmonds	lbw, b Lawson	12
L.B.Taylor	not out	1
Extras	b 13, lb 11, nb 26	50
		464

	O	M	R	W
Lawson	29.2	6	101	4
McDermott	31	2	108	4
Gilbert	21	2	96	1
Bennett	32	8	111	1
Border	2	0	8	0
Wessels	3	0	16	0

FALL OF WICKETS
1-20, 2-371, 3-376, 4-403, 5-405, 6-418, 7-425, 8-447, 9-452, 10-464

AUSTRALIA

FIRST INNINGS

			SECOND INNINGS	
G.M.Wood	lbw, b Botham	22	b Botham	6
A.M.J.Hilditch	c Gooch, b Botham	17	c Gower, b Taylor	9
K.C.Wessels	b Emburey	12	c Downton, b Botham	7
A.R.Border*	b Edmonds	38	c Botham, b Ellison	58
D.M.Wellham	c Downton, b Ellison	13	lbw, b Ellison	5
G.M.Ritchie	not out	64	c Downton, b Ellison	6
W.B.Phillips†	b Edmonds	18	c Downton, b Botham	10
M.J.Bennett	c Robinson, b Ellison	12	c and b Taylor	11
G.F.Lawson	c Botham, b Taylor	14	c Downton, b Ellison	7
C.J.McDermott	run out	25	c Botham, b Ellison	2
D.R.Gilbert	b Botham	1	not out	0
Extras	lb 3, w 2	5	b 4, nb 4	8
		241		129

	O	M	R	W	O	M	R	W
Botham	20	3	64	3	17	3	44	3
Taylor	13	1	39	1	11.3	1	34	2
Ellison	18	5	35	2	17	3	46	5
Emburey	19	7	48	1	1	0	1	0
Edmonds	14	2	52	2				

FALL OF WICKETS
1-35, 2-52, 3-56, 4-101, 5-109, 6-144, 7-171, 8-192 9-235, 10-241
1-13, 2-16, 3-37, 4-51, 5-71, 6-96, 7-114, 8-127, 9-129, 10-129

Umpires: H.D.Bird and K.E.Palmer

Gower made errors in selection, none bigger than the omission of John Emburey from the Headingley Test. He was let down by his bowlers in both innings, but his admission that he was swayed against his better judgement to field first after winning the toss, reveals why his approach to captaincy sometimes appeared to lack incisiveness.

History has still to reach a final verdict about Gower. Perhaps it never will, because it would be easier to capture moonbeams than make a judgement about someone who is well nigh unjudgeable.

What is in no doubt is that he has given enormous pleasure to cricket followers the world over. It is equally certain that he should have played in more Tests, particularly in the early 1990s. That he did not is a loss to England as much as to the player. He might not be the sort of batsman to whom you would entrust your life, but his choice of 'the innings of my life' reflects a philosophy in life and cricket that deserves to endure, even if his choice did not impress *Wisden*. His self-created problem is that brilliance and consistency cannot, by definition, go hand in hand. He has created a level of expectancy which can rarely be fulfilled. Burned by his own flame perhaps?

TOM GRAVENEY

151 on the second and third days of the second Test between England and India at Lord's, 23 and 24 June 1967.

Graveney's score was the cornerstone of England's first innings total of 386. Overnight he was 74 out of 252 for three and, on a rain-freshened pitch he scored 77 out of 107 added before he was sixth out. While batsmen of the calibre of D'Oliveira, Close and Murray were all at sea against the Indian spinners, Graveney was at his most majestic, with 92 of his runs coming in boundaries. The first innings lead of 234 he secured for England under difficult conditions was enough to secure victory in four days by an innings and 124 runs.

T homas William Graveney, OBE, was born on 16 June 1927 in Riding Mill, Northumberland. He played for Gloucestershire from 1948 to 1960 and then, after missing a full season for qualification purposes, he played for Worcestershire from 1962 to 1970. He completed a magnificent career by playing the last of his 732 first-class matches for Queensland in 1972 during a three-year coaching engagement in Brisbane. He played 79 times for England - the last 25 of which were consecutive Tests played between the ages of 39 and 42. He scored 75 at Old Trafford against the West Indies in his last appearance in 1969, and was then suspended for three matches for leaving the Test on the rest day to play in a benefit game in Luton. The match had been arranged eight months previously, but the Test & County Cricket Board's disciplinary sub-committee refused to accept Graveney's account of four conversations in that period between the player and Alec Bedser, chairman of selectors, and a distinguished Test career sadly ended under a cloud.

His career aggregate of 47,793 is the second highest among post-war batsmen - 633 behind Boycott. Similarly, among batsmen who have scored 100 hundreds since the Second World War, Graveney's total of 122 has been exceeded only by Boycott. He scored 11 Test hundreds, with six of them in excess of 150, and most of his runs were hallmarked with a beautifully orthodox technique that was a study in effortless elegance.

He affected the course of many games around the world with quality innings, so I was curious as to which one he would pick as 'the innings of my life' and why.

I had to think about a performance which still gives me most satisfaction when I look back. It has to be one when, not only did I play well, but I did so when conditions were difficult. There are plenty of knocks on flat pitches which called for lengthy concentration, but it was always the challenge of coming out on top against the best bowlers when things were in their favour which appealed to me most.

Some of my hundreds for England come into this category, as well as my 96 against Wes Hall and Charlie Griffith on my comeback at Lord's after three years out of the side. In the end, I have gone for my 151 against India at Lord's - or rather the second half of that innings, which was played on a rain-affected pitch with Chandrasekhar, Bedi and Prasanna making the ball hum like a top. We had gone off for rain on Friday afternoon when I was 74 and Basil D'Oliveira was 27. We were already 100 ahead at 252 for three after Kenny Barrington scored 97 as an opener.

England had beaten India in the first Test at Headingley by six wickets after India came back from a follow-on first innings arrears of 386, thanks to 148 from Pataudi. This was the game in which Boycott scored 246 and was then dropped for slow scoring. The Yorkshireman's first hundred took him five hours and 41 minutes, during which he faced 316 deliveries. His subsequent acceleration, 146 more runs in eight minutes under four hours from 239 balls, failed to prevent a disciplinary decision which cost him his place.

Compared with that side, Amiss replaced Boycott, and Warwickshire's fast bowler, Brown, came in for Higgs, and took three good wickets as India were bowled out for 152 in under four hours. Wicketkeeper Murray, on his home ground, took six catches to equal the then Test record held jointly by Wally Grout of Australia and South Africa's Dennis Lindsay.

On the second day, England progressed from their overnight 107 for two to 252 for three with little trouble, although Barrington and Graveney drew this comment from *Wisden* about the pace of their batting - a part of the game which was now in the spotlight after the Boycott affair on his home Headingley ground two weeks earlier. 'The batsmen proceeded with utmost care during the three hours of cricket which was possible on the second day. A crowd of 12,000 watched almost silently while Barrington, Graveney and D'Oliveira treated Chandrasekhar, and the two left-arm bowlers, Surti and Bedi with such respect that only 145 runs were added for the loss of Barrington.'

Chandrasekhar bowled Barrington as soon as he returned for his second spell. It was the second consecutive Test where he had been dismissed in his 90s, and prevented him, yet again, from achieving a Lord's century. That gap in Barrington's career was filled five weeks later, when he scored 148 against Pakistan and shared a then record third-wicket stand of 201 between those two countries with Graveney - whose 'Indian summer' was to yield 471 runs in nine innings.

Unlike Barrington, Graveney had already scored a hundred at Lord's - 153 against Pakistan towards the end of his 'first' career in the England side. However, he realised that, after the rain which ended play on the second day when he was 74, a second one was no formality. He and his Worcestershire colleague, D'Oliveira, had added 67 on Friday, but now conditions were different. Never a man of many words, England captain Brian Close was always sparing with praise, which makes this opinion one to value: 'A storm had left the wicket wet. Chandrasekhar made the ball bite and lift, but Tom mastered both the conditions and the bowlers. He was as valuable as he was stylish.'

Ask any cricketer about the ground on which he would most like to score a Test hundred, and the majority will say Lord's. And if they are then asked on which day, they will choose Saturday - the day on the ground which combines to produce the best atmosphere in international cricket. Usually a full house, the crowd is made up of many people to whom a pilgrimage to Lord's on the Saturday of a Test match is sublime.

Graveney, a traditionalist to his fingertips, walked out of the Long Room that Saturday morning, and sniffed the redolent atmosphere that never failed to stir him. His partner, D'Oliveira from Signal Hill in Cape Town, was playing in his second Lord's Test and his sixth for England.

What came next thrilled the crowd, delighted the critics as well as the England team, and showed why Graveney chose the pre-lunch session as 'the innings of my life'. *Wisden* was in no doubt. 'The early cricket on Saturday belonged almost entirely to Graveney. Fifteen years previously he had hit his first Test hundred against India in Bombay, and now he progressed towards his ninth in Tests and the 113th of his career.' At the other end, D'Oliveira struggled to find his form - scoring only six in an hour. But Graveney was in complete control until he was stumped in the first over after lunch, having made 151 in five hours. After his dismissal, the last five wickets fell in 45 minutes for 27 runs. Graveney says:

The Friday rain had given their spinners something to bowl on, and I knew that they could easily get on top unless I stopped them. I thought that off-spinner Prasanna would be the biggest danger, so I hit him into 'Q' Stand for six as soon as he came on, and Pataudi took him off. The day before I had swept Bedi into the Grandstand for six, but although the spiteful pitch was different, I had a morning when

everything hit the middle of the bat. It turned and lifted, and of course Chandra was genuine medium pace. He bowled all morning, but having been brought up on uncovered pitches, I was equipped to take advantage of anything that was not bowled exactly in the right area. That is why uncovered pitches are a must, if modern batsmen and bowlers are to have any chance of completing an education that is bound to be unfinished if they never play on a rain-affected pitch.

THE SHOT FOR SIX OFF PRASANNA WHICH STARTED GRAVENEY'S DOMINATION, ON A RAIN-AFFECTED PITCH, OF THE WORLD'S BEST SPIN ATTACK. *(TOPHAM PICTURE SOURCE)*

Partner D'Oliveira remembers how inadequate he felt, as he struggled to lay bat on ball for an hour, while

Graveney stroked the ball over Lord's. 'Twice I walked down and asked him to stop making me look a novice.'

Graveney believes that another word was used instead of 'novice', but agrees that he never played better. In the two-hour session, he scored 77, while his three partners scrambled a total of 20, and this against a trio of spin bowlers who, between them, bowled over 8000 overs in 174 Tests, and took 697 wickets at an average of just under 30. Once Graveney was stumped by Engineer off Bedi, the last four wickets were swept aside to emphasise the gulf in class on the day between the 40-year-old, and his partners D'Oliveira, Close and Murray.

ENGLAND V INDIA (2ND TEST)

PLAYED AT LORD'S, LONDON, ON 22, 23, 24, 26 JUNE 1967.
TOSS: INDIA. RESULT: ENGLAND WON BY AN INNINGS AND 124 RUNS.

INDIA

	FIRST INNINGS		SECOND INNINGS	
D.N.Sardesai	c Murray, b Illingworth	28	absent hurt	
F.M.Engineer†	c Murray, b Brown	8	(1) c Amiss, b Snow	8
A.L.Wadekar	c Illingworth, b D'Oliveira	57	b Illingworth	19
C.G.Borde	b Snow	0	c Snow, b Close	1
Nawab of Pataudi, jr*	c Murray, b Brown	5	c Graveney, b Close	5
R.F.Surti	c Murray, b D'Oliveira	6	c D'Oliveira, b Illingworth	0
V.Subramanya	c Murray, b Brown	0	c Edrich, b Illingworth	1
B.K.Kunderan	c Murray, b Snow	20	(2) lbw, b Illingworth	47
E.A.S.Prasanna	run out	17	(8) c D'Oliveira, b Illingworth	0
B.S.Bedi	c Amiss, b Snow	5	(9) b Illingworth	11
B.S.Chandrasekhar	not out	2	(10) not out	3
Extras	b 2, lb 2	4	b 11, lb 4	15
		152		**110**

	O	M	R	W	O	M	R	W
Snow	20.4	5	49	3	8	4	12	1
Brown	18	3	61	3	5	2	10	0
D'Oliveira	15	6	38	2				
Illingworth	2	2	0	1	22.3	12	29	6
Hobbs					6	1	16	0
Close					15	5	28	2

FALL OF WICKETS
1-12, 2-24, 3-29, 4-45, 5-58, 6-102, 7-112, 8-144, 9-145, 10-152
1-8, 2-60, 3-67, 4-79, 5-80, 6-86, 7-90, 8-101, 9-110

Umpires: J.S.Buller and A.Jepson

ENGLAND

	FIRST INNINGS	
J.H.Edrich	c and b Surti	12
K.F.Barrington	b Chandrasekhar	97
D.L.Amiss	b Chandrasekhar	29
T.W.Graveney	st Engineer, b Bedi	151
B.L.D'Oliveira	c and b Chandrasekhar	33
D.B.Close*	c Borde, b Prasanna	7
J.T.Murray†	b Chandrasekhar	7
R.Illingworth	lbw, b Chandrasekhar	4
R.N.S.Hobbs	b Bedi	7
D.J.Brown	c Pataudi, b Bedi	5
J.A.Snow	not out	8
Extras	b 5, lb 18, w 1, nb 2	26
		386

	O	M	R	W
Surti	31	10	67	1
Subramanya	7	1	20	0
Chandrasekhar	53	9	127	5
Bedi	31.2	13	68	3
Prasanna	32	5	78	1

FALL OF WICKETS
1-46, 2-107, 3-185, 4-307, 5-334, 6-359, 7-365, 8-372, 9-372, 10-386

A comparison of the two parts of Graveney's innings reveals the merit of his blazing performance on Saturday morning. In three hours on the previous day, he hit a six and ten fours on a good surface, but on a rain-affected pitch the next morning, he also hit a six and ten fours, but in two hours and out of 107 compared with 145 on Friday.

Graveney is the only batsman to score 10,000 first-class runs for two counties, and was the first post-war batsman to score 30,000 runs and 100 hundreds. He scored a hundred in each innings on four occasions, including once against Warwickshire at Edgbaston in 1957. This one made me unpopular with my colleagues because of a remark I made to Graveney before our match at Bristol in early June. I happened to mention to him that I had never seen him score a hundred. Within two weeks, I had seen three - and all from close quarters. He got 122 at Bristol, followed by 106 and an unbeaten 101 two weeks later.

Tom Graveney represented a quality in desperately short supply in the modern game: class. He oozed it from the moment he took guard. And never more so than that Saturday morning at Lord's, when he played what he now says is 'the innings of my life'.

GORDON GREENIDGE

*134 on the first day of the third Test
between England and West Indies at
Old Trafford, 8 July 1976.*

In his tenth Test, the Bajan opener leapt into second place behind Charlie Bannerman in the list of the highest percentage of a total scored by an individual. Bannerman scored 67.3 percent in the first Test ever played (165 out of 245), with Greenidge logging 63.5 percent (134 out of 211). It was an innings which had a big influence on the result, as only Collis King (32) and number eleven Wayne Daniel (10) reached double figures.

Middlesex seamer Mike Selvey made a sensational debut with three for six in his first 20 balls, and at 26 for four, with Fredericks, Richards, Kallicharran and Lloyd dismissed for six runs between them, Greenidge was the West Indies' last hope. His response was to cement a magnificent international career, and so give his side a platform from which they won the game and then the next two Tests. A hundred in the second innings made him the first batsman to score two hundreds in a Manchester Test.

Cuthbert Gordon Greenidge was born on 1 May 1951 in Barbados. He went to St Peter's School before his parents emigrated to Berkshire when he was 14. His cricket was already attracting notice and, the year after he played for England Schoolboys at the age of 16, he signed for Hampshire in 1968 to begin a career in county and international cricket that brought him 37,354 first-class runs when he made his last - but, still he insists, not final - appearance in 1992. No other overseas batsman has scored so many runs, and his aggregate of 7558 Test runs is threatened only by his distinguished partner, Desmond Haynes, as the most recorded by a West Indies opener.

He played in 108 Tests, two fewer than Clive Lloyd, with whom he shares third place in the West Indies list of Test century-makers - 19, with only Sobers (26) and Richards (24) ahead of them.

Unlike many heavy run-scorers, Greenidge had the ability to shape the course of games, and turn many which were going against his side. It is doubtful if there has been a more savage square-cutter or puller in post-war cricket, as testified to by John Thicknesse, the cricket correspondent of the *Evening Standard*. 'In his early days, Greenidge's main ambition sometimes appeared to be to knock the cover off the ball - perhaps to avoid being outshone by the artistic Barry Richards, his county opening partner.

'The 1970s were littered with examples of Greenidge's devastation, notably his 273 not out against the Pakistanis at Eastbourne, described by Barry Richards as his conception of the perfect innings. For 4½ hours, every bad ball went for six (13) or four (31) and by the end of that decade, he held the record score in all three English one-day competitions.'

He opened the innings with Haynes for West Indies in 89 games, which is easily a record, and their success was often the basis of the victorious reign of the West Indies from the end of the Packer revolution in 1979 throughout the 1980s, for which most of the credit is normally given to whichever quartet of fast bowlers was pulverising the opposition at the time. Haynes and Greenidge averaged 47 for the first wicket every time they opened together, and they put on fifty 26 times, a century on 16 occasions and 200 four times. The last of these double-century partnerships was in Antigua in April 1990, when their record 298

ended only when Greenidge was run out - painfully for him, sauntering a second run for Haynes.

GREENIDGE ATTACKING UNDERWOOD AT OLD TRAFFORD IN 1976. *(PATRICK EAGAR)*

He scored a career-best 226 in his penultimate Test against Australia in Bridgetown and, curiously for such a well-established pair, both he and Haynes were run out in Antigua in his final game and his last international innings. He also scored over 5000 runs in one-day internationals, and for Hampshire he scored 6344 Sunday League runs, including 11 hundreds - a record he then shared with Graham Gooch.

Perhaps because he spent so much time in English cricket, his character and manner lack the typical West Indian flamboyance, and his best friends would never claim that he is an extrovert. Occasionally, reports would surface of differences with senior Test colleagues, but his value to any side he played for is emphasised by the length of his career.

In contrast to his sledgehammer batting, he picks his words almost painstakingly, which is why his choice of 'the innings of my life' was made only after careful consideration.

I nearly went for my 93 in my debut in Bangalore, because that was a difficult pitch after rain got on it. And it was my first game for my country when I was only 23 - although I suppose that I could not have been expected to shoulder a great deal of responsibility in my first match. I played well and would probably have got a hundred had I not been run out. It was my call to Sunil Gavaskar at mid-on, but Alvin Kallicharran sent me back and that was that.

The other innings I thought about was my 104 in Adelaide in 1989. It was special because it was my first hundred in Australia and came in my last innings there. It was my fifth tour and my 32nd innings there, so I was pleased to end the jinx with my 16th Test hundred. But that was a good pitch and we drew the game, so I must go for a game which I know I helped to win - and on a difficult pitch.

For that reason, he decided upon his first innings at Old Trafford in 1976. He was then in his third series, and he took guard with a record of 533 runs from 17 innings. The great form of his debut Test (93 and 107) had not been sustained and, after 11 runs from four innings in Australia, including a pair at Brisbane, he was very much on trial in England. Scores of 22 and 23 at Trent Bridge, and 84 and 22 at Lord's - both Tests were drawn - added to the importance of the pivotal match of the series at Old Trafford.

As far as I am concerned, although it was my tenth Test match, that was where my career started. I had to concentrate and did so in a way that showed everyone I was not just a hitter, but that I could fashion a big innings when it was important in other ways. I was still a new boy in the side, and it was my first chance to rescue the side from trouble. And we were really up against it at 26 for four. It was a reasonable pitch, but the ball swung a lot and seamed as well. Selvey got the early wickets and bowled well, but so did Mike Hendrick, who I rated as a dangerous new-ball bowler.

Somehow Collis King and I weathered the storm, and what pleased me was that, although I was concentrating hard on defence, I was able to switch to attack when I received anything off line. I had one bit of luck when I was 26 and I mistimed a hook off Bob Woolmer. It was probably Derek Underwood's catch but Alan Knott went after it and, in the end, neither got to it. I hit the next three balls for four and Tony Greig took Woolmer off. Collis and I put on 111, but when he got out to Underwood, I just picked up what runs I could to try to get us somewhere near 200.

Greenidge did this so successfully that, when he was ninth out, the score was 193, with his partners for the sixth, seventh and eighth wickets scoring ten out of 56 added with the young opener. He was finally bowled by Underwood for a priceless 134, and the cricket world knew that a new batting star had arrived. His innings lasted for 250 minutes, with the first hundred coming in 170 minutes, which illustrates the care with which he batted throughout.

His experience in English county cricket undoubtedly completed his batting education, and was another example of the double-edged result of employing overseas cricketers in the English domestic game. The Caribbean has been a productive source of supply of big names who have delighted English crowds with their talents and, on balance, the price of reaping the consequences at Test level of improving their techniques, while reducing the opportunities for English qualified players, was probably worth paying at the time. Certainly, the advantages of employing long-term cricketers from abroad were many, and Greenidge was one of six West Indians who spent well over ten years in county cricket - Malcolm Marshall, Clive Lloyd, Viv Richards, Joel Garner and Alvin Kallicharran were the others.

When Underwood took the final wicket, a score of 211 gave the West Indies fast bowlers something to bowl at on a pitch with a slight variability of bounce, which is always magnified by extra pace. In 2½ hours Holding, Roberts and Daniel bundled the home side out for 71 - their lowest-ever score against any country other than Australia, with the last eight wickets going down for 25 in an hour. *Wisden* says, 'Some balls lifted at frightening speed and Greig and Underwood both had narrow escapes from what could have been serious injury. Woolmer and Hayes received balls which were all but unplayable and even the greatest of batting sides would have been severely taxed.'

Greenidge was back at the crease before lunch on the second day to begin a different sort of innings in a changed match situation. Selvey could not repeat his first innings form and the opening stand of 116 came in only 29 overs. Greenidge completed his second hundred of the match - only George Headley had previously done it against England - and with Richards hitting his sixth hundred of the year, West Indies established a massive superiority before the end of the third day.

A declaration set the scene for an hour of fast bowling which was blatantly intimidatory. The brutal fast bowling aimed at John Edrich and Brian Close that evening led to the former's announcement that he would retire from Test cricket. *Wisden* noted that 'the fast bowling was too wild and too hostile to be acceptable'.

ENGLAND V WEST INDIES (3RD TEST)

PLAYED AT OLD TRAFFORD, MANCHESTER, ON 8, 9, 10, 12, 13 JULY 1976.
TOSS: WEST INDIES. RESULT: WEST INDIES WON BY 425 RUNS.

WEST INDIES

	FIRST INNINGS		SECOND INNINGS	
R.C.Fredericks	c Underwood, b Selvey	0	hit wicket, b Hendrick	50
C.G.Greenidge	b Underwood	134	b Selvey	101
I.V.A.Richards	b Selvey	4	lbw, b Pocock	135
A.I.Kallicharran	b Selvey	0	(5) c Close, b Pocock	20
C.H.Lloyd*	c Hayes, b Hendrick	2	(4) c Underwood, b Selvey	43
C.L.King	c Greig, b Underwood	32	not out	14
D.L.Murray†	c Greig, b Hendrick	1	not out	7
M.A.Holding	b Selvey	3		
A.M.E.Roberts	c Steele, b Pocock	6		
A.L.Padmore	not out	8		
W.W.Daniel	lbw, b Underwood	10		
Extras	lb 8, nb 3	11	b 5, lb 30, w 1, nb 5	41
		211	(5 wickets declared)	411

	O	M	R	W	O	M	R	W
Hendrick	14	1	48	2	24	4	63	1
Selvey	17	4	41	4	26	3	111	2
Greig	8	1	24	0	2	0	8	0
Woolmer	3	0	22	0				
Underwood	24	5	55	3	35	9	90	0
Pocock	4	2	10	1	27	4	98	2

FALL OF WICKETS
1-1, 2-15, 3-19, 4-26, 5-137, 6-154, 7-167, 8-193, 9-193, 10-211
1-116, 2-224, 3-356, 4-385, 5-388

ENGLAND

	FIRST INNINGS		SECOND INNINGS	
J.H.Edrich	c Murray, b Roberts	8	b Daniel	24
D.B.Close	lbw, b Daniel	2	b Roberts	20
D.S.Steele	lbw, b Roberts	20	c Roberts, b Holding	15
P.I.Pocock	c Kallicharran, b Holding	7	(10) c King, b Daniel	3
R.A.Woolmer	c Murray, b Holding	3	(4) lbw, b Roberts	0
F.C.Hayes	c Lloyd, b Roberts	0	(5) c Greenidge, b Roberts	18
A.W.Greig*	b Daniel	9	(6) b Holding	3
A.P.E.Knott†	c Greenidge, b Holding	1	(7) c Fredericks, b Roberts	14
D.L.Underwood	b Holding	0	(8) c King, b Roberts	0
M.W.W.Selvey	not out	2	(9) c Greenidge, b Roberts	4
M.Hendrick	b Holding	0	not out	0
Extras	b 8, nb 11	19	b 4, lb 1, nb 20	25
		71		126

	O	M	R	W	O	M	R	W
Roberts	12	4	22	3	20.5	8	37	6
Holding	14.5	7	17	5	23	15	24	2
Daniel	6	2	13	2	17	8	39	2
Padmore					3	2	1	0

FALL OF WICKETS
1-9, 2-36, 3-46, 4-48, 5-48, 6-65, 7-66, 8-67, 9-71, 10-71
1-54, 2-60, 3-60, 4-80, 5-94, 6-112, 7-112, 8-118, 9-124, 10-126

Umpires: W.E.Alley and W.L.Budd

Clive Lloyd admitted after the match that 'our fellows got carried away', which begs the question why, as captain, he did not intervene, at least from a tactical standpoint if not to pre-empt criticism about clear intimidation. It was unnecessary as well, as the West Indies pace trio showed when they pitched a more acceptable length on the fourth day.

David Steele was the only England batsman to reach double figures in each innings, and Mr Extras' match aggregate of 44 was comfortably the highest home score - a unique occurrence in Test cricket. A final victory margin of 425 was an astonishing reversal of fortunes from when Greenidge was joined by King, 40 minutes after the start of the first day with four wickets down.

Born on 1 May, Greenidge answered his country's 'Mayday' distress call with a performance that leaves no doubt about his decision to choose it as 'the innings of my life'.

Michael Manley pays this tribute to Greenidge: 'Few would dispute that Gordon Greenidge, along with Gavaskar, was the finest opener of the 1980s, and none argue that he is not the best-ever opener from the Caribbean.'

DESMOND HAYNES

143 on the fourth day of the fourth Test between Australia and West Indies at Sydney, 29 January 1989.

On a bare pitch off which the ball turned throughout the match, Allan Border returned his best match figures of 11 for 96 to inflict on the West Indies their first defeat in 11 Tests. They lost 18 wickets to spin, with Haynes playing one of the best innings under the conditions ever seen by both captains. It was Haynes's 11th Test hundred in a remarkable performance for a man with the reputation of fallibility against spin. His judgement of line and length was such that he never missed the chance to punish any loose delivery. Haynes's match aggregate of 218 represented 45 percent of his side's total of 480, a massive effort under the unusual conditions.

Desmond Leo Haynes was born on 15 February 1956 in Holder's Hill, Barbados, and was educated at Federal High School. He made his debut for Barbados at the age of 20, and his first-class career began so well that he was capped by the West Indies in March 1978 in the first home Test against Australia at Port-of-Spain. He scored 61, and followed with 66 and 55 on his home Kensington Oval ground two weeks later.

The significant feature was that these games provided the first pairing of Haynes with Gordon Greenidge, who went on to form an opening partnership which became the most prolific in history: 6846 runs as a partnership. The next heaviest run-scoring duo is the Australian pair, Bill Lawry and Bobby Simpson, whose 62 innings in 34 Tests brought them 3596, although their average of 59.93 is appreciably ahead of Haynes and Greenidge. Their most prolific series came at home against Australia in 1984 when they managed 29, 250*, 35, 132, 21*, 0, 162 and 55*. They also put on over 500 runs together in series against India and England.

With Haynes on the verge of a successful international career, his involvement with Kerry Packer's World Series cricket meant a break of nine Tests before the West Indies Board of Control would pick their 'rebel' players, and Haynes's next three official appearances for the West Indies were undistinguished, with scores of 42, 4, 29, 9*, 28 and 27, but history beckoned for the 23-year-old at Dunedin in 1980. The West Indies were embroiled in one of the most controversial of all Test matches, and lost by one wicket after a record-equalling 12 LBW decisions, with seven going to Richard Hadlee whose match figures were 56-22-102-11. Such a performance would have brought the home side a crushing win - but for the effort of Haynes, who became the first man to bat through both innings of a Test match. Had he not been injured during his second innings of 105 out of 212, and therefore unable to field, he would have been the first West Indies cricketer to be on the field throughout a Test match. This game established Haynes in the side and led to a run of 72 consecutive appearances which ended in June 1988 when he suffered a damaged hamstring against England. Throughout the 1980s and into the 1990s, he often held together a batting order which became brittle, and his adaptability is shown by the fact that, in addition to his aggregate of 7250 Test runs by the end of the 1993 series between the West Indies and Pakistan, he had also scored more runs in one-day international cricket than any other batsman - 8194 in 225 matches.

Originally a dashing batsman, Haynes altered his method to suit the needs of his side, and such an instinctive awareness of team cricket made his signing by Middlesex in 1989 one of the shrewdest of overseas

A TYPICAL PIECE OF CARIBBEAN IMPROVISATION. WICKETKEEPER KNOTT LOOKS ON IN DISBELIEF DURING HAYNES'S 184 AT LORD'S IN 1984.
(PATRICK EAGAR)

acquisitions. He rewarded them with 2346 runs in 1990 and, although in 1993 he was 37, he was still regarded as one of the leading batsmen in world cricket. In fact, according to the Coopers and Lybrand world ratings, he was the leading batsman, following his two match-winning hundreds against Pakistan. Those innings improved his standing from seventh to first - ahead of his captain Richie Richardson, who had succeeded Viv Richards in that role when many people thought Haynes would be appointed. To date he has led his country four times, including the notorious game against England in Trinidad in 1990, when go-slow tactics resulted in his bowlers getting through only 17 overs in 105 minutes to ensure a draw.

He did not find it easy to choose his best innings and, unusually among the great players featured in this book, two performances which he remembers with satisfaction were in Test matches that the West Indies lost. Many of the other featured batsmen have chosen a particular innings because it either won or saved a match. Not so with Haynes, although analysis of the two Tests under consideration shows that, but for his contributions, his side would have lost both games by much wider margins.

It was a real toss-up between my first Test match against New Zealand in 1980 and one ten years later against Australia at the SCG. The World Series cricketers were brought back against Australia in Brisbane earlier that season, where Deryck Murray skippered the side because Clive had had a knee operation. It was a three-match series which we won 2-0, but I never got going, and badly needed a good performance in New Zealand. The Dunedin pitch was not great - slow and low - and although we won the toss, we were soon in real trouble at four for three, with Richard Hadlee getting rid of Gordon Greenidge, Lawrence Rowe, and Alvin Kallicharran.

Lloyd (24), Collis King (14) and David Parry (17) were the only other players to reach double figures while Haynes played a superb, technical, defensive innings to score 55 before he was last man out when he was caught and bowled by Lance Cairns. That performance alone might not have caused Haynes to hesitate about choosing 'the innings of my life', although he came within a whisker of carrying his bat. But his second innings was even better. A first innings lead of 109 for New Zealand seemed more than enough when Hadlee

AUSTRALIA V WEST INDIES (4TH TEST)

PLAYED AT SYDNEY CRICKET GROUND, ON 26, 27, 28, 29, 30 JANUARY 1989.
TOSS: WEST INDIES. RESULT: AUSTRALIA WON BY SEVEN WICKETS.

WEST INDIES

	FIRST INNINGS		SECOND INNINGS	
C.G.Greenidge	c Waugh, b P.L.Taylor	56	c and b Hughes	4
D.L.Haynes	c Boon, b Hohns	75	c M.A.Taylor, b Border	143
R.B.Richardson	c P.L.Taylor, b Border	28	c Hughes, b P.L.Taylor	22
C.L.Hooper	c Marsh, b Border	0	c Jones, b Hohns	35
I.V.A.Richards*	c Boon, b Border	11	c Jones, b Hohns	4
A.L.Logie	b Border	0	c P.L.Taylor, b Hohns	6
P.J.L.Dujon†	c Hughes, b Border	18	run out	9
R.A.Harper	c P.L.Taylor, b Border	17	lbw, b Border	12
M.D.Marshall	c Marsh, b Border	9	c P.L.Taylor, b Border	3
C.E.L.Ambrose	c Jones, b P.L.Taylor	1	c Boon, b Border	5
C.A.Walsh	not out	4	not out	7
Extras	b 1, w 1, nb 3	5	b 1, w 1, nb 4	6
		224		256

	O	M	R	W	O	M	R	W
Alderman	10	2	17	0	2	0	6	0
Hughes	10	3	28	0	18	6	29	1
P.L.Taylor	25.2	8	65	2	29	4	91	1
Hohns	24	8	49	1	34	11	69	3
Border	26	10	46	7	18.4	3	50	4
Waugh	4	0	18	0	3	0	10	0

FALL OF WICKETS
1-90, 2-144, 3-156, 4-174, 5-174, 6-174, 7-199, 8-213, 9-220, 10-224
1-17, 2-56, 3-167, 4-188, 5-198, 6-225, 7-232, 8-244, 9-247, 10-256

AUSTRALIA

	FIRST INNINGS		SECOND INNINGS	
G.R.Marsh	c Dujon, b Marshall	2	b Richards	23
M.A.Taylor	b Ambrose	25	c Haynes, b Ambrose	3
D.C.Boon	c Dujon, b Walsh	149	c Harper, b Marshall	10
D.M.Jones	b Richards	29	not out	24
A.R.Border*	b Marshall	75	not out	16
S.R.Waugh	not out	55		
I.A.Healy†	c Logie, b Marshall	11		
P.L.Taylor	lbw, b Marshall	0		
T.V.Hohns	b Marshall	0		
M.G.Hughes	c Dujon, b Walsh	12		
T.M.Alderman	run out	9		
Extras	b 6, lb 14, nb 14	34	b 3, lb 1, nb 2	6
		401	(3 wickets)	82

	O	M	R	W	O	M	R	W
Marshall	31	16	29	5	8	2	17	1
Ambrose	33	5	78	1	7	1	16	1
Harper	37	9	86	0				
Walsh	22.5	5	48	2	3	0	9	0
Hooper	37	10	72	0	10.3	2	24	0
Richards	31	1	68	1	7	2	12	1

FALL OF WICKETS
1-14, 2-43, 3-114, 4-284, 5-335, 6-355, 7-357, 8-357, 9-388, 10-401
1-3, 2-16, 3-55

Umpires: L.J.King and T.A.Prue

repeated the dose with three quick wickets, and with Kallicharran completing a pair, West Indies were 29 for four - still 80 adrift.

It was then that Haynes showed a rare combination of guts and technique with a maiden Test hundred. It took Hadlee & Co 108.4 overs to bowl West Indies out for an improbable 212, with Haynes again denied the feat of carrying his bat by number eleven Colin Croft. He batted for 7¼ hours in the innings, and nine minutes short of 12 hours in the match. Surely it was the best single-handed performance in modern cricket, and one which came within one wicket of winning the game when New Zealand's last pair, Gary Troup and Stephen Boock, needed to make four to win when they came together in the tensest of finishes.

I was proud of that match, because it showed I could get my head down as well as hit the ball around. But I have chosen my Sydney knock because of the pitch, which turned square all through. They had picked two spinners, and so had we, bringing in Roger Harper instead of Patrick Patterson. The experts had always said I couldn't play spin very well, so I proved them wrong by top-scoring in both innings.

Gordon and I put on 90, and when Richie and I were going well at 144 for one, it looked as though we would get the sort of big score which would put us in charge. We played the front-line two spinners so well that Border brought himself on, and he turned the game inside out. Richie got out to a long-hop, as did three more of our guys, and we lost five wickets, all to Border, for 30.

We scraped 224 and they grafted well for 401 - David Boon played a super knock for 149 - to give them a lead of 177. By now, it was turning a lot, and I knew we'd got a fight on our hands just to survive. Gordon was our only batsman to get out to seam in either innings - and the fact he was caught and bowled by Merv Hughes says something about the pitch. We had won the series with victories at Brisbane, Perth and Melbourne, but I regarded this as my biggest challenge. What pleased me most was that I was able to defend for so long, yet I never missed a bad ball. Playing spin is an art all on its own. You can't go looking for the ball. You have to play it with soft hands and a relaxed grip, and it is easy to get so bogged down that you miss runs when the chance is there.

Wisden confirms this: 'Again carelessness had much to do with the West Indies' downfall, especially in the case of Hooper and Richards, both caught at deep mid-off trying to hit Hohns for six. The one outstanding exception was Haynes, whose 143 was considered by both captains to be among the finest innings they had seen. Haynes batted almost faultlessly for 5¼ hours, assiduously smothering the spin and making good use of the loose ball.'

What Haynes considers to be the best innings he ever played was to be in vain, although for much of the West Indies second innings it seemed that his heroics would give their spinners something around 200 to bowl at. He dominated the scoring in remarkable fashion. When Hooper was third out at 167, Haynes had scored all but 61 from the bat and the deficit was nearly wiped out. The rash dismissal of Richards started a mid-order collapse which only further underlined the magnificence of Haynes.

As wickets tumbled at the other end, the Bajan opener battled on, determined the Australian spinners would have to get him out and that he would not contribute to his own downfall. Finally, Border pitched the perfect slow left-arm leg-break, which drew him forward and took the outside edge on its way to Mark Taylor at slip. This was his 11th wicket in the match, taking his Test total to 27 and it was the first time he had taken more than four wickets in a first-class match. He also batted for 386 minutes to score 75, making the slowest-ever fifty by a Australian batsman. Modern Test pitches are not often raging turners outside India, Pakistan and Sri Lanka, which is why big individual scores under such conditions are rare. All too often, the merit of an innings is in the ability of the batsman to withstand a battering from fast bowling, but not on that late January day in Sydney.

Haynes showed that he had become a complete player. Middlesex colleague John Emburey says this of a man who has contributed a lot, on and off the field, to county cricket in his first three seasons with Middlesex in 1989, 1990 and 1992: 'He has been a tremendous help to young players like Mike Roseberry, Mark Ramprakash and Matthew Keech. He is always encouraging them, and he provides the perfect example of when they should try to take charge, and when they should defend. He has changed a bit as a player, because when he started he was more of a strokeplayer.

'Now he is solid, with no weakness. He can play all sorts of bowling, and he is not so on-side as people think. I know he stands very open, but if the ball is there outside off-stump, he just opens the face beautifully. I rate him very highly, and it has been a pleasure to play with him.'

It is no coincidence that Haynes has worked his way up to the top of the world ratings since the retirement of his longstanding partner, Gordon Greenidge. When Haynes started his Test career, Greenidge was considered to be the senior partner, but Haynes has shown what steady maturity can achieve. To take the number one spot at the age of 37 is, arguably, the best of all his performances.

95 on the fourth and fifth days of the fifth Test between Australia and England at Sydney, 6 and 7 January 1983.

This innings by Hemmings was the fifth highest score by a nightwatchman in Test cricket. He top-scored in a last day rearguard score of 314 for seven to enable his side to draw the game.

Edward Ernest Hemmings was born on 20 February 1949 in Leamington Spa. He joined Warwickshire in 1965 and made a dramatic County Championship debut three years later against Hampshire at Basingstoke. Then a seamer, he took the first six Hampshire wickets for 36, and also had Barry Richards dropped in the covers. He switched to off-cutters in 1971, but did not establish himself in the first team until 1974, when 82 wickets brought him a county cap. He joined Nottinghamshire in 1979, eventually winning selection for England in 1982 against Pakistan at Edgbaston. At 33, he was the fourth oldest England debutant since 1946 - Tony Lewis was 34 and Robin Jackman and Ian Thomson were 35. He dismissed Javed Miandad with his fourth ball in Test cricket, and played 16 times for his country in nine different series, as well as in 33 one-day internationals.

A combative cricketer who is always prepared to have his say, on and off the field, he was released by Nottinghamshire at the end of the 1992 season, and was immediately snapped up by Sussex to play for them in 1993 at the age of 44. After 14 successful seasons at Trent Bridge, he had taken 1404 wickets in 482 first-class games and scored 9297 runs, including one hundred. This book mostly includes innings played by great batsmen, but there is room for a bowler who dominates an Ashes Test match in Australia with the bat, and that is what Hemmings did in the final Test of his first overseas tour for England.

It was his third match in the series - and his most successful with the ball. His figures of 74-26-184-6 prevented a powerful Australian batting order from running away with the game, and five of his wickets came from the first six - John Dyson, David Hookes and Allan Border in the first innings, and Greg Chappell and Kim Hughes in the second.

The game had got off to a controversial start, with Willis apparently running out Dyson by some distance in the first over, only for umpire Mel Johnson to rule for the batsman. In response to Johnson's subsequent claim that 'it was either six inches in or six inches out, and that is too close to call', one of the English management wondered if he was talking about LBWs, which underlines the tourists' thoughts on several marginal decisions in the match which went against them. A wonderful sporting cartoon next morning depicted the tall Johnson standing at the bowler's end with dark glasses, white stick and a guide dog. The bowler and non-striker were looking at him, and the caption had him saying: 'Now remember. It's one woof for out and two for not out.'

As Dyson scored 79 and Australia led England on the first innings by 77 - 314 to 237 - the decision shaped the course of a match which England needed to win to square the series and thus retain the Ashes. Hughes scored 137, but the England players were convinced he was out when, with the score 82 for three,

Hughes played a delivery from Geoff Miller off his boot to Geoff Cook at short leg. Well supported by Border, who scored 89 and 83 in the game, Hughes put the game out of England's reach, and also gave the tourists an awkward 30 minutes' batting at the end of the fourth day. Hemmings remembers:

As Geoff Cook and Chris Tavaré were about to go out, Bob Willis came over to me and asked me to do nightwatchman. I was very surprised, because Bob Taylor always did it, and I had done it only once

before, when I was still with Warwickshire. My style of batting is usually an attacking one, but I was still thinking of how I might play it when Cook was LBW and, after bowling nearly all day, I was back in the middle with 20 minutes to go.

'EXACTLY WHERE I MEANT IT TO GO,' FROM THE ACTING PRESIDENT OF THE UNION OF NIGHTWATCHMEN IN JANUARY 1983 AT SYDNEY.

(PATRICK EAGAR)

I will remember my first ball from Geoff Lawson to my dying day. I normally like to get forward, but it was short and I hit it over cover for three. Not quite your usual nightwatchman's start, but I survived with Tavaré and had not scored another run when I had to face the last three balls of the day. The crowd was noisy, and so were the Aussie close fielders as I set out to block for the morning. I got an absolute beauty - it nipped back and nearly cut me in two, but I got an inside nick and four runs.

Next morning, there were a few gaps with all the close fielders, so I decided to play some shots and hit Rodney Hogg for four fours - three to third-man and one to fine-leg. I got two comments: 'F------

slogger' from Hogg, and from my partner, 'We'll have won this by tea.' As we started the day needing 452 in just under six hours, I could see the funny side of things - which the Aussies clearly could not. It was turning a bit and 'Tav' was LBW to Yardley to make it 55 for two. I was now enjoying it, especially batting with David Gower, and I got to 54 by lunch, although I had then got two bad blows on the back of the hand from Lawson, and I was struggling against pace.

I didn't know it then, but I had broken a bone. However, as Gower got out to a remarkable catch at long-off by Hookes off Yardley, I knew I had to keep going for as long as I could. I had wondered about going off, but Gower encouraged me. He was as nice to me as anyone on my first tour, and he has always impressed me as a cricketer and as a person. At lunch, Bernard Thomas packed my bottom hand with ice, and although I still was not sure I could stay on, the sledging I got from the Aussie fielders

AUSTRALIA V ENGLAND (5TH TEST)

PLAYED AT SYDNEY CRICKET GROUND, ON 2, 3, 4, 6, 7 JANUARY 1983.
TOSS: AUSTRALIA. RESULT: MATCH DRAWN.

AUSTRALIA

	FIRST INNINGS		SECOND INNINGS	
K.C.Wessels	c Willis, b Botham	19	lbw, b Botham	53
J.Dyson	c Taylor, b Hemmings	79	c Gower, b Willis	2
G.S.Chappell*	lbw, b Willis	35	c Randall, b Hemmings	11
K.J.Hughes	c Cowans, b Botham	29	c Botham, b Hemmings	137
D.W.Hookes	c Botham, b Hemmings	17	lbw, b Miller	19
A.R.Border	c Miller, b Hemmings	89	c Botham, b Cowans	83
R.W.Marsh†	c and b Miller	3	c Taylor, b Miller	41
B.Yardley	b Cowans	24	c Botham, b Hemmings	0
G.F.Lawson	c and b Botham	6	not out	13
J.R.Thomson	c Lamb, b Botham	0	c Gower, b Miller	12
R.M.Hogg	not out	0	run out	0
Extras	b 3, lb 8, w 2	13	lb 7, nb 4	11
		314		382

	O	M	R	W	O	M	R	W
Willis	20	6	57	1	10	2	33	1
Cowans	21	3	67	1	13	1	47	1
Botham	30	8	75	4	10	0	35	1
Hemmings	27	10	68	3	47	16	116	3
Miller	17	7	34	1	49.3	12	133	3
Cook					2	1	7	0

FALL OF WICKETS
1-39, 2-96, 3-150, 4-173, 5-210, 6-219, 7-262, 8-283, 9-291, 10-314
1-23, 2-38, 3-82, 4-113, 5-262, 6-350, 7-357, 8-358, 9-382, 10-382

ENGLAND

	FIRST INNINGS		SECOND INNINGS	
G.Cook	c Chappell, b Hogg	8	lbw, b Lawson	2
C.J.Tavaré	b Lawson	0	lbw, b Yardley	16
D.I.Gower	c Chappell, b Lawson	70	(4) c Hookes b Yardley	24
A.J.Lamb	b Lawson	0	(5) c and b Yardley	29
D.W.Randall	b Thomson	70	(6) b Thomson	44
I.T.Botham	c Wessels, b Thomson	5	(7) lbw, b Thomson	32
G.Miller	lbw, b Thomson	34	(8) not out	21
R.W.Taylor†	lbw, b Thomson	0	(9) not out	28
E.E.Hemmings	c Border, b Yardley	29	(3) c Marsh, b Yardley	95
R.G.D.Willis*	c Border, b Thomson	1		
N.G.Cowans	not out	0		
Extras	b 4, lb 4, nb 12	20	b 1, lb 10, w 1, nb 11	23
		237	(7 wickets)	314

	O	M	R	W	O	M	R	W
Lawson	20	2	70	3	15	1	50	1
Hogg	16	2	50	1	13	6	25	0
Thomson	14.5	2	50	5	12	3	30	2
Yardley	14	4	47	1	37	6	139	4
Border					16	3	36	0
Hookes					2	1	5	0
Chappell					1	0	6	0

FALL OF WICKETS
1-8, 2-23, 3-24, 4-146, 5-163, 6-169, 7-170, 8-220, 9-232, 10-237
1-3, 2-55, 3-104, 4-155, 5-196, 6-260, 7-261

Umpires: R.A.French and M.W.Johnson

settled it for me. They were all at it, including their captain. I was told I was slower than Boycott and other uncomplimentary things which made me even more determined to hang around and annoy them as much as I could.

The abuse from the close fielders never stopped - the only exception was Rod Marsh - and there were times I felt like wrapping the bat round Chappell's neck. I know Test cricket is played hard, but I reckon it went beyond the pale. It was therefore not a pleasant innings to play, but what kept me going was that I was doing a good job for England by getting right up the noses of the Aussies.

I still had not quite given up hopes of winning the game, because with Lamb, Randall and Botham to come, anything could happen. When we got to 155 for three, with Lamb starting to motor, we were still not out of it, but then he got caught and bowled by Yardley for 29, and that set us back. It brought Derek Randall in, and so it was Australia against Nottinghamshire.

We put on 41, and I had scored virtually half of our 196, so was more than hopeful of bringing off a fantastic double, because I had made my maiden first-class hundred a few months earlier against Yorkshire at Worksop.

His parents, sitting hardly daring to breathe in the stand to the right of the SCG press box, shared his hopes. Sniffing a 'colour piece' for the *Birmingham Post*, I went to join them when Eddie got into the 90s, and his mother was immediately sure that I would bring a change of luck. She never actually blamed me when he was given out under yet more controversial circumstances - caught at the wicket off Yardley, but it did not need a clairvoyant to guess who she blamed most - not the bowler, nor the keeper nor the umpire, but the *Birmingham Post* cricket correspondent. Hemmings says:

I swear I never hit the ball. It pitched in the rough and caught both my pads, and when I got home at the end of the tour and put the video on freeze frame, it is quite clear that my bat did not make contact. At least the innings proved to a lot of people that I could bat, and it was satisfying to know that I didn't give a chance in 226 minutes' batting. It was a genuine innings and helped save the game. We could still have lost it, especially when Jeff Thomson got Randall and Botham in three balls, but Geoff Miller and Bob Taylor played out time.

In one way, it was almost a relief to get out, because of the sledging and the determination of their quicks to pitch everything short, but I can look back now and rate it as one of my proudest moments. In another way, it led to one of my biggest disappointments too, because I was not picked again until 1987, but I have learned to take whatever cards are dealt to me.

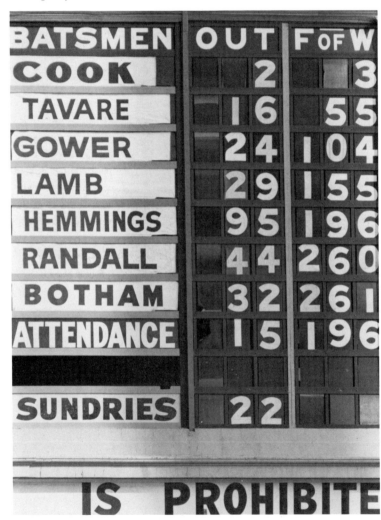

BATSMEN	OUT	F OF W
COOK	2	3
TAVARE	16	55
GOWER	24	104
LAMB	29	155
HEMMINGS	95	196
RANDALL	44	260
BOTHAM	32	261
ATTENDANCE	15	196
SUNDRIES	22	

IS PROHIBITE

95 OUT OF 196 SHOWS IT WAS MUCH MORE THAN A TAILEND KNOCK.

(PATRICK EAGAR)

Not all cricketers are so philosophical, but then not every player lasts in the physically demanding modern game for nearly 30 years, still as enthusiastic as Hemmings was when he believed he could take all ten on debut at Basingstoke in 1968. The game has been good to Hemmings, and he has been good for cricket.

GRAEME HICK

178 on the first and second days of the third Test between India and England at Bombay, 19 and 20 February 1993.

Hick came in to bat at 58 for four, with England on the verge of further disaster against an Indian spin attack which had already won the first two Tests and the series. It was Hick's 22nd innings in his 14th Test and seemed as unlikely to produce his first hundred as the previous 21, which included just two fifties and a highest score of 64.

Hick's 178 in the first innings included 20 fours, and he faced 319 deliveries in one of his longest innings - 6½ hours - in which his runs came out of 297 scored while he was at the crease. It revived the fortunes of his side and it proved that the Indian spinners were far from unplayable, even on a turning pitch.

Graeme Ashley Hick was born on 23 May 1966 in Salisbury, Rhodesia, and educated at Prince Edward's High School in the same city, now named Harare. His prodigious heavy-scoring feats - 68 hundreds in 377 innings at the start of the 1993 English season - were in evidence at the age of six when he scored 102 for Banket Primary School (24 fours), and he hit three-figure scores at every level of cricket in his formative years. The son of a tobacco farmer who was a keen sportsman, Hick captained his country's Under-13 side in South Africa after creating a record by first playing for that team when ten years old.

Politics prevented his participation in South Africa's celebrated Nuffield Schools week, but his obvious talent earned him a place, for experience only, in Zimbabwe's party for the 1983 World Cup in England, and he signed for Worcestershire the following year. His debut at The Oval in the last match of the season was his 12th first-class innings, following 11 knocks for Zimbabwe against Young West Indies, Sri Lanka and Young India. His unbeaten 82 against Surrey helped to save the game, and was then his highest score. For a batsman who was soon to average two hundreds every 11 innings, the first one was a long while coming - in his 26th innings, two years after his debut. Typically, it was a double, 230 for Zimbabwe against Oxford University at the Parks; and when he followed with 192 against Glamorgan, a new batting star had begun to twinkle.

He was capped in 1986, when he scored Championship double hundreds against Nottinghamshire and Glamorgan, and other three-figure scores against Surrey, Sussex, Gloucestershire and once more against Glamorgan. From then, until his international debut on his birthday in 1991, he rewrote the record books, completing his 49th and 50th hundreds with unbeaten innings of 252 and 100 at Abergavenny in 1990. Of those three-figure scores, six were double hundreds and 13 were scores of 150 or better. In addition, there was his unbeaten 404 in 9¼ hours at Taunton in 1988, when he broke two pieces of new ground. It was the highest score in English cricket for 93 years, and he had never before batted for longer than 305 minutes.

That innings encapsulated, perfectly, Hick's metronomic approach to batting. His progress to one, two and three hundred came off 126 balls, 152 and 133, with only the tempo of the fourth markedly different - it took him 58 balls. His clinical approach to batting might not please the aesthetes, but the fact that the slowest of his first 50 hundreds, in terms of deliveries faced, took him 197 balls illustrates a relentless quality possessed by few.

His ability to strike boundaries through a wide 'v' between extra-cover and mid-wicket, allied to a productive square-cut, meant that, of his first 10,000 runs, close to 50 percent came in boundaries, scored at a personal run-rate of four runs off every six balls faced.

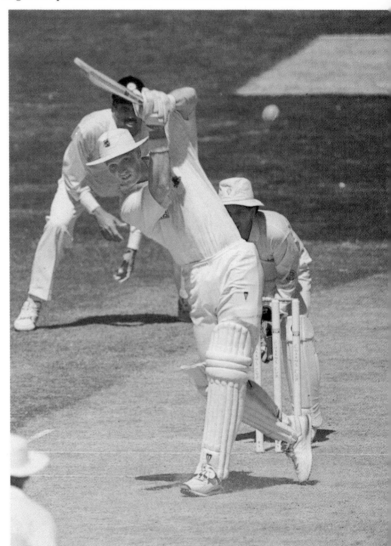

THE PAY-OFF FROM POSITIVE STROKEPLAY. A WELL-EXECUTED LOFTED DRIVE DURING HICK'S 178 IN BOMBAY. (ALLSPORT/BEN RADFORD)

He returned from the 1993 tour of India and Sri Lanka needing a handful of runs to pass 20,000 - all done in his first ten years in first-class cricket. He is a proud man, whose best innings may well prove to be the turning point of a career which had been staggeringly successful at every level other than Test cricket. He considered two other performances for Worcestershire as among his best, and had I approached him before Bombay, he would have probably settled for either his 212 against Lancashire at Old Trafford in 1988, or the dramatic 172 against the West Indies five weeks later, when he grasped his final opportunity on 28 May to become the eighth batsman to complete 1000 runs before the end of May. Only W.G.Grace and Don Bradman achieved this in fewer innings than the 11 taken by Hick.

'That innings was special because of three factors: it was my last chance to get to 1000 before the end of May; the pitch was lively and the quality of the West Indies pace attack meant I had to fight for my runs.' Patterson, Ambrose, Walsh and Bishop certainly peppered a man who they knew they would eventually face in Test cricket but, as umpire Ken Palmer says: 'He stood up to it very well, and it was a fine innings.'

I saw the other performance he rates highly, his 212 on a slow, low turner at Old Trafford. Worcestershire scored 409 for seven and won the match by ten wickets, but none of Hick's colleagues reached fifty. Skipper Phil Neale scored 40 out of a match-turning partnership for the fourth wicket of 202, and Hick's boundary count of 124 is reflected in a revealing split of the strike and runs scored. Hick's 212 came from 312 balls, with the other 197 coming from 552 deliveries.

That innings remains one of my best, because the ball turned sharply on the first morning and I had little experience of such a pitch. The year before I had been stumped by yards at Old Trafford, so this time I played everything from my crease and it worked well. I know some of the Lancashire players thought I would be easy meat on a turner, so I was especially pleased to prove them wrong.

However, he finally went for his maiden Test century. An aggregate before the Bombay Test of 397 at an average of 18.90 can only be compared with the early England records of Bill Edrich and Mike Gatting - two other batsmen who finally repaid a long-term faith by the selectors denied to many. Edrich scored 88 in his first 11 innings, and was playing in his eighth Test before he broke through with his famous 219 in the timeless Test in Durban in 1939, while Gatting scored 427 in his first 21 innings for England.

The difference between Hick and every other early 'failure' for England was his massive batting achievements at county level before his long-awaited Test debut against the West Indies at Edgbaston in

INDIA V ENGLAND (3RD TEST)

PLAYED AT WANKHEDE STADIUM, BOMBAY, ON 19, 20, 21, 22, 23 FEBRUARY 1993.
TOSS: ENGLAND. RESULT: INDIA WON BY AN INNINGS AND 15 RUNS.

ENGLAND

	FIRST INNINGS		SECOND INNINGS	
G.A.Gooch*	c More, b Kapil Dev	4	b Prabhakar	8
A.J.Stewart	run out	13	lbw, b Prabhakar	10
M.A.Atherton	c Prabhakar, b Kumble	37	c More, b Prabhakar	11
R.A.Smith	c More, b Raju	2	b Kumble	62
M.W.Gatting	c Kapil Dev, b Raju	23	st More, b Chauhan	61
G.A.Hick	c Kapil Dev, b Prabhakar	178	c Amre, b Kumble	47
R.J.Blakey†	lbw, b Kumble	1	b Kumble	0
C.C.Lewis	lbw, b Kumble	49	c More, b Raju	3
J.E.Emburey	c More, b Kapil Dev	12	c Tendulkar, b Kumble	1
P.A.J.DeFreitas	lbw, b Kapil Dev	11	st More, b Raju	12
P.C.R.Tufnell	not out	2	not out	2
Extras	b 4, lb 5, w 2, nb 4	15	(b 4, lb 6, w 1, nb 1	12
		347		229

	O	M	R	W	O	M	R	W
Kapil Dev	15	3	35	3	7	1	21	0
Prabhakar	13	2	52	1	11	4	28	3
Raju	44	8	102	2	26.5	7	68	2
Kumble	40	4	95	3	26	9	70	4
Chauhan	23	7	54	0	12	5	32	1

INDIA

	FIRST INNINGS	
N.S.Sidhu	c Smith, b Tufnell	79
M.Prabhakar	c Blakey, b Hick	44
V.G.Kambli	c Gatting, b Lewis	224
S.R.Tendulkar	lbw, b Tufnell	78
M.Azharuddin*	lbw, b Lewis	26
P.K.Amre	c DeFreitas, b Hick	57
Kapil Dev	c DeFreitas, b Emburey	22
K.S.More†	c Lewis, b Emburey	0
A.Kumble	c Atherton, b Tufnell	16
R.K.Chauhan	c Atherton, b Tufnell	15
S.L.V.Raju	not out	0
Extras	b 5, lb 14, w 5, nb 6	30
		591

	O	M	R	W
DeFreitas	20	4	75	0
Lewis	42	9	114	2
Emburey	59	14	144	2
Tufnell	39.3	6	142	4
Hick	29	3	97	2

FALL OF WICKETS

1-11, 2-25, 3-30, 4-58, 5-116, 6-118, 7-211, 8-262, 9-279, 10-347
1-17, 2-26, 3-34, 4-155, 5-181, 6-181, 7-206, 8-214, 9-215, 10-229

FALL OF WICKETS

1-109, 2-174, 3-368, 4-418, 5-519, 6-560, 7-560, 8-563, 9-591, 10-591

Umpires: P.D.Reporter and S.Venkataraghavan

1991. He would certainly have played Test cricket much earlier, but for an enforced seven-year wait to comply with the rules of qualification, which is why expectations were understandably high in 1991, for by that time he had become the youngest cricketer to score 50 hundreds.

It was the most important innings of my life, because of the position of the match and the series, and the fact that it was my first hundred in a Test. When Mike Atherton and Richard Blakey got out, we were 118 for six and I knew that if I followed, the innings might not last much longer, because the ball was turning.

I had actually been playing well since my 25 in the second innings in Calcutta, so I felt confident enough. The innings took on different perspectives as it developed. It turned more before lunch on the first day than later, perhaps because it was damp. I went in 15 minutes before lunch and the odd one bit and kicked, but after the break it seemed a bit easier. Only the odd one went, and I decided to stay in a positive frame of mind. I have never had any trouble hitting the spinners over the top - after all, it's only an extension of an on-the-ground shot - so I went for it. I got away with one that was close to mid-on, but it still went for four, and I was pleased with the rest of my shot-selection. I find that if you bat that way, positively, they bowl differently at you, which is what you try to do - make the bowlers do something different.

I even tried to play Kumble in the same way, because after the first Test I had come to terms with his drift, which was more or less always into me. I was 96 when he started the last over of the day, and naturally I was keen to get to a hundred that night. I thought I had when I got one away to long-leg, but Kapil's boot meant it was three and I lost the strike. It would be silly to pretend I did not think about it overnight. If I had got one more run I could have celebrated properly with the lads, and also if I got out next morning after scoring the single, I would not have counted that as a great achievement.

I slept reasonably well, although I couldn't help but think of different ways I might get out. As it happened, I pushed a single off Kapil's third ball, and that really came from watching their batsmen play, and how well they kept the score ticking over with singles. Once they pushed the ball past the close fielders they were off, and I tried to do the same. I tried to think each phase of my innings through, and play accordingly. John Emburey is a good partner, because he can look after himself, and I was able to concentrate on getting as many runs as possible. We put on 51 before he was caught at the wicket, and then I decided to open out. I think in the last hour or so of my innings, I came as near as I have ever done to bat for England in the same way I do for Worcestershire. I felt in control, and we managed another 85 from the last two wickets.

As should be the case with a class batsman, the longer Hick was at the crease, the more dominant he became, and his shot-selection was so well executed that his last three partners, Emburey, DeFreitas and Tufnell contributed 25 of the 136 scored in partnerships for the eighth, ninth and tenth wickets, respectively. It was a triumph for a man who had failed against West Indies and Pakistan, and proved that his temperament was sound, and that his technique could be successful against any bowling short of top pace. England's final total of 347 should have ensured at least a draw, but relatively innocuous bowling resulted in India gaining a lead of 244 and completing a 3-0 clean sweep of the series by an innings and 15 runs. Hick completed his best Test to date with 47 in the second innings, and the wickets of Prabhakar and Amre to underline his potential as a useful off-spinner.

This innings was a source of relief both to him and the selectors, and also confirmation that the most voracious appetite for runs in modern cricket could gorge at the international table. David Frith hailed the breakthrough, albeit with a note of caution. 'England could at least delight in the emergence of Graeme Hick, whose maiden Test century provided relief from two years of unbearable tension. "Give me two years to prove myself," Hick had asked when his qualification period was complete. Expectations had been so high, and performances so low, that such patience was too much to expect. The slow pitches of India were always likely to serve him well, but before his class is established, he will need to achieve similar batting standards against Australia and the West Indies.'

So he does, but there can be little argument that, by scoring 20,000 first-class runs by the age of 27 years and 20 days - another record, beating that of Wally Hammond by almost a year - Hick's place in the record books is already secure.

JAVED MIANDAD

116 in the final of the Austral-Asia
Cup between Pakistan and India at
Sharjah, 18 April 1986.*

Needing 246 in 50 overs, Pakistan were taken to a spectacular victory by Javed Miandad, whose unbeaten century included a six off the final ball of the match. He came in to bat at 29 for two and, after the fourth wicket went down with the score at 110, he played one of the best one-day innings ever seen.

His masterly exhibition of placement and running between the wickets won him not only the Man of the Match award, but also many other gifts, including a new Mercedes-Benz car, a diamond-encrusted bracelet, reputedly worth over twice the winning team's prize-money of $40,000, and various gifts of cash from admirers.

Javed Miandad was born on 12 June 1957 in Karachi. He made his Test debut for Pakistan in Lahore against New Zealand in October 1976, and scored 163 at the start of a three-match series in which he scored 504 runs in four completed innings. This included an innings of 206 in the third Test in Karachi, which made him, at the age of 19 years and 141 days, the youngest to score a double hundred in Test cricket. It was the start of a distinguished, if sometimes stormy, international career in which he had played in 121 Tests and over 200 one-day internationals at the end of Pakistan's tour of the West Indies in May 1993.

He has captained his country 34 times, winning 14 Tests and losing six, and his aggregate of Test runs is third only to that of Allan Border and Sunil Gavaskar. Thanks to two successful periods in English county cricket with Sussex and Glamorgan, he has scored nearly 30,000 first-class runs and is one of only two modern batsmen - Allan Border is the other - to average over 50 in both Test and first-class cricket. His batting method is based on an unorthodox stance which is far from sideways-on, but succeeds because of a hawk-like watchfulness and a minimal backlift. He is a great adjuster, with an instinctive ability to play the ball later than most batsmen. An abrasive cricketer, he has been at the centre of several incidents, notably when he and Dennis Lillee clashed physically in Perth in 1981, and when he was captain in Faisalabad in 1987 in the 'Gatting-Shakoor Rana' Test. Although not on the field at the time of the flare-up, it is widely believed that he was influential in preventing any further play until the England captain issued a public apology. Like John McEnroe in tennis, Javed pushes officials and opponents to the limit if he thinks he can gain a tactical advantage, and he was fortunate to escape censure at Old Trafford in 1992 when umpire Roy Palmer was harassed, following a warning given to Aqib Javed.

He charms, then infuriates; he delights and then offends. However, he is content to be judged on a playing record that is of the highest quality. His horizons are such that, in 1987 at The Oval, when he was finally dismissed for 260 - one of only two three-figure scores against England in 22 Tests - he expressed his disgust because he believed that the Garry Sobers record score of 365 was there for the taking.

He is a battler, and because no game is won or lost while he is batting, he has a string of innings from which to pick one as the best of his life. For nearly two decades he has taken on and beaten the world's best bowlers, so his choice must be a special one.

I have picked my hundred against India in Sharjah which won us the Austral-Asia Cup off the last ball of the match. I count that as my best innings for several reasons: it was a five-nation tournament, and a final between us and India was what the locals wanted most. We had knocked Australia and New Zealand out with two comfortable wins by eight and ten wickets, but we looked beaten when India were 216 for one. Imran and Wasim Akram got us back into it with a couple of wickets each and, although they finished with 245 for seven, we still had a chance on what is always a good pitch.

An interesting shuffle of the Indian batting order failed, as six wickets fell for 29 and, even though Mohammad Azharuddin had then been in Test cricket for only two years, it seems unbelievable that, with quick runs the priority, he did not bat after being relegated behind Chetan Sharma, Ravi Shastri and Chandu Pandit.

The Sharjah Stadium was built by a wealthy Arab who spent his university days in Pakistan, and became a cricket fanatic. Abdul Raman Bukhatir decided that a 'neutral' cricket ground in Sharjah was the answer to political problems which usually affected games between Pakistan and India in their own countries. A decisive factor was the number of Asian ex-patriates working in Sharjah, and an initial ground capacity of around 15,000 was tested so many times that it was recently increased by at least 50 percent.

The ground is well appointed, with British names like umpire 'Dickie' Bird and television commentator Tony Lewis full of praise for the facilities. Bird says: 'It is a lovely well-grassed field in the middle of grey

THE MOST BELLIGERENT STROKEMAKER OF THE 1980S - AS DAVID GOWER REALISES DURING JAVED'S 260 AT THE OVAL IN 1987.

(PATRICK EAGAR)

sand, and the changing-rooms and umpires' accommodation are first class.'

Lewis was commentating during the closing overs of the game Javed has chosen, and remembers the crowd atmosphere: 'It was electric, with the loyalties of an all-ticket crowd evenly divided. There was a roaring black-market trade for what was a dream final, and the noise was more like that of a football match than a game of cricket.

'The ground is about four miles out of Sharjah, and the only buildings nearby are blocks of flats and often you can only see the city through a haze of grey sand. What adds to the atmosphere is the fact that more betting takes place on the Sharjah ground than anywhere else I have seen. More people than not have mobile telephones which they use to contact the Bombay bookmakers sometimes two or three times an over.'

Cricket in England has admitted the bookmakers at all the Test grounds, but the business done is nothing compared with Bombay, which I can confirm handles more and bigger commissions on a ball-by-ball basis than in England, where business is usually suspended once play is in progress.

The Indian supporters on that April day in 1986 must have been counting their rupees when Mudassar Nazar (5), Mohsin Khan (36), and Ramiz Raja (10) were back in the pavilion with the score only 61. Salim Malik hit 21 out of 49 added for the fourth wicket with Javed before he was run out and, with over half the overs gone, so, apparently, had Pakistan's winning chances.

An initial asking rate of just under five an over was now nearly double that, and it needed something exceptional if the Pakistan supporters were not to contribute to the profits of the BBF - the Bombay bookmaking fraternity. But Javed was still there - running like a prairie cat and chivvying partners to play their part by being at the non-striker's end as often as possible.

The return of Kapil Dev did for Qadir, who had been promoted up the order and hit 34 in a fifth-wicket partnership of 71. But when Imran and Manzoor went quickly to Madan Lal and Chetan Sharma, the Indian supporters pressed their international dial numbers like expert touch-typists. Wasim Akram, then only 19, scored three out of a frantic eighth-wicket partnership of 20, but 11 were still needed when Chetan began the last dramatic over. He bowled Zulqarnain before Tausif scored one of the most important singles of his career to give the strike to Javed.

His last five partners had contributed just 15 between them. Javed himself had scored 70 percent of the runs required after the fall of the fourth wicket, with hardly a boundary being hit, which emphasises his unrivalled ability to take charge of a game with brilliant improvisation. Despite this low boundary count, he kept his side in the game in the face of a required run rate in excess of nine during the last ten overs.

Let Javed and Tony Lewis describe the climax as they saw it from standpoints over 100 yards apart. Javed first:

We were so near, yet I had to hit boundaries. Even though I managed one off Chetan, we needed another off the last ball of the match. There seemed to be masses of team-talks going on, but you could not hear a word because of the crowd noise.

Lewis remembers: 'I had Asif Iqbal with me, and he hardly dared to look as Chetan ran in for death or glory. The odds were with him because, magnificently though Javed had played, he had still hit only one six and two fours, and now he had to hit another. Three runs would have tied the game but Pakistan had lost more wickets so it had to be a boundary.

'Poor Chetan! I assume he tried to get the ball up into the block-hole, but he overdid it and it arrived at Javed's end as a full toss, about knee-high. I can still see the ball disappearing over mid-on and over the fence for six, and it seemed as though the entire desert became an echo-chamber.'

Back to Javed:

I have witnessed many crowd scenes, but nothing like that. Many of them were in tears [a coup at 5-1 can do that - even to hard-bitten gamblers!] and I got the biggest reception of my life. I have always thought that Sharjah is the perfect place for India and Pakistan to meet, because there is no crowd segregation, and never any trouble.

Emotional and happy memories in plenty for one of cricket's toughest characters, and his bank manager would not have been too displeased either. As for the 'Merc', presumably it was that car to which Imran referred in his book *All Round View* when he wrote about the delayed appearances of Javed and Qadir at the start of the 1987 tour of England. 'We started the tour badly when Kent beat us by an innings. Javed and Qadir had still not joined us for personal reasons - Qadir because his wife was ill, Javed because he was trying to release his car from Customs.'

Javed also considered one of his two hundreds against New Zealand in Hyderabad in 1984 for 'the innings of my life', but his final comment about cricket in the desert reveals it was hardly a contest. 'Nobody's cricket education is complete until they have played in Sharjah.'

He and Imran have not always thought and acted together as one, so when Pakistan's World Cup captain has this to say of a man who has been both colleague and rival, it can be considered to be a reasonably definitive assessment.

INDIA V PAKISTAN (AUSTRAL-ASIA CUP FINAL)

PLAYED AT SHARJAH, ON 18 APRIL 1986.
TOSS: PAKISTAN. RESULT: PAKISTAN WON BY ONE WICKET.

INDIA

K.Srikkanth	c Wasim, b Qadir	75
S.M.Gavaskar	b Imran	92
D.B.Vengsarkar	b Wasim	50
K.Azad	b Wasim	0
Kapil Dev*	b Imran	8
Chetan Sharma	run out	10
R.J.Shastri	b Wasim	1
C.S.Pandit†	not out	0
M.Azharuddin		
Madan Lal	did not bat	
Maninder Singh		
Extras	lb 6, w 2, nb 1	9
	(50 overs, 7 wickets)	245

	O	M	R	W
Imran	10	2	40	2
Wasim	10	1	42	3
Manzoor	5	0	33	0
Mudassar	5	0	32	0
Qadir	10	2	49	1
Tauseef	10	1	43	0

FALL OF WICKETS
1-117, 2-216, 3-216, 4-229, 5-242, 6-245, 7-245

PAKISTAN

Mudassar Nazar	lbw, b Chetan	5
Mohsin Khan	b Madan Lal	36
Ramiz Raja	b Maninder	10
Javed Miandad	not out	116
Salim Malik	run out	21
Abdul Qadir	c sub (R.Lamba), b Kapil Dev	34
Imran Khan*	b Madan Lal	7
Manzoor Elahi	c Shastri, b Chetan	4
Wasim Akram	run out	3
Zulqarnain†	b Chetan	0
Tauseef Ahmed	not out	1
Extras	lb 11	11
	(50 overs, 9 wickets)	248

	O	M	R	W
Kapil Dev	10	1	45	1
Chetan	9	0	51	3
Madan Lal	10	0	53	2
Maninder	10	0	36	1
Shastri	9	0	38	0
Azharuddin	2	0	14	0

FALL OF WICKETS
1-9, 2-39, 3-61, 4-110, 5-181, 6-209, 7-215, 8-235, 9-241

Umpires: D.M.Archer and A.Gaynor

In 1988: 'There is no doubt that Javed is our top batsman now. He is a real street-fighter, and the displays he puts on are an indication of his competitiveness. He learned his cricket in a hard school, and he always tries, whatever the importance of the fixture. I ran some six-a-side matches for my benefit in 1987, and found it difficult to get involved with this sort of knockabout cricket, but Javed was always in there, fighting like a tiger. He is an excellent player of spin bowling, even on bad pitches. He likes taking risks and loves to improvise.'

After the bitter series in the Caribbean in 1991, Imran added this about his senior player. 'He gave me his complete co-operation. He is an out-and-out team man who tries to help on and off the field, and my respect for him went up during the series.'

I bracket Javed with Geoffrey Boycott as a man who I would pick, if pressed, to play an innings for my life. And, as he took guard, I would be dialling Bombay.

*Walter Hammond's 240 on the first
and second days of the second
Test between England and Australia
at Lord's, 24 and 25 June 1938.*

Hammond rescued England's first innings from 31 for three with 240 out of 494. It was his seventh score of 200 or more for England, and took him within striking distance of becoming the first batsman to score 6000 Test runs - a feat he accomplished three games and five innings later in Johannesburg. It was his highest Test score in England, and is the innings which BBC cricket commentator Brian Johnston has picked as 'the best I ever saw'. Then a teenager, the doyen of the Test Match Special commentary box was spellbound at the performance of a man who had always been his boyhood hero.

Walter Reginald Hammond was born on 19 June 1903 in Buckland, Dover, and died on 1 July 1965 in Durban. He was England's supreme all-round cricketer of the first half of the 20th century and, nearly 30 years after his death, he still has many records to his name, some of which are unlikely ever to be beaten. In 1928, he took 78 catches in a season, including ten in a match at Cheltenham against Surrey. He has by far the highest career average - 56.10 - of the seven batsmen who scored over 50,000 first-class runs, and his 167 hundreds in 1005 innings give him the lowest ratio (one in 6.1) among English batsmen who scored 100 hundreds. Only Bradman bettered him in this revealing statistic.

At Test level, he still holds several partnership records. In his era, performances in Ashes Test matches outranked those against other countries, which makes his aggregate of 905 runs in the 1928-29 series the most remarkable individual performance by any Englishman in history.

Brilliance is rarely twinned with consistency, but his stepping-stones to 7000 Test runs showed that it was possible for genius to span three decades. He reached 1000 in 18 innings, 2000 in a further 21, 3000 in another 22, 4000 in an additional 15, 5000 in another 21, 6000 in 17 more, with the final march to 7000, achieved after the Second World War, also taking him 17 innings. He was the first man to score double hundreds in successive Test innings - at Sydney and Melbourne in 1928-29 - and he still holds the record for the fastest triple hundred - 288 minutes at Auckland in 1933, which beat, by 48 minutes, Bradman's innings at Headingley in 1930. Of his final unbeaten 336, 295 came in one day - again a record.

He is the only Englishman to score four triple hundreds, and still holds the records for most

Championship hundreds in one season (13) and most Championship double hundreds (22). In an historic week of Championship cricket at Cheltenham in 1928, he took 15 wickets for 128 against Worcestershire and, in addition to his record of ten catches against Surrey the same week, he scored 139 and 143.

Small wonder that he was the idol of schoolboys between the wars, and small wonder that Brian Johnston has picked a Hammond epic as 'the best innings that I ever saw'. And epic it certainly was, played on cricket's greatest stage in an Ashes Test, with England at crisis point when Hammond walked in to bat.

Where schoolboys and their idols are concerned, hopes and expectations are rarely fulfilled. That morning at Lord's, the young Johnston scarcely dared to watch as Hammond emerged from the pavilion, with the scoreboard showing 20 for two. Hutton had been caught at short-leg off McCormick, while Edrich had played on, trying to hook the same bowler. It was part of a miserable sequence of scores for that summer of 5, 0, 10, 12, 28 and 12. Johnston remembers that June day in 1938.

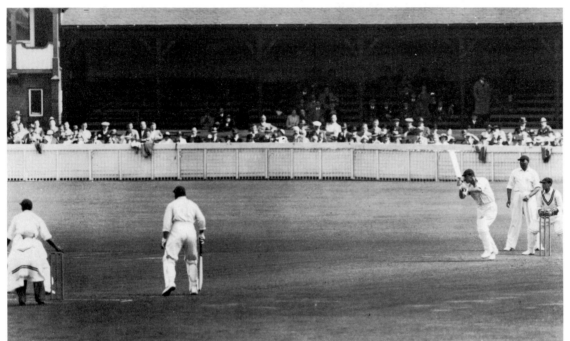

I worshipped Hammond because he was head and shoulders above his contemporaries in England, and he had such style. He had a commanding presence and there was an aura of majesty in the way he walked to the wicket. 'Like a ship in full sail,' R.C.Robertson Glasgow once wrote. He was strong and beautifully built, and, like a boxer, was light on his feet.

HAMMOND PLAYS HIS FAVOURITE OFF-DRIVE. (*HULTON-DEUTSCH COLLECTION*)

His trademark was his dark blue handkerchief showing out of his right hip pocket - like the Arnie Palmer golf glove, nonchalantly tucked there whenever he putted. Remember, the Aussies had the Ashes and we had to win the series to get them back. The first Test at Trent Bridge was drawn, with Paynter and McCabe scoring double hundreds, and Barnett, Hutton, Compton, Brown and Bradman hitting hundreds in a game in which 1496 runs were scored from 502.3 overs - and all in four days.

My hero joined his Gloucestershire partner, Charlie Barnett, at 20 for two, and I held my breath. Another disaster, with Barnett out to McCormick, also at short-leg and, at 31 for three, not an Englishman at Lord's thought we would lose only another couple of wickets that day. Well, perhaps there was one - dear old Neville Cardus. He watched Wally stride out, and murmured, 'He's going to get a hundred.' Not often was he wrong, but he was that day - he got a double.

It was marvellous to watch. He leaned back and cracked McCormick off the back foot through the covers many times, and he played the perfect captain's innings. Eddie Paynter was the ideal partner - unselfish and, as a left-hander, he unsettled the Australian attack, of whom Bill O'Reilly was easily the best.

McCormick had taken his three wickets for 15 in 25 balls, but Wally changed everything in the next few hours. He got to a hundred in 145 minutes, and put on 222 (double Nelson, but I wonder if anyone noticed in those days) in just over three hours with Paynter, before Bill O'Reilly got him and Denis Compton out LBW before tea and, when Les Ames joined Wally at 271 for five, the innings was back in the balance.

They were terrific! Wally and Les - they both eventually got 100 hundreds, and what a bonus for England it was to have a wicketkeeper who was good enough to play as a batsman. At the close of play, England were 409 for five, and I knew that I had seen one of the great innings at Lord's. Not just because it was from my hero, but because it was a double hundred scored when his side was in trouble, and it was a real captain's innings. It was only his second game as captain, because he had now turned amateur, and he and Ken Farnes were referred to on the scorecard as 'Mr', with the other nine professionals prefaced only by their initials.

Hammond got out the next day, bowled leg stump by McCormick to end one of the great Test match innings. He hit 32 sumptuous fours and batted for just seven minutes more than six hours. It was a funny game in many ways, because Les Ames fractured a finger and Eddie Paynter kept wicket. Also Ken Farnes should have had a hat-trick, but Fleetwood-Smith was dropped in the slips after he got O'Reilly and McCormick with successive deliveries.

In the end, the game was drawn, but Bill Brown had to carry his bat in the first innings for 206, and Bradman scored a fine unbeaten 102 in the second to do it. At 31 for three on that agonising first day, Wally and I would have settled for that, but not after we turned the tide. I say 'we', because I played every ball with him. He may not have known it, but there were two of us partnering Paynter and Ames on that Friday and Saturday.

I knew then there would never be another cricketer like him. He had such style and bearing. He was handsome, and had such a strong and athletic build. The crowds for the four days totalled a record 100,933, thanks to a record attendance for one day on the Saturday, when the official attendance was 33,800.

Lord's has seen many great games and been the stage for many great innings, but Wally's 240 was the best I ever saw. I considered one other innings - and that was on the same ground and was in the same attacking mould: Ted Dexter's 70 against Wes Hall and Charlie Griffith in 1963 was brilliant. It was possibly even more thrilling than Hammond's innings, but one was 70 and the other 240. Also I saw the one before I was out of my teens, and Wally was my hero. I love those few cricketers who have something about their appearance which is pure charisma. Wally was one, Ted was another and so was Garry Sobers.

My one regret is that I never spoke to him or interviewed him when I was the television commentator for the two London Tests in 1946 against India. It just didn't happen in those days. No interviews on the prospects of the match at the close of play, nor even at the end of the game. I made up for it in December 1964 in Durban, when I saw him watching England practise. I introduced myself and he could not have been more charming. My lasting memory is of him holding court in the team hotel, with all the players hanging on to his every word. I thought after he died how glad I was that he came back into the fold, so to speak, after an unhappy time in his life.

The manager of that tour, Donald Carr, remembers inviting Hammond into the dressing-room during the Test. 'I played with him in a Victory Test in 1945, but he always tended to be a little distant. He had had a bad car accident in South Africa, and the doctors reckon he only survived because he was such a strong man.' England captain M.J.K.Smith remembers Hammond's physical appearance. 'He looked so strong, even though he was then 61 and had had the accident. He was around six feet tall, and had the same sort of stocky build as Ken Barrington with massive forearms.'

Carr adds: 'After the Test, the boys were so impressed by him that they clubbed together to fly him to the last Test in Port Elizabeth two months later. He came, and it was immensely sad to hear that he died five months later. He was a wonderful player of spin bowling, and there are all sorts of stories about how he used to play Tom Goddard in the Bristol nets with the edge of the bat, if the pitch was turning.

ENGLAND V AUSTRALIA (2ND TEST)

PLAYED AT LORD'S, LONDON, ON 24, 25, 27, 28 JUNE 1938.
TOSS: ENGLAND. RESULT: MATCH DRAWN.

ENGLAND

	FIRST INNINGS		SECOND INNINGS	
C.J.Barnett	c Brown, b McCormick	18	c McCabe, b McCormick	12
L.Hutton	c Brown, b McCormick	4	c McCormick, b O'Reilly	5
W.J.Edrich	b McCormick	0	(4) c McCabe, b McCormick	10
W.R.Hammond*	b McCormick	240	(6) c sub (M.G.Waite), b McCabe	2
E.Paynter	lbw, b O'Reilly	99	run out	43
D.C.S.Compton	lbw, b O'Reilly	6	(7) not out	76
L.E.G.Ames†	c McCormick, b Fleetwood-Smith	83	(8) c McCabe, b O'Reilly	6
H.Verity	b O'Reilly	5	(3) b McCormick	11
A.W.Wellard	b McCormick, b O'Reilly	4	b McCabe	38
D.V.P.Wright	b Fleetwood-Smith	6	not out	10
K.Farnes	not out	5		
Extras	b 1, lb 12, w 1, nb 10	24	b 12, lb 12, w 1, nb 4	29
		494	(8 wickets declared)	242

	O	M	R	W	O	M	R	W
McCormick	27	1	101	4	24	5	72	3
McCabe	31	4	86	0	12	1	58	2
Fleetwood-Smith	33.5	2	139	2	7	1	30	0
O'Reilly	37	6	93	4	29	10	53	2
Chipperfield	8.4	0	51	0				

FALL OF WICKETS
1-12, 2-20, 3-31, 4-253, 5-271, 6-457, 7-472, 8-476, 9-483, 10-494
1-25, 2-28, 3-43, 4-64, 5-76, 6-128, 7-142, 8-216

AUSTRALIA

	FIRST INNINGS		SECOND INNINGS	
J.H.W.Fingleton	c Hammond, b Wright	31	c Hammond, b Wellard	4
W.A.Brown	not out	206	b Verity	10
D.G.Bradman*	b Verity	18	not out	102
S.J.McCabe	c Verity, b Farnes	38	c Hutton, b Verity	21
A.L.Hassett	lbw, b Wellard	56	b Wright	42
C.L.Badcock	b Wellard	0	c Wright, b Edrich	21
B.A.Barnett†	c Compton, b Verity	8	c Paynter, b Edrich	14
A.G.Chipperfield	lbw, b Verity	1		
W.J.O'Reilly	b Farnes	42		
E.L.McCormick	c Barnett, b Farnes	0		
L.O'B.Fleetwood-Smith	c Barnett, b Verity	7		
Extras	b 1, lb 8, nb 6	15	b 5, lb 3, w 2, nb 1	11
		422	(6 wickets)	204

	O	M	R	W	O	M	R	W
Farnes	43	6	135	3	13	3	51	0
Wellard	23	2	96	2	9	1	30	1
Wright	16	2	68	1	8	0	56	1
Verity	35.4	9	103	4	13	5	29	2
Edrich	4	2	5	0	5.2	0	27	2

FALL OF WICKETS
1-69, 2-101, 3-152, 4-276, 5-276, 6-307, 7-308, 8-393, 9-393, 10-422
1-8, 2-71, 3-111, 4-175, 5-180, 6-204

Umpires: E.J.Smith and F.I.Walden

'When I joined Derbyshire, I heard a lovely story about their pre-war leg-spinner, Tommy Mitchell. Wally had given him some almighty tap for three or four years, and all Tommy wanted was to get him out once. He ran up to bowl at him at Burton and watched in horror as Wally, still on nought, smashed a catch into the covers, which went down. So did Tommy, full length on the ground as he burst into tears. He feared the worst and was right - nought for plenty again.'

Let Brian Johnston have the last word:

My favourite cricket photograph is of him playing his famous cover drive, from a yard outside his crease, with that dark blue handkerchief showing out of his trouser pocket. He was in the perfect position for the stroke as he followed through with the bat. It must have been four.

'Johnners' is the best. So was Walter Reginald Hammond.

ALVIN KALLICHARRAN

124 on the first and second days of the first Test between India and West Indies at Bangalore, 22 and 23 November 1974.

Kallicharran's century came out of a West Indies total of 289. Other than 93 from Gordon Greenidge, only Roy Fredericks and Clive Lloyd reached double figures on a rain-affected pitch which helped the seamers on the first day and, after more overnight rain, the Indian spin trio of Chandrasekhar, Prasanna and Venkataraghavan on a drying pitch on the second day. It was Kallicharran's fifth Test hundred in his 16th Test match, and his masterly performance gave his side a platform from which they went on to win the game comfortably by 267 runs. The victory set the pattern for a thrilling series, in which all five matches provided results, and West Indies won 3-2.

Alvin Isaac Kallicharran was born on 21 March 1949 in a small sugar plantation in Port Mourant, Berbice, Guyana. His early schooling was at St Joseph Anglican School, although his boyhood heroes - born in the same village - Basil Butcher, Rohan Kanhai and Joe Solomon went to the Roman Catholic School. Kallicharran is a typical product of back-street cricket in the Caribbean, where his improvised bat was a coconut branch and the ball was made from empty tins squashed together. Cricket has been his life.

When I was about five, we kids used to listen to cricket on the radio. The whole street would go into our one big shop, and we would listen to local boys who had made good. When the radio finished, we would run and play any sort of cricket we could and, like kids all over the world, we would pretend to be one of our heroes. I was always Rohan Kanhai - he is 14 years older than me, which seems nothing now, but when I was five he was like a god to me.

Small wonder that Kallicharran named his son after Kanhai and, although there was a break in their relationship for a few years, their longstanding friendship is now happily restored.

All my early cricket was barefooted, even when I got into the school side. My first big break came in 1965 in the first inter-island schoolboy tournament ever organised in the West Indies. I was made captain, and what a thrill it was to leave Berbice for the first time, and go to Georgetown - the first time I had ever been to a city. If that opened my eyes, what about when I sat in my first plane a few days later?

I had a good tournament and was immediately invited to the Guyana trials, where I got three hundreds and I played for the island team under the captaincy of Lance Gibbs in 1966. What a batting line-up they had then, and I got my first chance only because Clive Lloyd broke a hand. There I was, a little chap, playing with Rohan, Roy Fredericks, Steve Camacho and Basil Butcher. I stayed in the side, and although I got plenty of runs, the West Indies batting order was so strong that I could not force my way in until April 1972 against New Zealand on my home Bourda ground.

He became only the fourth West Indian to score a hundred in his first innings in Test cricket. Kallicharran went on to play in 66 Tests and scored 4399 runs, including 12 hundreds, at an average of 44.43. He signed

for Warwickshire in 1972, and became one of the most successful and influential overseas players in English county cricket until his retirement in 1990. Only Gordon Greenidge, Viv Richards, Zaheer Abbas and Glenn Turner from abroad have scored more runs than Kallicharran's first-class aggregate of 32,650, and his total of 87 hundreds has only been bettered by the above quartet and Bradman.

At his best, he was a stylish left-hander, capable of a brilliance which destroyed the best bowlers. At The Oval in the 1975 World Cup, his contemptuous treatment of Dennis Lillee had to be seen to be believed, and his match-winning hundred in a limited-overs match at Taunton was highlighted by a ferocious back-foot onslaught on Joel Garner such as his international colleague had rarely experienced. In that innings, he and Dennis Amiss put on 153 for the third wicket - the former England batsman scored 59 - and the little left-hander was in such crashing form that he hit 102 out of 141 in boundaries, one six and 24 fours.

He took over his country's captaincy during the Packer revolution. Kallicharran thought this honour was

A PERFECTLY EXECUTED HOOK   taken away from him in unseemly haste as soon as the 'rebels' returned, and
SHOT BY KALLICHARRAN, WITH THE   this led to a disaffection with authority which ended his Test career at 31.
BACK FOOT HAVING SWIVELLED   When he was omitted from the West Indies party to tour Australia in 1981-82
THROUGH NEARLY 180 DEGREES.   - he claims he was told that he would be selected - he signed to coach and
(PATRICK EAGAR)   play in South Africa where he spent several English winters. This resulted in

a temporary excommunication from his native Guyana, and it is sad that such a happy, talented cricketer should have departed the international scene so prematurely.

Like all great batsmen - and that is what he was in the 1970s - the choice of his best innings is difficult, and he narrowed it down thus:

The game before our World Cup match against Australia in 1975, four Sri Lankans had been put in hospital by Lillee and Thomson, and we knew we had a problem against them. Once you hit them, you know they will come again - and again. It was also the first time I had faced them as a pair. At that time I loved to hook and pull, and so I took them on. I middled a couple of hooks and actually scored 35 off ten balls.

That was special, but you have to look at an innings which helped win a Test match. That is why I go for Bangalore, because my 124 came on a drying pitch against the best spinners in the world. Also it was the first Test match ever played in Bangalore and there was a crowd of over 50,000 who knew I was of Indian origin, so it was almost like going home. They were very fair to me, even though my batting helped beat their side.

Because of overnight rain, we didn't start until 20 minutes before lunch, and that delay was extra nerve-wracking for Gordon Greenidge, who was making his debut. We were put in to bat and, with rain having got on the pitch, batting was bound to be difficult. Viv Richards also made his debut in that game, and it was Clive Lloyd's first game as captain.

The new ball went all over the place, but Abid Ali and Solkar couldn't take advantage, and Pataudi soon turned to spin. Roy Fredericks and Gordon Greenidge batted well, but to show you how lively the pitch was, Roy was hit by a Chandrasekhar bouncer, bang in the middle of his forehead. He could hook, but he had no chance, and remember Chandra was a leg-spinner. He was one of the best bowlers I ever faced, because he was so quick and aggressive - always at you and even more difficult for left-handers, because his googly and bouncing top-spinner would leave the bat.

Although the scorebook shows the opening stand was worth 177, I had to go in when we were 38, because Roy sprained an ankle and was only able to bat again next day, and then took no further part in the match. I could not afford to defend against Chandra, because there were four of the best close catchers in Test cricket around me.

We would have been in real trouble had Bishen Bedi played, but he was banned for that match as a disciplinary measure for giving a live television interview in England earlier that year. I had to gamble, so I swept Chandra over mid-wicket for one of my two sixes, and with Gordon playing well in his first Test innings, we had a good couple of sessions. I couldn't get down the pitch to Chandra, but I did against the two off-spinners, and it unsettled them.

India took their first wicket in the final session, but the credit - or blame - did not belong to a bowler. Greenidge, within seven runs of emulating Kallicharran by scoring a hundred in his first Test innings, was run out. As usual, there are two slightly differing versions of the incident. Greenidge insists that 'Kalli was ball-watching'. Nearly 20 years later, the official party line of Guyana and Barbados is still at variance. 'It was never a run,' comments Kallicharran, accompanied, it must be said, by a giggle.

In came Richards for his first Test innings and, after one boundary, out he went for the first of two dismissals in the match by Chandra. It was a rare consolation for the leg-spinner, who was successfully attacked by Kallicharran that evening and next day.

I was 64 not out overnight and Clive Lloyd was on 21, and we were well on top with 212 for two, considering how the pitch behaved that first day. We couldn't start until after lunch because of more rain, and we soon knew that the drying pitch was at its worst.

Wisden's comments were full of praise. 'The Indian spinners, Venkataraghavan and Chandrasekhar in particular got the ball to bite and turn, and the remaining eight West Indies wickets went down for only another 77 in less than two hours. Of these runs, 60 were scored by Kallicharran whose faultless innings lasted four hours and 40 minutes, with two sixes and 15 fours. He played with supreme skill on a pitch from which the ball turned and lifted and, adding to the merit of his innings, was the fact that he had to face two of the world's finest off-spinners in these conditions.'

Once Lloyd was out for 30 at 230 for three, the next seven batsmen scored eight out of 59, and Kallicharran was devastating. Chandra wiped out the tail, but at a cost which was crucial. He was hit for 112 from 28 overs, while the two off-spinners conceded 121 from 52.2 overs.

To spot the danger bowler is one thing, but to take him on with an innings of that quality is something else. It called for high-class technique and, even more important, the nerve to use that technique in an attacking vein.

I could not get down to Chandra, but I could square-cut him, because I 'picked him' and so I could play it late. All our other players were lunging at him, because they did not read him. I played a lot of leg-spinners when I was growing up in Guyana, and that was when I learned to play off the back foot. Once you do that, they pitch it up a bit further, so you have forced them to do something different. I used to attack Derek Underwood, so he would bowl quicker. Then he would turn it less and I could square-cut him. It is always a battle with class spinners to see who can get on top, and I succeeded quite a lot.

The pitch was one of the most difficult I ever played on. After starting wet, as it dried out it went

INDIA V WEST INDIES (1ST TEST)

PLAYED AT KARNATAKA STATE C.A. STADIUM, BANGALORE, ON 22, 23, 24, 26, 27 NOVEMBER 1974.
TOSS: INDIA. RESULT: WEST INDIES WON BY 267 RUNS.

WEST INDIES

	FIRST INNINGS			SECOND INNINGS	
R.C.Fredericks	c Patel, b Venkataraghavan	23			
C.G.Greenidge	run out	93	(1) c Gavaskar, b Venkataraghavan	107	
A.I.Kallicharran	c Engineer, b Prasanna	124	lbw, b Prasanna	29	
I.V.A.Richards	c Prasanna, b Chandrasekhar	4	c Abid Ali, b Chandrasekhar	3	
C.H.Lloyd*	c Abid Ali, b Venkataraghavan	30	c Solkar, b Chandrasekhar	163	
D.L.Murray†	c Solkar, b Venkataraghavan	0	(2) lbw, b Abid Ali	0	
K.D.Boyce	b Chandrasekhar	4	(6) c Pataudi, b Venkataraghavan	4	
A.G.Barrett	c Patel, b Chandrasekhar	2	not out	5	
V.A.Holder	b Chandrasekhar	0	(7) not out	26	
L.R.Gibbs	c Solkar, b Venkataraghavan	2			
A.M.E.Roberts	not out	0			
Extras	b 5, lb 1, nb 1	7	lb 15, nb 4	19	
		289	(6 wickets declared)	356	

	O	M	R	W	O	M	R	W
Abid Ali	8	1	21	0	19	1	92	1
Solkar	7	1	28	0	2	0	7	0
Chandrasekhar	28	5	112	4	23	3	102	2
Prasanna	22.2	4	46	1	18	3	57	1
Venkataraghavan	30	8	75	4	21	4	79	2

FALL OF WICKETS
1-177, 2-181, 3-230, 4-236, 5-245, 6-255, 7-255, 8-264, 9-289, 10-289
1-5, 2-71, 3-75, 4-282, 5-301, 6-340

INDIA

	FIRST INNINGS			SECOND INNINGS	
S.M.Gavaskar	c Richards, b Holder	14	c Murray, b Boyce	0	
F.M.Engineer†	c Richards, b Roberts	3	absent hurt	-	
H.S.Kanitkar	st Murray, b Barrett	65	(2) c Kallicharran, b Holder	18	
G.R.Viswanath	lbw, b Gibbs	29	b Holder	22	
N of Pataudi,jr*	c Lloyd, b Holder	22	absent hurt	-	
B.P.Patel	c Murray, b Holder	2	(5) lbw, b Roberts	22	
E.D.Solkar	run out	14	(3) c Murray, b Boyce	15	
S.Abid Ali	run out	49	(6) c sub (D.A.Murray), b Boyce	1	
S.Venkataraghavan	b Roberts	1	(7) lbw, b Roberts	7	
E.A.S.Prasanna	c Kallicharran, b Roberts	23	(8) not out	12	
B.S.Chandrasekhar	not out	5	(9) b Roberts	0	
Extras	b 4, lb 8, w 4, nb 17	33	b 1, lb 5, nb 15	21	
		260		118	

	O	M	R	W	O	M	R	W
Roberts	22	5	65	3	10.5	4	24	3
Holder	20.5	7	37	3	10	3	8	2
Gibbs	15	4	39	1	1	0	1	0
Boyce	12	1	51	0	13	3	43	3
Barrett	14	3	35	1	8	3	11	0

FALL OF WICKETS
1-23, 2-23, 3-112, 4-154, 5-157, 6-163, 7-197, 8-199, 9-241, 10-260
1-5, 2-25, 3-54, 4-69, 5-71, 6-96, 7-118, 8-118

Umpires: M.V.Nagendra and J.Reuben

brown. Sometimes that sort of pitch dries into a good one, but this one became crusty, which is why it bounced a lot and took so much bite.

Such a pitch offers greater problems to smaller men, because they do not have a long reach, yet Kallicharran, the smallest West Indian batsman, was the only man to answer the questions set by world-class spinners in the stiffest examination in world cricket - a spiteful pitch in India with 50,000 extra umpires to help the official pair to give every bat-pad deflection out.

It was not bad for a barefooted youngster from Port Mourant. He travelled the world and played on every big cricket ground around the world. He gave rich entertainment to spectators from Berbice to Bloemfontein to Birmingham, where he now lives. He always valued skill and courage, which is why he is able to choose a performance which, above all others, really was 'the innings of my life'.

ALAN KNOTT

73* on the sixth day of the fifth Test between West Indies and England at Georgetown, Guyana, 3 April 1968.

Knott went in at 41 for five, with Edrich, Boycott, Graveney, Barrington and D'Oliveira all out, and batted for nearly four hours, much of it with tailenders for company, to save the match and thus secure the series for England.

Alan Philip Eric Knott was born on 9 April 1946 in Belvedere. Son of a club wicketkeeper, he joined the Kent staff as a batsman-cum-offspin bowler, but did not take long to show a talent with the gloves which made him the best post-war wicketkeeper/batsman to play for England. Impish in appearance, and only 5ft 8in tall, he brought a new dimension to his art with a combination of mental and physical application that was a source of wonder and envy to his contemporaries.

He played 95 Test matches, including a record run for England of 65 consecutive appearances which was broken only when he joined the Kerry Packer World Series cricket circus in 1977. Only Australian Rodney Marsh won more caps as a wicketkeeper. 'Knottie', as he was universally known, ended a magnificent career in 1985 with 269 Test victims, the third highest in history, and his total of 1344 first-class victims in 511 games places him fourth in the all-time list, behind Bob Taylor, John Murray and Herbert Strudwick. Knott's average of 2.62 wickets per match is the highest of the quartet.

His wicketkeeping was without weakness and, like Lester Piggott, Bobby Moore, Bjorn Borg, Nick Faldo and Steve Davis when at their peaks, he rarely made an avoidable error. Like all specialists in sport, a wicketkeeper has to be something of an eccentric, and Knott was no exception, devising a range of exercises and a diet which may have caused a few smiles, but showed the world what an unshakable self-belief he had - one which was the cornerstone of a batting method which earned him more runs than any other Test wicketkeeper, 4389 at an average of 32.75.

If his wicketkeeping was mostly orthodox, his batting was certainly not, relying on improvisation, wonderful reflexes and an eye of unrivalled keenness which brought him five Test hundreds and 30 fifties to establish him as one of the greatest all-rounders ever to play for England. Not only that, but the value of his runs is underlined by one fact: he walked to the crease 149 times for his country, but on only ten occasions did he bat higher than number six, including a nightwatchman stint against the West Indies at Lord's in 1973. In all first-class cricket, he scored 18,105 runs at an average of 29.63 and, as he scored 17 hundreds and passed fifty 97 times, he clearly has many performances from which to choose 'the innings of my life'.

Reluctantly he discarded his unbeaten 106 at Adelaide in 1975. It was Australia's fourth thumping victory in five Tests, the margin being 163 runs:

> I have always believed that batting against real pace is the ultimate test, and Lillee and Thomson were at their peak, although Jeff could not bowl in the second innings because of an injury sustained in a

game of tennis on the rest day.

THIS SHOT JUST ELUDED
GARRY SOBERS AT SLIP AS
KNOTT CONTINUED TO CAUSE
THE WEST INDIES PROBLEMS
IN 1968.
(*TOPHAM PICTURE SOURCE*)

As Knott became the second England wicketkeeper to make 200 dismissals in Test cricket - Godfrey Evans was the first - that match was one of his most memorable, even before he went in to bat at 76 for five towards the end of the fourth day's play with his side 325 runs in arrears. His runs came out of 165 added for the last five wickets, and he became only the second wicketkeeper to score a hundred in an Ashes Test. Again, he followed a Kent cricketer into the record books - this time it was Leslie Ames, who scored 120 in 'Verity's Match' at Lord's in 1934.

The other front-runner for Knott was his 116 at Headingley against the West Indies in 1976 which included another milestone when he caught Richards to equal Evans's total of 219 Test victims.

An attack of Roberts, Holding, Daniel and Holder was something special, which is why I count that knock as one of my best. But, in the end, I have to go for one in which the match situation was the tensest I have ever known. I may have scored only 73 not out, but it saved the final Test against West Indies in Guyana in 1968, and so we won the series - something no England side has done since.

Knott has picked one of the most dramatic Test matches in history in a series bedevilled by controversy and accusations of time-wasting. The only win in the previous four matches came in Trinidad when Sobers, apparently provoked by go-slow tactics, gambled by leaving England a target of 215 in 165 minutes, despite lacking the services of fast bowler Charlie Griffith. West Indies bowled 52.4 overs at a rate of just under 19 an hour, and thus became only the fourth side in 631 Tests to lose a match after making a second innings declaration.

Knott's match was of six days duration, the final day comprising 5½ hours in which Sobers and Gibbs bowled 71 of the 120 overs sent down at a rate which would make the modern cricketer gasp in disbelief. Despite a superlative effort from Snow, 150s from both Kanhai and Sobers took the home side to 322 for three with every possibility of topping 500.

Snow and Lock responded by taking five of the last six wickets to fall, and a total of 414 gave England a much less demanding task to avoid the follow-on on a pitch which offered spin, but only slowly. Boycott's fourth hundred for England held the innings together with the aid of Cowdrey in a second-wicket partnership worth 172. But with the next five wickets going for 74, including a modest seven from Knott, England's chances of winning the series looked slim with 2½ days remaining. It was then that Surrey Past and Present, in the persons of Lock and Pocock, flown in five weeks earlier after Titmus lost four toes in a boating accident, came to the rescue with innings of a vividly contrasting nature.

Lock hit 76 of 93 scored in 100 minutes before the end of the fourth day, while Pocock stayed on nought for 82 minutes - the second longest instance in Test cricket - and so helped England to a total of 371 which seemed to have saved the game, but the real drama was still to unfold.

Another fine performance from Snow held West Indies in check, and only Sobers, with an unbeaten 95, ensured that England were left with a victory target of 308, which was an academic one with the pitch now offering more spin to Sobers, Gibbs and Holford.

At the start of the final day, six days short of his 22nd birthday, the Kent tyro did not dream that history beckoned in what was only his fourth game for England. He had played a full part in the previous victory, scoring an unbeaten 69 to help his side from 260 for five to 404 in reply to the West Indies' seemingly invincible first innings score of 526 for seven declared.

England has not fielded a more powerful-looking first six batsmen since the war than Boycott, Edrich, Cowdrey, Graveney, Barrington and D'Oliveira, and such was the confidence in the dressing-room that the draw was, if not quite a formality, the likeliest result, that number eleven, Jeff Jones from Glamorgan asked for, and was given, permission to leave the ground and return to his hotel to pack in readiness for the trip home. He recalls:

'The skipper told me he didn't mind, provided I listened in to the radio in case I would be needed. Needed? How could I with that sort of batting order and a short day?' Had Cowdrey thought to inquire of his fast bowler why he had not already packed, he would have been told that he had accompanied Denis Compton and Colin Milburn on a tour of Georgetown's not over-bountiful supply of nightspots and did not return to his hotel until 6.30am that morning, feeling 'rather rough'.

At number seven, Knott thought he might get a knock,

but naturally hoped he would not. A slightly tense dressing-room settled down to watch what they hoped would be a comfortable last-day ride, but the wheels clattered all over the Bourda as Gibbs wove a wonderful pre-lunch spell, taking four for 12 in 14 overs, and plunging England from the relative comfort of 33 without loss to 41 for five, thus bringing in Knott.

In the first innings, it was Surrey who had saved England, now it was Kent, with Cowdrey a hugely comforting figure to Knott. Another wicket then, and history would tell a different story, but Knott survived a chance to Murray off Gibbs to defy the wildly excited crowd, and only marginally less excitable West Indies cricketers. Sobers and Gibbs twirled away to close-set fields through which the bowlers could just about thread each delivery, but the inexperienced Knott showed the mixture of determination and eagle-eyed technique which was to characterise a marvellous career. Lunch came and went and, to the growing relief of the England dressing-room, so did tea.

Jones, having made a hasty return from the hotel to the Bourda ground by taxi, was slowly recovering his colour - until Cowdrey was LBW to Gibbs for 82. Just 76 minutes to go, and Snow, Lock, Pocock and Jones to stand firm with Knott and bring the ultimate reward.

The first two quickly went to Sobers, whose magnificent match - 247 runs for once out and a match analysis of 68-31-125-6 - deserved a victory that was to be denied in agonising fashion. Snow was given out

LBW padding up, and Lock was caught at mid-off off a stroke which was not quite in keeping with the demands imposed by the tense match situation. By this time, Knott was in command:

Colin Cowdrey helped me so much, particularly in how to cope with Sobers when he took the new ball. He told me not to put my front foot down the pitch, but to wait for the ball to swing. He had got me out at Canterbury in 1966, so this time it was extra sweet to stay there when a Test series was at stake. How many chances do you get to share in a triumph like that?

Cowdrey is on record as saying 'it was the longest day of my life. We couldn't win, so runs were of little value. All that mattered was the minute hand creeping round the clock. I remember Knott leaning back to cut a four off the top of off stump, and I said to him, "Thank God there is still one batsman in the world who intends to hit every bowler out of sight." Alan grinned and acknowledged the point. It was the last risk he took. "Perce" Pocock stuck for a time and I really thought we were home when he was given out to what looked like a bump ball.'

Pocock is more emphatic: 'I squeezed one from Gibbs to Clive Lloyd at forward short-leg and he immediately threw it up and started the war dance. I was definitely not out, but had to go. Mind you, I suppose it was a rough sort of justice, because the previous over I got the faintest nick from Gibbs, but only Murray appealed. I turned and glared at him as though to tell him not to try anything on, but it was such a faint one, nobody else heard it. I often wonder what our dressing-room would have said had I walked.'

With the game's temperature now white-hot, Jones went out to meet a date with destiny that he now believes was preordained when he, Compton and Milburn were painting Georgetown as near scarlet as they could a few hours previously.

'I was nervous, in fact I am not sure how I got to the middle. My previous innings in the series were 2, 0*, 1*, 1 and 0*, and I seemed an awful long way from home in West Wales.' Not many cricketers take more wickets than they score runs in a career - Bill Bowes and Eric Hollies were two - but Jones came within two of so doing, 515 runs and 513 wickets.

Knott advanced to meet England's last hope, and went part of the way towards settling his partner by the message he calmly conveyed. It was nothing to do with the pitch, the bowling or the state of the game. 'He simply put an arm round my shoulders and gave me the first two lines of "We'll keep a welcome in the hillsides".'

Pocock was out to the final ball of the 39th Gibbs over, and Knott carefully played out a maiden from Sobers. After five balls, Knott called Jones down the pitch, much to the annoyance of the crowd and home players who were desperate to get in at least two more overs. The gist of the chat was that Jones expressed so much doubt about his ability to cope with the chinamen and googlies of Sobers that it was agreed they would not change ends. So when, off the final ball of the over, Knott and Jones would normally have looked for a single, Jones stood with both feet behind the non-striker's crease and made no attempt to back up. Knott remembers that he refused a single in the next over when Jones edged the fourth delivery from Gibbs past slip.

I know it looked odd because it turned out to be the last over of the game. But I really thought there would be another over from Sobers, and I had to face that. As it turned out, I could have taken the single and faced the last two balls instead of Jeff.

Jones again: 'I might have been nervous, but so was Gibbs. It was not a great over and I was able to pad a couple off.'

Knott could hardly bear to watch, and several of his team-mates hid themselves away. Pocock says that 'there were three cubicle toilets in the dressing-room, and Cowdrey, Graveney and Parks locked themselves away in traps one, two and three. Experienced players like them and Barrington and Edrich reckon they have never encountered such tension. Somehow, at times like that, it is worse watching than being in the middle.'

Knott was so sure there would be another over, he actually took guard as the West Indies team ran to their places: 'I had looked at the clock, and that minute hand seemed just short of 5.30pm. It was the biggest surprise of my life when umpire Kippins suddenly announced the end of the game and took the bails off.'

WEST INDIES V ENGLAND (5TH TEST)

PLAYED AT BOURDA, GEORGETOWN, GUYANA, ON 28, 29, 30 MARCH, 1, 2, 3 APRIL 1968.
TOSS: WEST INDIES. RESULT: MATCH DRAWN.

WEST INDIES

	FIRST INNINGS		SECOND INNINGS	
S.M.Nurse	c Knott, b Snow	17	lbw, b Snow	49
G.S.Camacho	c and b Jones	14	c Graveney, b Snow	26
R.B.Kanhai	c Edrich, b Pocock	150	c Edrich, b Jones	22
B.F.Butcher	run out	18	(6) c Lock, b Pocock	18
G.St A.Sobers*	c Cowdrey, b Barrington	152	not out	95
C.H.Lloyd	b Lock	31	(4) c Knott, b Snow	1
D.A.J.Holford	lbw, b Snow	1	(8) b Lock	3
D.L.Murray†	c Knott, b Lock	8	(7) c Boycott, b Pocock	16
L.A.King	b Snow	8	b Snow	20
W.W.Hall	not out	5	b Snow	7
L.R.Gibbs	b Snow	1	b Snow	0
Extras	lb 3, w 2, nb 4	9	b 1, lb 2, w 1, nb 3	7
		414		**264**

	O	M	R	W	O	M	R	W
Snow	27.4	2	82	4	15.2	0	60	6
Jones	31	5	114	1	17	1	81	1
D'Oliveira	8	1	27	0	8	0	28	0
Pocock	38	11	78	1	17	1	66	2
Lock	28	7	61	2	9	1	22	1
Barrington	18	4	43	1				

ENGLAND

	FIRST INNINGS		SECOND INNINGS	
J.H.Edrich	c Murray, b Sobers	0	c Gibbs, b Sobers	6
G.Boycott	c Murray, b Hall	116	b Gibbs	30
M.C.Cowdrey*	lbw, b Sobers	59	lbw, b Gibbs	82
T.W.Graveney	c Murray, b Hall	27	c Murray, b Gibbs	0
K.F.Barrington	c Kanhai, b Sobers	4	c Lloyd, b Gibbs	0
B.L.D'Oliveira	c Nurse, b Holford	27	c and b Gibbs	2
A.P.E.Knott†	lbw, b Holford	7	not out	73
J.A.Snow	b Gibbs	0	lbw, b Sobers	1
G.A.R.Lock	b King	89	c King, b Sobers	2
P.I.Pocock	c and b King	13	c Lloyd, b Gibbs	0
I.J.Jones	not out	0	not out	0
Extras	b 12, lb 14, nb 3	29	b 9, w 1	10
		371	(9 wickets)	**206**

	O	M	R	W	O	M	R	W
Sobers	37	15	72	3	31	16	53	3
Hall	19	3	71	2	13	6	26	0
King	38.2	11	79	2	9	1	11	0
Holford	31	10	54	2	17	9	37	0
Gibbs	33	9	59	1	40	20	60	6
Butcher	5	3	7	0	10	7	9	0

FALL OF WICKETS
1-29, 2-35, 3-72, 4-322, 5-385, 6-387, 7-399, 8-400, 9-412, 10-414
1-78, 2-84, 3-86, 4-133, 5-171, 6-201, 7-216, 8-252, 9-264, 10-264

FALL OF WICKETS
1-13, 2-185, 3-185, 4-194, 5-240, 6-252, 7-257, 8-259, 9-368, 10-371
1-33, 2-37, 3-37, 4-39, 5-41, 6-168, 7-198, 8-200, 9-206

Umpires: H.B.de C.Jordan and C.P.Kippins

There was an explosion of emotion. The West Indies were dazed, hardly comprehending that victory had been snatched from their grasp. Knott and Jones returned to an ecstatic dressing-room in which the corks were popping.

Knott went on to have a magnificent career in which he sustained sky-high standards for another 20 years. Contemporaries are still full of admiration for one of the best craftsmen ever to play for England. Fast bowler David Brown says: 'He was the best. He had a brilliant, fast pair of hands, and hardly ever made a mistake. I remember one stumping in Karachi, when he was going down leg-side and the ball was deflected off the batsman's pad past off stump. He brought off a one-handed stumping which was simply stunning.' Tom Graveney agrees that Knott was the best of his era, although he would not draw any comparison between him and Evans. 'I only ever remember Alan having one bad day for England. He was a wonderful keeper with lightning reactions.'

His record speaks for itself. To serve county and country with equal diligence is rarely possible for most players, but Knott could not stay true to himself if he coasted in lesser matches. It was not his style. He had class and ability, and he always made the most of both qualities, which is why he remembers 3 April 1968 in Georgetown with such pride and affection: 'It had to be the innings of my life.'

ALLAN LAMB

157 on the third day of the Britannic Assurance County Championship match between Sussex and Northamptonshire at Hastings, 1 July 1986.

The Sussex attack that day included Imran Khan, who rated the innings as one of the best he had seen on a broken pitch. Sussex captain Ian Gould declared at the end of the second day, because the state of the pitch convinced him that a target of 321 in a full day was not over-generous and it would give his bowlers maximum time in which to win the match.

Lamb walked to the wicket with the score one for two. Then, in a magnificent display of selective hitting, Lamb faced only 153 deliveries from which he hit 27 fours. When he was finally caught off Pigott for 157, the score was 260 for four, and his side was poised to achieve a remarkable victory. In the end the last pair, Mallender and Walker, had to score 20 to ensure that Lamb's brilliant display was not in vain. *Wisden* described the pitch as 'dubious', but Lamb's onslaught was so fierce that his side scored their 321 runs off only 74.5 overs.

Allan Joseph Lamb was born on 20 June 1954 in Langebaanweg, Cape Town. He went to Wynberg High School and made his debut for Western Province in 1972. Born of English parents, Lamb decided to qualify for England, and threw in his lot with Northamptonshire, for whom he made his debut in 1978. He had to serve a four-year period of qualification before he played his first Test match for England against India in 1982. He scored the first of 14 Test hundreds at The Oval in his fourth innings, and played 79 times for his adopted country before he was omitted from England's tour of India and Sri Lanka in 1993.

This was only the second tour he had missed in ten years - the first being the ill-fated one of Pakistan following the World Cup in India in 1987. Both winters he returned to South Africa and had successful seasons with Orange Free State and Western Province, playing for both sides as an overseas player in order to protect his qualification for England. For Free State he hit a career-best 294 to earn around £25,000 for hitting the highest score in the history of the Currie Cup, sharing a record partnership of 355 with Joubert Strydom, and for reaching 150 off fewer than 300 balls and 200 in under 400 balls.

His firm-footed technique is heavily dependent upon cutting, pulling and on-driving, with considerable strength of forearm bringing him within reach of 30,000 first-class runs at the start of the 1993 English season. He became captain of Northamptonshire in 1989, and led them to a NatWest Trophy win against Leicestershire in 1992, as well as third place in the Britannic Assurance County Championship.

Lamb soon earned a reputation of possessing a big-match temperament, and his 80 first-class hundreds have usually been scored quickly and in a counter-attacking mode which influences the course of a game. At his best against hostile fast bowling, he scored three hundreds against the West Indies in 1984, with one in 1988 and two more at Kingston and Bridgetown in 1990 taking his total to six. This is more than any other Englishman except Colin Cowdrey, who also scored six. Cowdrey played 22 times against the West Indies - one more than Lamb - but a difference in level of achievement is that Lamb invariably had to contend with four out-and-out fast bowlers, whereas Cowdrey faced more spin.

Lamb became the second England batsman, after Gooch, to reach 4000 runs in one-day internationals, and there were few batsmen in world cricket in the 1980s with the same facility to score quickly without hitting boundaries. A good example of this

A SWIVEL-PULL OFF BAPTISTE ON THE WAY TO 100 AT HEADINGLEY IN 1984.

(PATRICK EAGAR)

is when, in Australia in 1987, he hit 18 from the final over of the match bowled by Bruce Reid. He won the game scoring 77 at nearly a run a ball yet, so well did he work the ball around, his first boundary only came in that final dramatic over.

How near did Lamb come to picking one of his innings against the West Indies as 'the innings of my life'?

They are all special, because they have such a unique form of attack. It's hard to describe the difficulties of batting against four fast bowlers. You've always got two fresh ones coming at you and, unless you are careful, an innings becomes an exercise in survival. Take away the bouncers and the short balls, plus the odd wide one and there aren't many scoring opportunities. I've always gone in to look to score off the short ball around off stump, but even if you get a few fours, the match situation is usually in their favour, so they don't break the field up. I remember on a cracked pitch in Kingston in 1986, Patrick Patterson was a real physical threat. He broke Mike Gatting's nose and floored Phil Edmonds. The bounce was up and down and all you could do was to play for the end of his spell. Finally, he took his sweater and I was just breathing a sigh of relief when I heard Viv say: 'Malcolm, come and have a bowl.'

I didn't get a hundred then, but I did on the next tour in 1990, and that was one of my best for England. I scored 132 at Sabina Park and batted for 364 minutes to help us beat them for the first time in nearly 20 years. We had bowled them out cheaply and it was vital we got a big lead. I concentrated as hard as I have ever done. I have also thought about one or two other innings, but in the end I have to go for the one at Hastings, because of the pitch and because I hit such a big score at a run a ball without slogging.

I'd had a poorish season and hadn't got a hundred. In eight previous innings for my county, I'd managed only 221 and before the first two Tests, in which I scored a total of 65, I landed a duck and 45 in the two Texaco games. Then I heard I was dropped for the third Test against India, and so I was at a pretty low ebb when I went in to bat.

Sussex were overwhelmingly in charge, as they had been from the start of the game, after Ian Gould won what seemed destined to be a crucial toss. Sussex struggled to 283 for nine declared and then bowled the visitors out for 136 after, at 111 for eight, they seemed certain to follow-on. Imran Khan then completed his second fifty of the game and was 62 not out at the end of the second day when his side were 173 for three, giving them an overall lead of 320.

The pitch had deteriorated to such an extent that Gould was happy he had enough runs in the bank, and when the first two wickets went for one run, a home victory seemed assured, with over 100 overs in which to take the other eight wickets. Opener Larkins, who had just been called up for England, broke a finger as he was dismissed for nought by Pigott and Boyd-Moss had also failed to score. Lamb says:

The pitch had become a minefield, and it looked as though we'd be on the way home by lunchtime. Imran was a really nasty proposition, and bowlers like Colin Wells and Dermot Reeve were just the sort of accurate medium pacers to exploit the broken surface. The bounce was anyhow - one up and one down. Although I hit a couple of early boundaries, there looked to be little hope of getting the runs. Think about it: we had to score 38 more on the last day than Sussex managed on the first when the pitch was relatively good.

Anyway, I let fly at anything up or wide and it worked. David Capel got his head down and played a great supporting role, and suddenly anything seemed possible. So often in cricket, there is only a fine line between success and failure, and I have always worked on the theory that a positive approach succeeds more often than not. It's either dictate or be dictated to, and I have always done my best to stop bowlers getting on top. Hit a few boundaries and suddenly they bowl differently, and often matches which look lost are won.

That is what happened so gloriously at Hastings. When Capel was bowled by Imran, a score of 173 for three had revived the spirits of a dressing-room which had been prepared to accept the inevitable. Much depended upon the next partnership with Bailey, who promptly emulated his senior partner with 57 off 52 balls, with the already furious run-rate accelerating still more. The Sussex attack was close to disintegration when, as can always happen, both batsmen went in quick succession, to start a collapse which took the score from 260 for three to 288 for eight. Mallender and Walker kept their nerve at the end, and one of the best wins of the season was thus achieved - entirely due to Lamb's innings, described by *Wisden* as 'magnificent'.

His 157 did more than win a game. It turned his season right round, and he scored three more hundreds for his county as well as topping 80 three times in 11 innings. He was also recalled to the England side in the final Test against New Zealand at The Oval and, although he got a duck, he was chosen to go with Gatting's side to Australia. A fine international cricket career was thus resurrected on a day when he fought and won another 'Battle of Hastings'.

SUSSEX V NORTHAMPTONSHIRE (BRITANNIC ASSURANCE COUNTY CHAMPIONSHIP)

PLAYED AT HASTINGS, ON 28, 30 JUNE, 1 JULY 1986.
TOSS: SUSSEX. RESULT: NORTHAMPTONSHIRE WON BY ONE WICKET.

SUSSEX

	FIRST INNINGS		SECOND INNINGS	
D.K.Standing	c Cook, b Harper	22	c Harper, b Capel	16
A.M.Green	b Harper	55	lbw, b Capel	28
P.W.G.Parker	c and b Cook	26	b Wild	54
Imran Khan	c Waterton, b Capel	59	not out	62
C.M.Wells	c Lamb, b Harper	11	not out	12
A.P.Wells	lbw, b Capel	44		
R.I.Alikhan	not out	27		
I.J.Gould†*	b Cook	1		
D.A.Reeve	c Walker, b Cook	10		
A.C.S.Pigott	c Boyd-Moss, b Mallender	10		
A.M.Bredin	did not bat			
Extras	b 8, lb 5, nb 5	18	lb 1	1
	(9 wickets declared)	283	(3 wickets declared)	173

	O	M	R	W	O	M	R	W
Mallender	13.5	3	28	1	12	5	26	0
Walker	11	2	37	0	13	4	42	0
Capel	12	0	30	2	12	0	48	2
Harper	29	8	79	3	5	1	9	0
Cook	34	11	72	3	16	6	30	0
Boyd-Moss	4	1	14	0				
Wild	3	0	10	0	6	0	17	1

FALL OF WICKETS
1-72, 2-83, 3-133, 4-148, 5-232, 6-235, 7-236, 8-258, 9-283
1-43, 2-52, 3-146

NORTHAMPTONSHIRE

	FIRST INNINGS		SECOND INNINGS	
D.J.Capel	c Parker, b Pigott	13	b Imran	54
W.Larkins	c Gould, b Imran	9	c C.M.Wells, b Pigott	0
R.J.Boyd-Moss	c Gould, b C.M.Wells	17	b Imran	0
A.J.Lamb	c Standing, b Imran	20	c sub, b Pigott	157
R.J.Bailey	c Alikhan, b Reeve	7	c Gould, b C.M.Wells	57
D.J.Wild	lbw, b Reeve	0	c Reeve, b C.M.Wells	18
R.A.Harper*	lbw, b C.M.Wells	22	lbw, b C.M.Wells	0
S.N.V.Waterton†	lbw, b C.M.Wells	9	run out	3
N.G.B.Cook	b Imran	18	b C.M.Wells	1
N.A.Mallender	not out	7	not out	8
A. Walker	c Standing, b C.M.Wells	1	not out	13
Extras	b 3, lb 7, nb 3	13	b 1, lb 6, nb 3	10
		136	(9 wickets)	321

	O	M	R	W	O	M	R	W
Imran	16	2	44	3	18.5	1	66	2
Pigott	9	3	19	1	15	4	61	2
Reeve	11	5	26	2	10	3	46	0
Standing	6	1	14	0	8	1	35	0
C.M.Wells	7.2	2	23	4	17	2	72	4
Bredin					6	2	34	0

FALL OF WICKETS
1-25, 2-25, 3-46, 4-57, 5-57, 6-94, 7-99, 8-111, 9-135, 10-136
1-0, 2-1, 3-173, 4-260, 5-282, 6-282, 7-285, 8-288, 9-301

Umpires: A.A.Jones and R.Julian

Lamb may not go down in history as the best batsman to play for England, nor even the best looking, but he deserves to stand with Maurice Leyland, Bill Edrich, Trevor Bailey and Eddie Paynter in a group of cricketers who proved there is a place in Test cricket for raw courage. None of them ever ducked a challenge; indeed, they positively relished one. Lamb always resents any mention of his birthplace, because of his pride in playing for England. He should not, because he has done himself and his country proud. What you see is what you get: a no-nonsense, strong, squat man who gives his all and asks the same from other cricketers.

Tactically unsubtle? Maybe, but tell him at your risk. He is not a man to trifle or argue with, but a man who cricketers would rather play with than against, as his Battle of Hastings proved.

WAYNE LARKINS

73 on the third day of the Britannic Assurance County Championship match between Warwickshire and Northamptonshire at Edgbaston, 4 August 1987.

Northamptonshire, having been set to get 222 from minimum of 31 overs, were given a tremendous start by Larkins who scored his 73 from 50 deliveries and, in an innings that was eventually reduced by rain to 26 overs, helped them to a score of 207.

Wayne Larkins was born in Roxton, Bedfordshire, on 22 November 1953, and moved to Durham in 1992, after playing for Northamptonshire for 20 seasons. He is one of the most aggressive opening batsmen in English cricket, having played many thrilling innings in which he took apart some of the best bowlers of his day. At the end of the 1992 season, he had scored 24,384 first-class runs, including 53 hundreds, with a highest score of 252. He played 13 times for England in five separate series, but was never able to play the sort of innings which would have established him, and passed fifty only three times in 25 innings. A man to whom fate dealt many unkind injury blows, Larkins has never complained, and earns the respect of his colleagues for his approach to batting, whatever the state of the pitch or the quality of the bowling. An unselfish, perfect team man, he has adorned the county scene throughout his career, and few batsmen have given more pleasure to crowds on the county circuit in that time.

When a man like Larkins has taken on the world's best fast bowlers unflinchingly for two decades, his choice of 'the innings of my life' assumes considerable significance. Many of his hundreds have been blazing innings, only playable by a batsman who can play with equal facility off back and front foot - a quality rare among English batsmen.

The impact a Larkins innings makes on a game goes far beyond figures, because his colleagues recognise that, after one of his special performances, their task in dealing with the suffering bowlers has been made incalculably easier. A batting gambler, he invites the all-too-easy charge of being an under-achiever, but Larkins has had only one approach to an innings, and sensible captains know that you can get what you see, and you take it with gratitude.

Director of Durham cricket Geoff Cook knew this when he unhesitatingly signed his former opening partner to play in Durham's inaugural first-class season at the age of 38. 'He plays every innings in the same way, whether it is a one-day game, one of three, four or even five days. If the ball is there to hit, he obliges, because he has the most simple approach to batting I have ever seen. Sometimes it is his undoing, but I put him in the same bracket as Graeme Hick, Graham Gooch, Robin Smith and Allan Lamb - they will win you three or four games a year, which is what any captain wants.

'He never moans, unlike a few batsmen I know, who, if the pitch looks as though it might do something at the start of a game, will always try to persuade the captain to field first. Wayne's philosophy is so simple: "You've got to bat sometime, so why not now?"'

Durham skipper David Graveney soon appreciated this quality: 'It helps a dressing-room so much to have someone like Wayne prepared to bat any time, anywhere against any bowler. He is a good pro, and a perfect role-model for young players.'

Larkins narrowed the choice of his best innings to one of two - both of which were on difficult pitches and against high-quality bowling.

At first I was inclined to pick an innings which really established me in the Northamptonshire side, four years after my debut in 1972. We played Worcestershire at Northampton, and I got 83 in 50 minutes on a raging turner against Norman Gifford. Roy Virgin and I put on 112 in 40 minutes for the sixth wicket, and in the end we won by scoring 247 in 2¼ hours.

I am a big supporter of uncovered pitches, because I reckon it makes for better batsmen and bowlers. Runs scored on them have to be earned and, if the bowlers are doing their stuff and bowling accurately, a batsman has to be able to combine a solid defence with the ability to make the most of the occasional ball which is short or wide.

So, although I have chosen my innings of 73 at Edgbaston in 1987 when county cricket was played on covered pitches, it came after we had had an interruption after tea on the last day when heavy rain got on the pitch before they could get the covers on. When we came back, Tony Merrick was bowling very fast and straight, and it was just like playing on one of the old, uncovered pitches. Also, at the time, we were second in the Championship table, a few points off the top with games in hand, so there was the extra pressure of trying for an impossible-looking eighth win of the season to take us top.

Larkins' old adversary, Norman Gifford, was again the opposing captain and, with typical shrewd caution, he exploited Northamptonshire's Championship hopes with a tough declaration which originally left them to score 222 from a minimum of 31 overs. Gladstone Small and Merrick shared eight wickets in the first innings on a well-grassed pitch, but the England fast bowler was injured after only four overs on the final afternoon, and Gordon Parsons was also absent with a leg injury. Even so, it was a very daunting target, and one which only a title-chasing side with attacking batsmen like Larkins and Lamb would even consider. Larkins recalls:

When we started our innings, it looked hopeless. Geoff Cook was soon LBW to Merrick, and then it became obvious we were in for a storm. It was almost eerie to play while the thunder and lightning over the city centre, just two miles away, came nearer and nearer. It was dark, but we stayed out there until, finally, it rained. It was heavy, and, as we ran off, I could see that plenty got on to the pitch before they could cover it - as if we hadn't got enough problems to cope with.

Former Warwickshire captain Andy Lloyd, who earlier in the game ran himself out on 99 to one of the world's most dangerous fielders, Roger Harper, agreed about the difficult conditions. 'It was really too dark to play, and the conditions were spooky. Even after we went back on, thunder and lightning rolled around the ground, but what followed was one of the most brilliant displays of correct hitting I have ever seen. I have seen people slog it around, but these were proper shots - cleanly hit hooks, cuts, drives and pulls. It underlined Ned's wonderful hand and eye co-ordination and, although the game was drawn, the innings made such an impact on our players that we talked about it every subsequent season when someone threatened to play a similar innings. Nobody did, thank goodness, and I will never forget what I saw that day.

'The rain took five overs out of the game, so what was originally virtually impossible, now definitely was. Our captain reckoned that, as there was no chance of losing, we might as well crowd the batsmen. So, when Paul Smith bowled the first over after the stoppage, Wayne was surrounded by slips, gullies and short legs. Four balls later, we were scattered everywhere, as he smashed Paul into the Members' Bar over extra-cover in an over which cost 16.'

All-rounder Smith, whose final analysis of 10-1-103-3 would mentally scar most bowlers for life, is equally generous in his praise of the biggest thrashing he has ever received as a bowler. 'The pitch was wet, and the ball flew through. In one way it was an advantage, but it also meant that if you didn't get the ball in the right place, it would disappear.'

Smith makes the perfect point to support playing on uncovered pitches. They make bowlers bowl accurately, and they also produce batsmen with more rounded techniques than is the case with bland, always dry, surfaces. The art of playing cricket on soft or wet pitches is a lost one, and the modern game is the poorer for it, as Larkins says.

That day took me right back to my early years in county cricket when I am sure I was made into a better batsman by occasionally playing on wet pitches. People forget that a wet pitch is not always dangerous. Often we would bat on puddings for as long as it took for the pitch to dry out. Even then, it was usually difficult only for a limited period, and the battle then between bat and ball was a fascinating one. It made for great spectating value and, because the run-ups were not covered, you couldn't always bowl the fast bowlers when play restarted.

LARKINS IN CHARACTERISTICALLY BELLIGERENT ACTION AT MELBOURNE IN 1990, SCENE OF TWO OF HIS THREE TEST FIFTIES. (ALLSPORT/BEN RADFORD)

It is no argument to say that, because Test cricket is played on covered pitches, there is no point in uncovering county pitches. It is no coincidence that leading batsmen of the 1980s like Geoff Boycott, Dennis Amiss and Keith Fletcher were brought up on uncovered pitches. It makes you more able to look after yourself on dodgy pitches - then when you get on flat pitches, you are better equipped to cash in. Anyway, I do not agree that every aspect of county cricket should be tailored to Test cricket.

After Smith was hit into the Members' Bar, he admits: 'I just did not know where to bowl. I can pay Wayne no higher compliment than to say that, although his innings only lasted a brief while, I rank it alongside the one of 322 scored by Viv Richards against us at Taunton in 1985 in terms of clean, scientific hitting.'

The bones of his innings are these. After losing Cook to Merrick at nine for one, Larkins scored 22 out of 38 in six overs when the thunder and lightning were finally compounded by rain. After the resumption, Larkins made a nonsense of his omission from the England World Cup preliminary squad when he got 51 out of 82 off 30 balls as he kept Northamptonshire in touch with the impossible dream.

WARWICKSHIRE V NORTHAMPTONSHIRE (BRITANNIC ASSURANCE COUNTY CHAMPIONSHIP)

PLAYED AT EDGBASTON, BIRMINGHAM, ON 1, 3, 4 AUGUST 1987.
TOSS: WARWICKSHIRE. RESULT: MATCH DRAWN.

WARWICKSHIRE

	FIRST INNINGS		SECOND INNINGS	
A.J.Moles	c Bailey, b N.G.B.Cook	33	lbw, b Davis	41
T.A.Lloyd	c Walker, b Capel	18	run, out	99
Asif Din	lbw, b Walker	27	(4) c Ripley, b Capel	10
D.L.Amiss	b Capel	42	(5) lbw, b Capel	60
G.W.Humpage	b N.G.B.Cook	16	(6) not out	35
P.A.Smith	c Davis, b N.G.B.Cook	0	(7) not out	4
G.A.Tedstone†	c Ripley, b Capel	51		
G.J.Parsons	c Lamb, b Capel	0		
G.C.Small	c Williams, b Capel	0	(3) b Davis	8
T.A.Merrick	lbw, b Walker	9		
N.Gifford*	not out	5		
Extras	lb 12, nb 22	34	lb 16, w 2, nb 5	23
		235	(5 wickets declared)	280

	O	M	R	W	O	M	R	W
Davis	18	4	55	0	28	7	75	2
Capel	16.4	3	45	5	28	4	92	2
Walker	14	5	25	2	9	2	34	0
Robinson	11	1	53	0	4	1	13	0
N.G.B.Cook	19	6	45	3	22	10	39	0
Williams					9	4	11	0

FALL OF WICKETS
1-27, 2-91, 3-91, 4-112, 5-112, 6-188, 7-188, 8-191, 9-221, 10-235
1-92, 2-122, 3-137, 4-218, 5-266

NORTHAMPTONSHIRE

	FIRST INNINGS		SECOND INNINGS	
G.Cook*	c Moles, b Small	47	lbw, b Merrick	8
W.Larkins	b Small	4	b Merrick	73
R.J.Bailey	b Merrick	29	b Smith	28
A.J.Lamb	lbw, b Small	85	c sub, b Smith	28
D.J.Capel	c Tedstone, b Merrick	4	b Smith	3
R.G.Williams	lbw, b Smith	7	c Tedstone, b Merrick	7
D.Ripley†	lbw, b Gifford	37	not out	13
N.G.B.Cook	c Humpage, b Merrick	15	(9) not out	1
W.W.Davis	b Small	0	(8) b Merrick	17
A.Walker	not out	41		
M.A.Robinson	c Tedstone, b Merrick	0		
Extras	b 1, lb 11, nb 13	25	b 8, lb 16, w 1, nb 4	29
		294	(7 wickets)	207

	O	M	R	W	O	M	R	W
Small	27	3	98	4	4	1	22	0
Merrick	30.5	1	102	4	12.5	0	58	4
Parsons	9	4	13	0				
Gifford	20	9	41	1				
Smith	7	1	28	1	10	1	103	3

FALL OF WICKETS
1-13, 2-79, 3-107, 4-114, 5-132, 6-228, 7-228, 8-228, 9-259, 10-294
1-9, 2-128, 3-128, 4-137, 5-172, 6-175, 7-206

Umpires: B.Dudleston and P.B.Wight

When the last 20 overs began, 184 were needed and, almost single-handedly, he reduced the target to 150 off 17, 137 off 15, 108 off 12 and finally 99 off 11 when he went to the well once too often against Merrick, and was bowled. The game ended in a draw, but the small Edgbaston crowd had seen one of the best innings of its type ever played on the ground. Larkins says:

I picked it, not just because I came off, but because of the pitch, the overhead conditions and the bowling of Merrick. The bad light, the thunder and lightning seemed to add to the drama of everything, and that is why I rate it the best knock I ever played.

My newspaper report for the *Birmingham Post* said this: 'Larkins cut loose with an innings which, for sheer destructive power and improvised audacity, could not have been bettered - even by an Ian Botham or a Viv Richards.' A writer often looks back on his report of a special event, and wishes he could rewrite a sentence. Not this time.

TONY LEWIS

125 on the third and fourth days of the fourth Test between India and England at Kanpur, 28 and 29 January 1973.

Lewis, playing in his fourth Test match, all as captain, went in to bat at 48 for two, with his side 2-1 down in the series. His previous scores were 0, 70*, 4, 3, 4 and 11, so his credibility as a batsman was at stake, as well as captain. The best way out of the problem, he decided, was through courageous attack. He succeeded magnificently on both counts. He scored a splendid 125 out of his side's total of 397. Although the game was drawn, Lewis's innings stemmed a tide which, on the sub-continent, can quickly wash away the opposition and his much-heartened side drew the final Test in Bombay.

Anthony Robert Lewis was born on 6 July in 1938 in Uplands, Swansea and, while still at Neath Grammar School, played two Championship matches for Glamorgan in 1955. After National Service, he spent three years at Cambridge University, winning three Blues and captaining the side in his final year in 1962. Always an attractive, rather than solid, batsman, Lewis's international ambitions were hardly helped by home pitches in South Wales. As a result, apart from being named twelfth man for England in the final Test against the West Indies in 1966 at The Oval, his representative cricket was limited throughout his best batting years in the 1960s to leading an MCC side to Asia in 1969-70. A natural captain, he led Glamorgan for six years, during which period they won their second Championship title in 1969. He had an old-style amateur approach to a game he never enjoyed when it became a joyless pursuit and, although a longstanding knee injury cut his career short when he was enjoying a belated run in the England side, his enforced early retirement in 1974 enabled him to launch one of the most successful broadcasting careers enjoyed by a former cricketer.

Blessed with a softly spoken and typically Welsh eloquence, he is in no greater danger of being mistaken for a belligerent Yorkshireman than is Brian Close of being labelled a native of the Valleys. His descriptive strengths, whether behind the typewriter or the microphone, soon earned him international fame on a level he never quite found while playing. He is equally at home on radio and television, and combined the two successfully until, in the mid-1980s, he concentrated on television. He was the natural successor to Peter West as front man for the BBC's summer coverage of English cricket in 1987. His writing ability earned him the distinction of compiling the most recent MCC history, the bi-centenary publication *Double Century* and he ended a long spell as the cricket correspondent for the *Sunday Telegraph* in 1992 - the same year as he was given the prestigious appointment of chairman of the Welsh Tourist Board.

As a batsman, Lewis never paid lip service to personal success, yet he still topped 20,000 first-class runs at an average of 32.42, more or less the same as for England, 457 runs in 18 innings at 32.64. Critics might argue his was an unfulfilled talent, but no more cheerful or affable man has captained a county side since 1946, and he did enough for England to show what might have been, had the call come earlier under different circumstances than those of caretaking the job because Ray Illingworth decided not to tour India.

The series had started well when England unexpectedly won the first Test in Delhi, thanks to match figures of nine for 91 by Arnold, but the Indian spinners hit back so effectively in the next two Tests in Calcutta and Madras that England were bowled out for 174, 163, 242 and 159 in a total of 359.1 overs, of which 21 were seam and the rest spin. Their aggregate of 738 runs at roughly two runs per over showed what a stranglehold Bedi, Chandrasekhar and Prasanna had on the England batsmen, of whom only three topped fifty in those four innings. Fletcher scored an unbeaten 97 in Madras, Denness 76 in the same Test, and Greig 67 in Calcutta.

England were dragged into a familiar rut. Crease-bound batsmen were surrounded by a posse of close fielders who, in the four innings, took 26 catches. Add nine LBWs, and it is clear that the tourists were in a tactical mess. Lewis was determined to reverse a trend which could only lead to further trouble and, despite his side's parlous position, he charged Bedi first ball, got away with it, and proceeded to take the attack to the hitherto dominant trio of spinners. Chandrasekhar had taken 16 wickets in the previous two Tests, Bedi 13 and Prasanna nine and, even though the Kanpur pitch was the flattest of the three, it took great courage for the England captain to set the example he did by refusing to be dominated.

Few choices in this book have confounded fellow-cricketers. There have been surprising ones - surprising, that is, until the player's reasons are given. However, several of Lewis's colleagues on that tour - Amiss, Arnold, Knott and Birkenshaw, for instance - found it difficult to understand why, to him, the innings in Kanpur counted as the best he ever played. Let Lewis tell the story.

After the second and third Tests, we were in the same sort of trouble as the England players on their last tour of India in early 1993. It doesn't take much for Indian spinners to dominate and, once they are on top, they never let go. It makes for exciting cricket of a type we never see in England. Each time the ball does something, the bowlers and fielders get more wound up - as do the crowd to whom every ball is life and death.

A BALANCED SWEEP BY LEWIS WITH THE WRISTS HAVING ROLLED OVER TO KEEP THE BALL DOWN.

(SPORT AND GENERAL)

Batsmen can hardly hear themselves think - communication with your partner has to be at close quarters - and it seems as though the pair of you haven't got a friend in the world.

You lose wickets in clusters, so you are never safe, and the dressing-room is always teetering on the edge of a combined nervous breakdown. For instance, in our second innings at Eden Gardens, we went from 17 for four to 114 for five, and then 138 for nine. In Madras we lost our first five wickets for

98, but then got to 242, and in the second innings we were 30 for three, 97 for four, 152 for six and 159 all out. It is an emotional roller-coaster you can laugh at when you have retired, but it is so easy for players to become demoralised when it is happening.

By the time we got to Kanpur, I felt the whole team was going down, and I had to do something, because we couldn't win the series by defensive batting. I did not sleep too soundly and a couple of phone calls didn't help - especially as they were not for me. Early on the morning of the match, I had breakfast with John Woodcock, the man from *The Times*, and we had a long chat about my fears if we continued to try to block it out. We agreed that although we won the first Test, we won it the wrong way, and someone had to get down the track. I know I got 70 not out and Tony Greig 40 not out to win the game after lunch on Christmas Day. However, we could have lost it as we had fallen to 107 for four earlier that day. They then overwhelmed us in the next two Tests.

Part of our problem was the difficulties Barry Wood and Dennis Amiss had found in trying to play the spinners, and I felt it best to leave them both out in Kanpur, and promote Alan Knott to number three. It was the sort of gamble that makes you look foolish if it misfires, but 'Knottie' has always batted with great character against the best bowlers - fast or slow.

Lewis's decision to try a new opening pair was taken after Wood and Amiss aggregated 191 in 12 innings in the first three Tests, with first-wicket partnerships of 61, 18, 18, 3, 33 and 14 denying the side a good start more often than not. Mike Denness had done as well as anyone with 197 in six innings, and Lewis promoted him and gave a Test debut to Surrey's Graham Roope.

Replying to a laboriously compiled Indian first innings total of 357 scored from 167 overs, Roope went for 11 at 37 for one, and Denness soon followed for 31 - both openers swallowed by Chandrasekhar. For Lewis, it was an all-too-familiar situation into which he walked with his mind self-programmed to challenge the Indian spinners: England had lost two wickets cheaply, the Indians were on top, and his side needed 110 to save the follow-on with the game still not halfway over. Brave thoughts, brave words - plenty of these in team talks, but now his bat had to do the talking.

It was as though there was a cassette in my head, but would I press the right button at the right time? 'Knottie' had only just gone in and another wicket then would have meant real trouble, with only Keith Fletcher left of the specialist batsmen, plus Tony Greig and Jackie Birkenshaw as all-rounders.

My mind was made up - there was no going back. Bishen Bedi ran in to bowl and off I charged. I was not quite to it, but I went through with the lofted shot and got away with it. It went for four, and it did exactly what I hoped for. It gave me confidence to attack and break up the close field, and I was soon in control. I hit a six over long-off and the field was soon spread. At one stage, there were actually five on the boundary, but the one field placement which pleased me the most was when I suddenly spotted Solkar at long-on. He had tortured us all from short leg in the previous three Tests in which he took 12 catches, but now he was back, and it seemed a different game.

Knott played a typically inventive innings for 40 before Fletcher came in to join his captain and complete the rehabilitation of the England batting. By the close of play on the third day, the tourists were 198 for three, with Lewis then 86, and next morning they extended their fourth-wicket partnership to 144, before Lewis was bowled by Abid Ali. The most pleasing part of the dismissal was that the England captain's positive approach during his maiden Test hundred had forced Pataudi to revert to seam. He batted for 267 minutes, with 70 of his runs coming in boundaries, and it was England's first hundred for 11 Tests.

Wisden paid this handsome tribute to the England captain: 'With a 2-1 lead, India were expected to take the initiative. Instead, Lewis and England called the tune, finishing the match with a flourish, forcing thoughts of defeat on India on the final afternoon. Lewis should have happy memories of the match. Apart from the manner in which his team performed, the captain himself scored a decorous century, his first in Test cricket and the first for the series. He took command with positive methods.

'His classic treatment of Bedi, stepping up the pitch and lifting him over the fielders' heads, set the tone for his innings. He played faultless cricket, unmarred by a single violent movement and completed his hundred in effortless style on the fourth morning, and then burst into a flurry of sparkling strokes.'

Lewis not only has happy memories of his best day in Test cricket, he has proud ones as well.

I don't think the team thought I could bat as well as that, and my innings did a lot for general morale. I got to my hundred with a three - and several students came on and garlanded 'Fletch'. I must have made a big impression on them, if they gave the wrong man the flowers. At least it made up for a bit of typical eccentric Indian hospitality - my hotel room had a double bed, but only single bedding.

We had a team room on the top floor, and I remember when we were having a drink one night and we heard the sound of a fire engine. Anything for a diversion - so we all crowded onto a roof-top balcony and looked down on the action. Within minutes we were spotted and a mass of people gathered to wave at us. Traffic could not get through, but it did not seem to matter - not even to the driver of the fire engine and his crew, who all got out and joined the waving crowd. Nice to know that a wave to the English was more important than some blazing building!

His colleagues still believe his unbeaten 70 to seal a victory in the first Test of that series was the better innings - but not Lewis. The real heroes are not those who know no fear, but those who recognise it and conquer it. As did Lewis, for himself and his side, in what he rightly calls 'the innings of my life'.

INDIA V ENGLAND (4TH TEST)

PLAYED AT GREEN PARK, KANPUR, ON 25, 27, 28, 29, 30 JANUARY 1973.
TOSS: INDIA. RESULT: MATCH DRAWN.

INDIA

	FIRST INNINGS		SECOND INNINGS	
C.P.S.Chauhan	c Old, b Underwood	22	c Roope, b Arnold	1
S.M.Gavaskar	c Greig, b Birkenshaw	69	c sub (B.Wood), b Underwood	24
A.L.Wadekar*	c Fletcher, b Greig	90	c and b Underwood	9
G.R.Viswanath	c Denness, b Old	25	not out	75
Nawab of Pataudi, jr	lbw, b Arnold	54		
E.D.Solkar	b Underwood	10	c Greig, b Birkenshaw	26
F.M.Engineer†	b Underwood	15	(5) c Old, b Birkenshaw	2
S.Abid Ali	b Old	41	(7) b Greig	36
E.A.S.Prasanna	c Knott, b Old	0	(8) not out	2
B.S.Bedi	not out	4		
B.S.Chandrasekhar	b Old	0		
Extras	b 1, lb 9, nb 17	27	b 5, lb 4, nb 2	11
		357	(6 wickets)	186

	O	M	R	W	O	M	R	W
Arnold	35	10	72	1	7	3	15	1
Old	24	5	69	4	11	3	28	0
Underwood	51	20	90	3	26	11	46	2
Greig	29	11	40	1	10	7	6	1
Gifford	8	2	17	0				
Birkenshaw	20	6	42	1	25	5	66	2
Roope					5	1	14	0

FALL OF WICKETS
1-85, 2-109, 3-179, 4-265, 5-292, 6-296, 7-326, 8-345, 9-357, 10-357
1-8, 2-33, 3-36, 4-39, 5-103, 6-181

ENGLAND

	FIRST INNINGS	
M.H.Denness	c Abid Ali, b Chandrasekhar	31
G.R.J.Roope	c Abid Ali, b Chandrasekhar	11
A.P.E.Knott†	c Gavaskar, b Prasanna	40
A.R.Lewis*	c Abid Ali	125
K.W.R.Fletcher	c Chandrasekhar, b Bedi	58
A.W.Greig	c Chauhan, b Bedi	8
J.Birkenshaw	c Abid Ali, b Chandrasekhar	64
C.M.Old	lbw, b Chandrasekhar	4
G.G.Arnold	b Bedi	45
D.L.Underwood	not out	0
N.Gifford	absent hurt	
Extras	b 1, lb 8, w 1, nb 1	11
		397

	O	M	R	W
Abid Ali	22	3	55	1
Solkar	5	0	14	0
Bedi	68.5	15	134	3
Chandrasekhar	41	12	86	4
Prasanna	34	4	87	1
Viswanath	2	0	10	0

FALL OF WICKETS
1-37, 2-48, 3-118, 4-262, 5-274, 6-288, 7-301, 8-397, 9-397

Umpires: M.V.Gothoskar and J.Reuben

PETER MAY

285* on the third, fourth and fifth days of the first Test between England and West Indies at Edgbaston, 1, 3 and 4 June 1957.

May's innings helped his side from 113 for three to 524 for four. It remained a career-best score, was the highest score by an England captain until Gooch's 333 against India in 1990, and his fourth-wicket partnership with Cowdrey of 411 remains England's highest for any wicket, and also the best for the fourth-wicket in Test cricket. It was his 16th game as England captain and, after a run of 14 Test innings without a hundred, it started a golden run of seven hundreds in 24 innings in two years in which he scored 1502 at an average of 71.52 and topped fifty on five other occasions.

Peter Barker Howard May, CBE, was born on 31 December 1929 in Reading. He was educated at Charterhouse and Cambridge where he gained a Blue in each of his three years. He made his first-class debut for the Navy during his National Service, and followed with his first appearance for Surrey in 1950 and for England the following year, while he was still at Cambridge. His 138 against South Africa at Headingley made him only the third batsman to score a hundred for England on debut in England, and the tenth in all. By the middle of the 1993 English season, the number had been increased to 14 by Arthur Milton, John Hampshire, Frank Hayes and Graham Thorpe.

Rated by most sound judges as the best English batsman since the war, May's career was short, but studded with many brilliant innings. When he retired from Test cricket at 31, his 4537 runs included 13 hundreds and 22 fifties, and were scored at an average of 46.77, and he captained his country for a record 41 times in the 66 Tests he played.

He played for Surrey until 1963, retiring with a career average of 51 - something achieved by nine other English batsmen, with Boycott the only other batsman to score all his runs since 1946. Among current batsmen, only Graeme Hick is in the same bracket. May scored 85 hundreds in his aggregate of 27,592 runs, passed 200 five times, and also topped 2000 runs in a season five times.

A man of purpose, it was unsurprising that he had the least difficulty of all the cricketers in this book in choosing the innings which, even in retrospect, still gives him most satisfaction.

It has to be my 285 at Edgbaston in 1957 for several reasons. I had had a poor tour of South Africa - at least as far as the Tests were concerned. I seemed to get a hundred every other time I batted, but scores of 6, 14, 8, 15, 2, 2, 61, 0, 24 and 21 explain why the selectors were reluctant to appoint me for the entire series at home against the West Indies. It was my fourth full five-match series, and the first one in which I did not score a hundred or get to fifty at least three times.

Then we had the Ramadhin problem. He got 23 wickets against us in the 1953-54 series, although we had played him and Valentine with fair comfort then, with conditions out there very different. Sonny was unusual with his quick loose wrist, rolled-down sleeves and, for a spinner, brisk pace and lowish trajectory. In English light it was hard to see the ball spinning in the air and no one could read him.

Another unknown factor was the Edgbaston pitch, as this was the first Test match played on the ground for 28 years, and the first five-day game ever. Selection was interesting - John Goddard left Valentine out and, compared with the last Test in Port Elizabeth three months earlier, we brought in Brian Close for Denis Compton, who had retired from Test cricket, and Fred Trueman and Brian Statham for Frank Tyson and Peter Loader.

As could be expected in a side containing several strong characters - Richardson, Close, Insole, Bailey, Lock, Evans and Trueman for example - and a left-handed pair of openers, there was more than one theory about how to play Ramadhin, and May's well-known reluctance to instruct batsmen on how best to play for England meant that each player was free to adopt his own approach.

The pitch was slow but true and, at 104 for two after lunch, the sun shone in the home dressing-room as well as on a good-sized crowd who were part of a total attendance of 91,447, including 26,500 members, who watched the return of Test cricket to Birmingham.

It was then that Ramadhin wove a spell that was too much for a batting order which featured Lock at number seven, Evans at eight and Laker at nine. In 31 overs, 16 of which were maidens, he took seven for 49. The slump to 130 for eight stunned the home players and supporters, and the little spinner had dismissed the top six in the order, except for Close who was caught by wicketkeeper Rohan Kanhai for 15 off Gilchrist. Richardson, May and Cowdrey were caught, while Insole, Bailey, Lock and Laker were all bowled - and this on a pitch which, even on the fourth and fifth days was nothing more than a slow turner.

Trueman and Statham scored 36 for the last wicket, otherwise the position would have been worse, although it all seemed irrelevant when West Indies ground out 474 from 191.4 overs. Even allowing for the amount of spin bowled in the match - 300 overs - the over-rate was far higher than would be the case nowadays. In the match, 1315 runs were scored from 599.2 overs, and in the only other game in the series to last for five days, the Trent Bridge Test produced 1422 runs from 537 overs - 177 of which were spin. Do the authorities realise how much they have let slip in this crucial area of Test cricket?

May had this to say about the Edgbaston pitch on the second and third days, when the West Indies were building a massive lead of 288:

The pitch, with its comfortable bounce, was no help to our bowlers - although they had five out for 197. There followed what seemed an interminable stand between Collie Smith and Frank Worrell which lasted from the middle of the afternoon on the second day until the last ball before lunch on the third.

Even home supporters must have sympathised with the West Indies opener, Bruce Pairaudeau. In his 12th and penultimate Test match, he was yorked by Trueman for one, and then spent the next 8¼ hours in the middle running, first for the injured Walcott, and then Worrell, who both pulled muscles.

England started their second innings with nearly half the match remaining, a deficit of 288, and near-certain defeat staring them in the face, especially when Richardson and Insole were out at 63 and 65. It was in to this nearly hopeless situation that May walked on the Saturday evening, having deserted his policy of non-intervention in the dressing-room.

As we prepared for the second innings, I talked to the other batsmen about how to play Ramadhin. It was no new subject, but I had never before been prepared to give batting orders. I was dubious about the theory that he lost heart if attacked, as by the Australians in 1951-52. What worked there was far from certain to work in England where he had more in his favour. When a bowler is on top, there are two ways of regaining the initiative - by hitting him out of the attack and breaking his confidence, or by taking no risks and wearing him down.

The first policy had been favoured by several batsmen in the first innings with marked lack of success. It seemed even more unsuited to the situation in which we now found ourselves. The difficulty which everyone had in picking Ramadhin made this aggressive approach unlikely to have more than passing success. Worrell would not be able to bowl, and the other West Indies bowlers seemed unlikely to cause many problems. Brian Close and I got through that evening, and I had all Sunday to think about how best to play.

It was vitally important that we should not lose the match and, on a personal note, I knew that I had a lot of catching up to do. Memories are short and although I made runs against Australia in 1956, I was only too aware that my shortage of them in South Africa could be said to have cost us the series. I thought we had a chance of a draw if we played sensibly.

MAY'S GREAT STRENGTH WAS THE ABILITY TO DRIVE ON-SIDE. NOTE THE OPEN POSITION OF THE FRONT FOOT WHICH FEW BATSMEN ARE ABLE TO ACHIEVE. THIS ENABLED HIM TO DRIVE ALONGSIDE, NOT AROUND, THE FRONT LEG.
(HULTON-DEUTSCH COLLECTION)

That hope was dented within 20 minutes of the start of Monday's play, when Close was caught at slip by Weekes off Gilchrist who, later in the day was to limp off and make England's task slightly easier. Only slightly, because by now Ramadhin was settling down to business.

May could not have wished for a more compatible partner than Colin Cowdrey. A great thinker about the game, May knew that the Kent batsman shared his view about the best way to combat Ramadhin - exclusively off the front foot and assuming that every delivery would be an off-spinner. Ramadhin was one of the few front-of-the-hand bowlers in the history of the game to deceive batsmen about the direction of his spin, and the treatment afforded him by Oxbridge's most successful pair of post-war batsmen, effectively saved the match, completely extinguished the spinner's threat, and established a platform for England to win comfortably a series they would otherwise have lost.

The events of the fourth and fifth days of the Edgbaston Test might be considered historic, but it was certainly at the expense of a premature end to the career of one of the most innovative spinners the game has ever seen. Compare his career figures before and after the start of the England second innings at Edgbaston:

Before: 28½ Tests,   120 wickets for 3240 runs, Average 27.00.

After: 14½ Tests,   38 wickets for 1339 runs, Average 35.24.

ENGLAND V WEST INDIES (1ST TEST)

PLAYED AT EDGBASTON, BIRMINGHAM, ON 30, 31 MAY, 1, 3, 4 JUNE 1957.
TOSS: ENGLAND. RESULT: MATCH DRAWN.

ENGLAND

	FIRST INNINGS		SECOND INNINGS	
P.E.Richardson	c Walcott, b Ramadhin	47	c sub (N.S.Asgarali), b Ramadhin	34
D.B.Close	c Kanhai, b Gilchrist	15	c Weekes, b Gilchrist	42
D.J.Insole	b Ramadhin	20	b Ramadhin	0
P.B.H.May*	c Weekes, b Ramadhin	30	not out	285
M.C.Cowdrey	c Gilchrist, b Ramadhin	4	c sub (N.S.Asgarali), b Smith	154
T.E.Bailey	b Ramadhin	1		
G.A.R.Lock	b Ramadhin	0		
T.G.Evans†	b Gilchrist	14	(6) not out	29
J.C.Laker	b Ramadhin	7		
F.S.Trueman	not out	29		
J.B.Statham	b Atkinson	13		
Extras	b 3, lb 3	6	b 23, lb 16	39
		186	(4 wickets declared)	583

	O	M	R	W	O	M	R	W
Worrell	9	1	27	0				
Gilchrist	27	4	74	2	26	2	67	1
Ramadhin	31	16	49	7	98	35	179	2
Atkinson	12.4	3	30	1	72	29	137	0
Sobers					30	4	77	0
Smith					26	4	72	1
Goddard					6	2	12	0

FALL OF WICKETS
1-32, 2-61, 3-104, 4-115, 5-116, 6-118, 7-121, 8-130, 9-150, 10-186
1-63, 2-65, 3-113, 4-524

WEST INDIES

	FIRST INNINGS		SECOND INNINGS	
B.H.Pairaudeau	b Trueman	1	b Trueman	7
R.B.Kanhai†	lbw, b Statham	42	c Close, b Trueman	1
C.L.Walcott	c Evans, b Laker	90	(6) c Lock, b Laker	1
E.de C.Weekes	b Trueman	9	c Trueman, b Lock	33
G.St A.Sobers	c Bailey, b Statham	53	(3) c Cowdrey, b Lock	14
O.G.Smith	lbw, b Laker	161	(7) lbw, b Laker	5
F.M.M.Worrell	b Statham	81	(5) c May, b Lock	0
J.D.C.Goddard*	c Lock, b Laker	24	not out	0
D.St E.Atkinson	c Statham, b Laker	1	not out	4
S.Ramadhin	not out	5		
R.Gilchrist	run out	0		
Extras	b 1, lb 6	7	b 7	7
		474	(7 wickets)	72

	O	M	R	W	O	M	R	W
Statham	39	4	114	3	2	0	6	0
Trueman	30	4	99	2	5	3	7	2
Bailey	34	11	80	0				
Laker	54	17	119	4	24	20	13	2
Lock	34.4	15	55	0	27	19	31	3
Close					2	1	8	0

FALL OF WICKETS
1-4, 2-83, 3-120, 4-183, 5-197, 6-387, 7-466, 8-469, 9-474, 10-474
1-1, 2-9, 3-25, 4-27, 5-43, 6-66, 7-68

Umpires: D.E.Davies and C.S.Elliott

May recalls the problems he and Cowdrey eventually solved in a partnership that lasted until after lunch on the final day.

> We were never sure about the leg-break. Sometimes we would think it was the one he bowled slightly slower, or higher or from wider of the stumps. We even tried to work out if there was a signal to the wicketkeeper, but again we were never sure.
>
> One stroke I ruled out against him was the one wide of mid-on to a ball slanting in towards the leg stump. It only had to straighten a little to have you in trouble. When you scored runs off him, he was adept at bowling the same ball again - but quicker. This, with the low trajectory which sometimes made the ball skid through, accounted for the high proportion of his victims who were bowled or LBW.

May and Cowdrey effectively eliminated the possibility of either dismissal by a use of the pads which reduced the bowler to despair and frustrated supporters so much that many queried the fairness of the ploy. For instance, Michael Manley wrote this in his *History of West Indies Cricket*:

'The partnership was important from every point of view. First, there was the sheer size of it - 411 runs. Secondly, it created a situation in which Ramadnin was eventually exhausted by being required to set a world record by bowling 98 overs in a single innings and 129 overs in the Test match. From the time he took Richardson's wicket early on the fourth day, he had no further success in the match. Yet, during this period, he must have had at least 50 appeals for LBW turned down by umpires Davies and Elliott. This arose because of another feature of the innings which profoundly influenced cricket in the years to come. In essence, May and Cowdrey tamed Ramadhin by a simple device. To anything pitched on or about the off-stump on a length just too short to drive, they simply stretched their left leg and pad far down the wicket and blocked the ball with the pad.

'Cricket fans in the West Indies listened for hour after hour as the commentator described one or other of the English batsmen stretching the leg down, Ramadhin and the fielders appealing for LBW and the umpire resolutely looking the other way. However *Wisden*, normally a provider of reasonably objective commentary on cricket worldwide, does not find a word to record this fascinating feature of the match. The justification of the umpire's attitude lay in the claim that, if the left leg is stretched well down the wicket, the batsman cannot be given out LBW because there must be an element of doubt as to whether some fractional deviation in the direction of the ball might have made it miss the wicket.

'What is interesting here is that May and Cowdrey were not defending with their pads outside the line of the stumps. Much of the time the left pad was in line with balls which seemed to be perfectly directed at the wicket.'

Much of that is opinion, but Manley's conclusion cannot be faulted. 'The May-Cowdrey partnership, which finally broke Ramadhin as a major force in Test cricket, was, for all practical purposes, the end of the series as a contest.' England went on to win three of the next four Tests by an innings, with only the third Test being drawn.

By the close of play on the fourth day, England were 378 for three - a total of 276 scored in the day, which seems to suggest that, occasionally, May and Cowdrey did put bat to ball as well as pad. May was the dominant partner, going from his overnight 21 to 193, when Cowdrey was 78.

A lead of 90 had brightened England hopes, but nothing more, unless the pre-lunch session on the fifth day could be negotiated safely. It was, and after Cowdrey was finally caught on the long-on boundary for 154 off Smith, May went on to seal the match from defeat, although he agrees he might have declared earlier.

When Colin got out, we were 236 ahead with 3¼ hours left, but the strength and depth of the West Indies batting decided me against it, and I eventually closed an hour later. The fact Laker and Lock got more out of the pitch and took five of seven wickets to fall, did not persuade me that I was wrong in not declaring earlier. The pitch was still good, and John Goddard defended so well that I am convinced it would have made no difference.

After Cowdrey was out, Godfrey Evans joined his captain, and immediately nearly ran him out on a call for a tight second run. Evans remembers May's reaction. 'He called me down the pitch, and said, "I admire the way you took my words to heart about scoring runs quickly, but please remember I have been batting for over eight hours."'

It was the beginning of a successful year for May. He won the series, and also led Surrey to their sixth successive County Championship in his first year as club captain. The longest innings he ever played - nearly ten hours - saved his country and reshaped history. Truly, the innings of his life.

BARRY RICHARDS

Hampshire won the toss and batted on a pitch which was rain-affected at one end and dry at the other, due to overnight rain penetrating the covers. The young Richards, then 22 years old, playing in only his second Championship game, came in to bat at five for two to face an international quartet of bowlers - Trueman, Illingworth, Wilson and Close - and a quality seamer in Nicholson. Under conditions he had never seen before, Richards scored 70 out of 109 added while he batted. Hampshire were bowled out for 122, and little further play was possible because of more rain.

Barry Anderson Richards was born on 21 July 1945 in Durban, and was educated at Durban High School, where he soon showed a brilliance at batting that was to mark one of the most frustrating careers in post-war cricket. Inevitable success in South Africa's unique Nuffield Schools week brought him the captaincy of the South African Schools side which toured England in 1963, and he made his debut for Natal the following year. In 1965, he and Mike Procter played second team cricket with Gloucestershire, but once special rules of registration for overseas cricketers were introduced in 1968, each county could have only one instant registration and, with Gloucestershire choosing Procter, Richards signed for Hampshire.

It was the start of a round-the-year career in first-class cricket which ended prematurely at the age of 36 when, starved of international competitive cricket, he retired mainly because he was bored with unfailing success at a level that failed to sustain his interest any longer.

He proved himself against the best bowlers in the world, but always felt unfulfilled after his brief taste of official Test cricket, which lasted for four Tests in 1970 in which he scored 29, 32, 140, 65, 35, 81 and 126. He thus became the first South African to score more than 500 runs in his first series - an achievement that was all the more remarkable because it was a four-match rubber against Australia.

He continued to play for Natal after a season with South Australia in 1970-71, and was a natural target for Kerry Packer's World Series cricket seven years later. He was often criticised in county cricket for playing long innings only when it suited him, but a career record of 28,358 runs, at an average of 54.74 and 80 hundreds which came at a ratio of one every seven innings indicates that some of the criticism was unjustified. He could be difficult, as he acknowledged in the mid-1980s when I heard him address the members of the Kingsmead Mynahs Club, a few months after he was appointed Director of Cricket for Natal.

THE POSITION OF WICKETKEEPER ENGINEER
INDICATES THIS RICHARDS OFF-DRIVE HAS BEEN
PLAYED 'INSIDE-OUT' FROM A LINE OF MIDDLE
AND LEG. THE BALANCE IS PERFECT - ACHIEVED
BY A STILL HEAD AND IMPECCABLE FOOTWORK.

(PATRICK EAGAR)

Outlining his plans for the players, he said, 'It was only when I sat on the other side of the negotiating table, that I realised what a s**t I must have been for most of my career.'

But what a career! What puts it into perspective is that he scored 43 more runs than Sobers, and played 33 fewer innings. When he retired from Natal, a Currie Cup aggregate of 1000 or more in a season had been achieved 12 times in history, five of them by Richards and four by Graeme Pollock. His six hundreds in his second season is still a record, and he and Dudley Nourse are the only two batsmen to score over 5000 Currie Cup runs at an average over 60. He reached fifty three times every seven innings for Natal and, although Pollock remains the highest run-scorer in the Currie Cup (12,409 compared with Richards' 7551), the left-hander hit his 35 hundreds in 261 innings compared with 26 in 140 by Richards.

His batting was touched by genius, and no more elegant batsman has graced a game which players like Richards turn into an art form. It is often said that the great players - and that is what he was - see the ball earlier than most, which is why they appear to play it later. Not so. What the best batsmen do is to stand still longer, which means they are not committed so early as the average batsman. Richards was the perfect example of a tall man who could play with equal facility of back and front foot. Add the ability to play either side of the wicket, and you have the altar of perfect orthodoxy at which spectators worshipped all over the world - as did many players he played with and against.

Would he choose one of dozens of destructive innings in which he destroyed Test bowlers, or would his sense of the aesthetic lead him to declare another kind of performance as 'the innings of my life'? No more fascinating conversation took place among the other subjects of this book.

I narrow it down to four. I must include my first Test hundred, because that was, and remains, extra special. Then I think about an innings I played for the Champion County against MCC at Lord's in 1974. Their attack included Mike Hendrick, Robin Jackman, Phil Edmonds, Roger Knight and David Acfield, and it was a freezing cold day. Right from the first ball, everything seemed to go off the middle and, when I got out half an hour before tea, I was 189 out of 249 for six.

His magnificent display included two sixes off Edmonds and 32 fours - leaving only 49 not scored in boundaries - so what fault could such a perfectionist find in a display which is still talked about by players of both sides?

> It was a decent pitch, but it was not a competitive match. I know it was played hard, but games with points at stake have a keener edge. The third innings I thought about, probably because it was my highest score, was my 356 for South Australia at Perth in 1970 and I scored the first 300 on the first day.

He actually put 325 runs on the board on day one, with a significant factor, according to the cynics, being an individual sponsorship afforded him of a dollar a run. Australian cricket historian Jack Pollard calls that performance 'one of the greatest innings known to Australian cricket'. That season was to be his only one in Sheffield Shield cricket, and he marked it with a massive aggregate of 1538 at an average of 109.86. It must have been a difficult decision for Richards to discard an innings of such quality, but all true artists have different criteria by which they judge their best work.

> I wanted a performance in which I played as well as I could under difficult conditions against a top attack. I therefore go for my third Championship innings for Hampshire, against Yorkshire at Harrogate, in my debut season.
>
> I started off with a duck and 50 against Sussex - LBW to Snow I think - and we had a very long car trip up to Harrogate. Roy Marshall took me and spent most of it trying to help me with advice. He said I must get forward more if the pitch was doing something, and also tried to prepare me for playing against 'the Yorkies'. At that time, they were the top team and had been champions four times in six years, and it was easy for sides to be overawed by them.
>
> It was a bit of a culture shock to arrive at our hotel in Harrogate at 3am, and find it was a temperance one. 'Marsh' reckoned it was a typical Yorkshire ploy to unsettle us, and the weather was gloomy and wet. I had seen nothing like it in Durban, and remember I had come to Hampshire straight from hard wickets in South Africa, so it was an even bigger shock when I saw the pitch next morning. Rain had got under the covers at one end, so it was wet there, and dry and green at the other.
>
> On top of that it was cold - and I had never been in a dressing-room before which had heaters. It was only a tiny room but we had them on, and I remember being so cold, I stood with my bare legs against the heater and was not even aware I was burning until there was a smell of singed hair. All the hairs off the back of my legs went up in smoke, so you can tell what state I was in when I walked out to bat. Fred had knocked our openers over - including 'Marsh' whose advice I was now beginning to wonder about.

So there was Richards, on the verge of playing what he now considers the best innings of his life: cold and singed in an environment that was cheerless and beerless, when the innocent from abroad was sent out to take on the best attack in county cricket, with tingling legs, involuntarily shaven, and a mountain of advice rattling around a confused mind. He was an obvious candidate for a quick return to the warmth of the dressing-room, but he chose that most unpropitious of situations to build an unforgettable innings.

> I then played as well, technically, as I ever did throughout my career. I came to terms with the different pace of both ends of what was a difficult pitch, and my shot selection was good. Considering the quality of the attack on that pitch, I was proud of how I played.

Wisden praised his 'watchful defence and skill in run-making under testing conditions'. It took Yorkshire 75 overs to bowl Hampshire out, with Richards playing through all but half a dozen overs. For well over three hours, he gave a model display of batting, which showed a maturity of technique that was difficult for watchers to assimilate.

A two-paced pitch and a quality attack need a defensive counter that takes years to learn, yet here was a young South African showing 'soft hands' and immaculate footwork and shot selection.

Richards' display made memorable an otherwise sterile match, and convinced the hard-bitten opposition that a rare talent was about to blossom in county cricket. To deal with the hostility of Trueman, the probing seam and swing of Nicholson and the spin of Illingworth and Wilson under such helpful bowling conditions called for the application of a technique that a young overseas batsman could hardly be expected to possess so early in his English career. Yet, as Illingworth recalls, 'it was the first of many innings he played against us that was out of the top drawer. I came to rate him among the top two or three batsmen I ever played against, although I always felt he gave me a chance, because he always responded to what he saw was a good challenge, and that kept him going once Test cricket was taken away from him. Why he gave me a chance was because he often tried to play me against the spin through the covers, and only a top batsman can do that against off-spin on a turner. He had everything: balance, which gave him the ability to play forward or back, and a lovely orthodox method which made the game look easy.'

YORKSHIRE V HAMPSHIRE (COUNTY CHAMPIONSHIP)

PLAYED AT HARROGATE, ON 4, 5, 6 (NO PLAY) MAY 1968.
TOSS: HAMPSHIRE. RESULT: MATCH DRAWN.

HAMPSHIRE

FIRST INNINGS

R.E.Marshall*	c Binks, b Trueman	0
B.L.Reed	c Binks, b Trueman	3
P.J.Sainsbury	b Illingworth	18
B.A.Richards	c Sharpe, b Wilson	70
D.R.Turner	c Close, b Illingworth	7
R.M.C.Gilliat	run out	2
K.J.Wheatley	c Close, b Illingworth	3
B.S.V.Timms†	c Binks, b Close	9
D.Shackleton	c Hampshire, b Wilson	3
D.W.White	c Close, b Wilson	2
R.M.H.Cottam	not out	3
Extras	w 1, nb 1	2
		—
		122

	O	M	R	W
Trueman	9	2	18	2
Nicholson	20	9	28	0
Close	11	7	14	1
Illingworth	19	6	34	3
Wilson	15	4	21	3
Boycott	1	0	5	0

FALL OF WICKETS
1-0, 2-5, 3-38, 4-58, 5-60, 6-71, 7-112, 8-114, 9-119, 10-122

Umpires: A.Gaskell and R.Aspinall

YORKSHIRE

FIRST INNINGS

G.Boycott	c White, b Cottam	5
P.J.Sharpe	c and b Cottam	18
D.E.V.Padgett	not out	12
J.H.Hampshire	not out	6
K.Taylor		
D.B.Close*		
R.Illingworth		
J.G.Binks†	did not bat	
D.Wilson		
F.S.Trueman		
A.G.Nicholson		
Extras		0
		—
(2 wickets)		41

	O	M	R	W
Shackleton	14	7	15	0
White	7	3	13	0
Cottam	7	3	13	2

FALL OF WICKETS
1-18, 2-28

England and Middlesex off-spinner John Emburey, like Ray Illingworth, is not given to over-praising batsmen, so his assessment of Richards is interesting. 'I have played most of my Test matches against Australia and the West Indies, and I seem to have spent most of my time bowling against either Allan Border or Viv Richards. So I suppose it is natural that I should consider them to be my most formidable opponents.

'In fact, if I had to name the best overseas batsman I have ever bowled against it would be neither of those two, great as they are. It would be Barry Richards, the incomparable South African opener. From what I have seen of him, he was not only the finest strokeplayer in the world, but had a batting technique every bit as good as Boycott's. There can be no higher praise than that.'

Agreed, which is why Richards received, from all quarters, a level of acclamation accorded to few cricketers. His achievements place him in the all-time top bracket of batsmen, and all done despite the canker of exclusion from Test cricket which gnawed away during his best years. The cricket world was privileged to watch a genius at work for over a decade. What they and he missed is incalculable. Barry Anderson Richards represents cricket's greatest gain and loss in the last 40 years.

VIV RICHARDS

61 on the fifth day of the first Test between West Indies and India at Kingston, Jamaica, 28 February 1983.
A seemingly certain drawn game at the tea interval was changed dramatically by fast bowler Andy Roberts, whose three wickets in his first over after the break gave the West Indies a faint hope of victory. A target of 172 from 26 overs looked impossible until Richards made the second fastest half-century in Test history. He hit four sixes and five fours in a blistering 61 off 36 balls, including his first 50 off 32 balls. Thanks to the Richards onslaught, the West Indies brought off a sensational victory, with Jeffrey Dujon hitting a six off the second ball of the final over, curiously bowled by Mohinder Amarnath. West Indies went on to win the five-match series 2-0, with their other victory coming, as usual, at the Kensington Oval in Bridgetown.

Isaac Vivian Alexander Richards was born on 7 March 1952 in St John's, Antigua, one of four sons of Malcolm, an acting-superintendent at the prison which adjoins the town's cricket ground. He was educated at the St John's Boys School and the Antigua Grammar School, where he became cricket captain at the age of 16. In 1968, he played in the Leeward Islands Tournament against St Kitts, and was suspended for two years after open dissent when given out. Richards says: 'It was probably my most important cricket match to that date. It taught me one mighty lesson and helped to curb my arrogance, which I must admit was pretty rampant at the time.'

During his two-year absence from representative cricket he played soccer, basketball and boxed a little, but not even a lengthy ban in his late teens could quench a fanatical enthusiasm for the game that was to launch one of the most spectacular careers cricket has ever known. He made his debut for the Leeward Isles in 1971, and first played for Somerset in 1974 before the first of his 121 Tests in Bangalore in November of the same year - the game chosen by Kallicharran in this book as the stage for his best-ever innings.

Richards developed into one of the most thrilling batsmen in the history of cricket, and the best compliment he can be paid is to say that he matched any West Indian batsman, the great Sobers included, for a variety of brilliant strokeplay that was not always strictly orthodox. He regarded each innings as an opportunity to impose himself on the game and the opposition, and it was the manner of his runs, as much as the quantity of them, which made him one of the greatest draw-cards of his time. Early in the 1993 English season, playing his last first-class season with his last club, Glamorgan, he passed 35,000 first-class runs in his

765th innings. He became the second overseas batsman to achieve this - Gordon Greenidge was the first - thanks to an unbeaten 109 against Oxford University, which was his 113th century, only four behind Bradman, who was then the leading overseas member of those to score 100 hundreds.

His aggregate of 8540 Test runs is the fourth highest, and only Sobers scored more hundreds for the West Indies - 26 compared with 24 by Richards. His heaviest run-scoring period in Test cricket came in 1976 when he scored a record 1710 runs in the calendar year. A remarkable average of 90.00 was achieved without the assistance of any not outs, and his 19 innings were considerably fewer than those played by four of the only other five cricketers who have scored more than 1250 runs in one year. Only Gooch played fewer - 17 for his 1264 - while Gavaskar had 32 and 27, Viswanath and Simpson 26, and Amiss 22.

The year included seven hundreds, the highest of which was his 291 at The Oval, scored off 386 balls in just under eight hours. He missed the Lord's Test in that series, but still scored 829 runs in seven innings, including 232 at Trent Bridge and 135 at Old Trafford.

Richards dominated the one-day game in the 1980s, hitting the highest-ever one-day international score - a magnificent unbeaten 189 at Old Trafford against England in 1984 - and also the highest individual score in a Benson and Hedges Cup final, when he hit an unbeaten 132 against Surrey in 1981. The 1993 *Wisden* index gives him a huge entry of 28 lines, but the name of Richards means much more than a statistical catalogue - impressive though it might be. Here are the views of two leading historians of the Caribbean, Michael Manley and C.L.R.James.

Manley first: 'It is impossible for Viv Richards to walk to the wicket in the presence of a West Indies audience without an argument starting as to whether he is the greatest West Indian batsman since the Second World War. Comparisons are never made with Headley as this would involve a form of lese-majesty too terrible to contemplate. Some people have put themselves beyond comparison not only because they are the best, but because the niche that they occupy has become profoundly symbolic of things that go beyond the boundaries of what they do. There can never be another Headley. It is as if one were to try to compare the later saints with St Paul. The one is seminal, and the others a part of an inheritance.'

Richards the batsman earns this from Manley: 'Everton Weekes, in his heyday and at his best, was quite simply the most electrifying batsman of our age, apart from Bradman before him and Richards after him, even though Englishmen might enter a caveat on behalf of Wally Hammond.'

James confines himself to the cricket field. 'Richards is undoubtedly a batsman who can be ranked with great batsmen of any time.'

That shrewdest of judges, Trevor Bailey, believed that Richards had an unequalled ability 'to destroy opposing attacks in both Tests and limited-overs cricket by a sustained tigerish assault, which combines brutality, bravado and beauty.'

His selection of the innings of his life is, on the face of it, a surprising one. There are Test hundreds all over the world. A triple hundred for Somerset against Warwickshire - he secured maximum batting points on his own in 1985 - and many other wonderful, match-tilting innings in county cricket. Then there are his one-day fusillades. Surely there has never been a more disdainful batsman? He would smash the ball through his favourite on-side and, before the umpire started the boundary wave, he would hammer a few blades of grass into place, as though to say to the poor bowler, 'pitch the next one here, please'. Strong of body with the classic build of a light-heavyweight - Peter Roebuck likens his physique to 'that of an egg-timer' - he must have had the strongest jaws in world cricket, such was the ferocity of his gum-chewing.

So many of his innings seemed personal vendettas - which one would he choose? 'I narrowed it down to two Test matches in which I scored very quickly to enable us to win. The first one was in Antigua against England in 1986 and my hundred off 56 balls gave us time to bowl England out and win the game.'

I saw that match, and I have never seen a press box in such disarray as it was either side of the tea interval on the fourth day. We were still checking out the fastest fifties in Test cricket - Richards got his off 33 balls - when, such was the breakneck speed of the local hero's progress, that we switched to the section listing the fastest hundreds. He hit seven sixes and seven fours and failed to score off only 15 balls in his 58-ball 110 not out. Giving himself an open cheque to score quickly or get out, Richards was at his savage best. Not for him the rapier - more the sledgehammer, although his occasional improvisation was breathtaking.

A soft-shoe shuffle of a feint against John Emburey ended with a shin-high full toss outside leg stump being smashed over the head of Neil Foster at long-off for an astonishing six - a carry I subsequently paced out as 95 yards. Emburey says this of Richards and that brutal day in Antigua, when he returned figures of 14-0-83-1 almost before he knew what and who had hit him.

'Richards will not allow any spinner to bowl to him for more than a few overs before he is trying to smash him all round the ground. If the wicket turns, he really goes on the rampage with a view to getting the spinner taken off - or, alternatively, making him wish he had been. I had first-hand experience of that kind of mayhem in Antigua in 1986. I felt, at long last, we were beginning to get on top and might even have a chance of avoiding a "whitewash" in the series, when Viv sauntered in as though he owned the place and

took the game by the scruff of the neck with the fastest century in Test history.

'He needed only 56 balls, but just one of those was enough to convince me of the impossibility of bowling against him on that day. I thought that I had completely deceived him in flight when he was shaping to give himself room and hit me for another six over long-off. I bowled it a fraction shorter, a little bit straighter and more towards middle and leg. For an instant, I had him in two minds. Then, halfway through his original shot, he decided not to hit the ball over long-off after all and just went round with the bat to pick it up and lift me nonchalantly over square leg for six. It was a great innings - unless you happened to be watching from where I was.'

A TYPICAL NO HOLDS BARRED OFF-DRIVE BY RICHARDS. THE WEIGHT DISTRIBUTION, ARCHED BODY AND HIGH FOLLOW-THROUGH COMBINE TO GENERATE TIMING AND POWER. (PATRICK EAGAR)

Even more brutal was a six into the top deck of the stand to the left of our press box off Ian Botham. Like the stroke against Emburey, it was 'inside-out', only this time the ball started outside off-stump and Richards hit it over extra-cover, over the rope, and over the first ten rows of the upper deck. The 11th row prevented the ball coming to ground but, had it been allowed to do so, it must have carried at least 125 yards.

However, even this was not good enough for 'the innings of my life' because:

It was a good pitch, and when I got to the wicket, we were 264 ahead, so there wasn't all that much pressure. I went for it and it came off, but if I hadn't somebody else would have and we might have had to declare a bit later, that's all. I've thought of a few other knocks, but in the end I go for my 61 at Sabina Park in 1983. It helped us beat India against all the odds - in fact it was an impossible-looking win.

It was a low-scoring game - Clive put them in and we bowled them out for 251. We got 254, but we lost time for rain, including the whole of the fourth day, and when they were 167 for six at tea on the last day, it looked a certain draw. When Andy Roberts got Kapil out earlier, we had a chance at 136 for six, but Shastri and Kirmani dug in and seemed to

HIS 189 AT OLD TRAFFORD IN 1984 WAS AMONG THE GREATEST ONE-DAY INNINGS OF ALL TIME. DEREK PRINGLE IS THE VICTIM THIS TIME. (PATRICK EAGAR)

have saved it. Then Andy proved what a great fast bowler he was. He got Kirmani first ball after tea, and off the last two balls of the same over, he had Sandhu and Venkat for ducks. Maninder Singh hung in for five more overs until Andy got him for his fifth wicket in the innings and his ninth in the match. Super bowling, but it all looked too late.

We wanted 172 from 26 overs, and that is not on in a Test match, where you can bowl your best bowlers and put your fielders where you want. Clive insisted we give it a go, and Desmond got us off to a terrific start, scoring 34 off 21 balls. Then he got out and Clive got only three, so I went in at 65 for two with the odds well against us. I had one of those days when everything clicked, and managed to keep us in touch with the rate. The crowd could hardly believe it, but of course we could have lost the game as well. Gordon was bowled by Kapil at 131 for three, and Andy Roberts got just one after coming in at number five. Jeffrey Dujon joined me, but I got out to Kapil at 156 and we still needed 16 in three overs.

It looked ours, but you never know, and when Kapil got his fourth wicket - Gus Logie, LBW - it was down to Jeffrey. I can still see that winning six in the last over, and we had pulled off one of the best wins I have ever known in Test cricket. I count my 61 as 'the innings of my life', because of the pressure of the match situation. Had I not come off, I doubt if we would have won, but it just shows that nothing is impossible.

Not for a man like Richards, whose refusal ever to wear a batting helmet says as much about his character as his technique. His batting horizons were limitless, and his natural attacking instincts often fuelled by a blaze of what some saw as pride, and others as arrogance. There has been no more destructive modern batsman, and perhaps it was inevitable that his fierce sense of nationalism led him into several situations of confrontation which were far from pretty. He seemed to believe that to compromise was to bend the knee, but it would be churlish to say that a few wild strokes of the brush spoiled one of the most vivid canvases ever created by a batting artist.

WEST INDIES V INDIA (1ST TEST)

PLAYED AT SABINA PARK, KINGSTON, JAMAICA, ON 23, 24, 26, 27 (NO PLAY), 28 FEBRUARY 1983.
TOSS: WEST INDIES. RESULT: WEST INDIES WON BY FOUR WICKETS.

INDIA

	FIRST INNINGS		SECOND INNINGS	
S.M.Gavaskar	c Dujon, b Marshall	20	b Holding	0
A.D.Gaekwad	c Dujon, b Holding	1	c Greenidge, b Marshall	23
M.Amarnath	c Dujon, b Garner	29	c Garner, b Marshall	40
D.B.Vengsarkar	c Richards, b Roberts	30	c Garner, b Marshall	20
Yashpal Sharma	c Haynes, b Garner	63	c Gomes, b Holding	24
R.J.Shastri	c Dujon, b Holding	1	not out	25
Kapil Dev*	c Marshall, b Roberts	5	c Dujon, b Roberts	12
S.M.H.Kirmani†	c Dujon, b Marshall	5	c Haynes, b Roberts	10
B.S.Sandhu	c Garner, b Roberts	68	c Garner, b Roberts	0
S.Venkataraghavan	hit wicket, b Roberts	0	c Greenidge, b Roberts	0
Maninder Singh	not out	3	c Holding, b Roberts	2
Extras	b 1, lb 15, nb 10	26	b 2, lb 4, w 1, nb 11	18
		251		174

	O	M	R	W	O	M	R	W
Holding	24	5	57	2	17	4	36	2
Roberts	22	4	61	4	24.2	9	39	5
Garner	15.4	4	41	2	13	6	16	0
Marshall	16	4	35	2	24	6	56	3
Gomes	9	0	31	0	7	2	9	0
Richards	1	1	0	0				

FALL OF WICKETS
1-10, 2-58, 3-66, 4-98, 5-99, 6-104, 7-127, 8-234, 9-238, 10-251
1-0, 2-68, 3-69, 4-112, 5-118, 6-136, 7-168, 8-168, 9-168, 10-174

WEST INDIES

	FIRST INNINGS		SECOND INNINGS	
C.G.Greenidge	c Venkataraghavan, b Shastri	70	b Kapil Dev	42
D.L.Haynes	c Amarnath, b Kapil Dev	25	b Kapil Dev	34
I.V.A.Richards	c Venkataraghavan, b Shastri	29	(4) c Kapil Dev, b Amarnath	61
H.A.Gomes	c Yashpal, b Shastri	4		
A.L.Logie	run out	13	(7) lbw, b Kapil Dev	10
C.H.Lloyd*	b Venkataraghavan	24	(3) c Amarnath, b Kapil Dev	3
P.J.L.Dujon†	lbw, b Kapil Dev	29	(6) not out	17
M.D.Marshall	c Yashpal, b Kapil Dev	23	not out	0
A.M.E.Roberts	c Sandhu, b Shastri	17	(5) c Kirmani, b Amarnath	1
M.A.Holding	c Kirmani, b Kapil Dev	1		
J.Garner	not out	0		
Extras	b1, lb 8, nb 10	19	lb 5	5
		254	(6 wickets)	173

	O	M	R	W	O	M	R	W
Kapil Dev	25.3	6	45	4	13	0	73	4
Sandhu	11	4	30	0	3	0	22	0
Venkataraghavan	25	3	66	1	7	0	39	0
Maninder Singh	31	6	51	0				
Shastri	24	8	43	4				
Amarnath					2.2	0	34	2

FALL OF WICKETS
1-36, 2-83, 3-91, 4-114, 5-157, 6-186, 7-228, 8-244, 9-254, 10-254
1-46, 2-65, 3-131, 4-132, 5-156, 6-167

Umpires: D.M.Archer and W.Malcolm

He received a farewell salute from the crowd at The Oval in 1991 which expressed genuine affection, and he clearly savoured every moment as he reluctantly departed a Test scene he had dominated for 17 years with pride and passion. Truly, Richards is one of a handful of sportsmen of whom we can say, 'We shall never see his like again'.

Peter Roebuck played, travelled and lived with the man. Let him have the last word: 'He has left cricket with much to remember, for he has been a majestic, charismatic, fit and explosive cricketer.'

*182 on the second and third days of
the second Test between West Indies
and Australia at Georgetown, Guyana,
24 and 25 March 1991.*

Richardson went in to bat at 10 for one in reply to Australia's 348. The first Test had been drawn after the home side conceded a first innings lead of 107 and two days were lost to rain. Australia had also dominated the one-day series, and it needed a special performance to stem and turn a tide which was running away from the West Indies. Richardson provided it with a dazzling 182 off 260 balls, and he hit two sixes and 26 fours. He was finally out third ball after lunch on the third day, having gone in in mid-afternoon the previous day. His innings of 5¾ hours swung the match, and with it the series, away from the previously rampant Australians.

Richard Benjamin Richardson was born on 12 January 1962 in Five Islands, Antigua, and made his debut for the Leeward Islands in 1981, and for the West Indies in Bombay in November 1983. After becoming yet another celebrated batsman to register a duck in his first innings, he was dropped for the next two Tests, but played in all five Tests at home against Australia three months later with considerable success. He scored 327 in five innings, including the first two of the 15 Test hundreds he had scored in 122 innings by the end of his second series as captain - against Pakistan in April 1993.

Despite those innings of 131* in Barbados and 154 on his home St John's ground in Antigua, which gave him two big hundreds in his first six Tests, he lost his place to Larry Gomes in England. Later in 1984, he toured Australia again and scored 138 at Brisbane to give him three hundreds in five Tests, and to establish him as one of the most exciting young batsmen in world cricket. A natural strokeplayer, he played one of his best innings for the West Indies in his 18th Test in Bridgetown against England, where he scored 160 out of 418 on a breaking pitch, and his refusal to compromise his natural style had brought him 5231 Test runs by May 1993 at an average of 46.70. When Viv Richards announced his retirement, Richardson was appointed captain ahead of Haynes, and soon won further respect for his calm and sportsmanlike leadership. He had a difficult series in Australia on which to cut his teeth in early 1993, but led his side to a 2-1 win in the five-match rubber - the highlight of which was a win by one run in the fourth Test at the Adelaide Oval when Australia looked certain to win the game and take the series. Earlier, he rectified the one gap in his record with a superb second tour of England in 1991. He topped 50 in at least one innings of every Test, and his two hundreds at Edgbaston and The Oval proved that he could play under any conditions. Of his 104 in the fourth Test at Edgbaston, *Wisden* said, 'His attacking strokes and defence throughout 4½ hours mocked those who thought he would never succeed in England, and his Man of the Match award was entirely justified.'

A quiet, almost studious man, Richardson was in no doubt about the innings he values most, although he was keen to talk about his 99 on a broken pitch in Trinidad against India in April 1989.

> I've got out three times on 99 in Tests, but I still can't tell you how I managed to be bowled out by Kapil. The pitch had gone on top, so you couldn't really trust much off the front foot. He bowled me one which pitched well up and outside leg stump. I just put the bat there to turn it for one, and suddenly I heard the rattle. It got through but I still don't know how.

No wonder he is proud of that innings. At one stage, his side were reeling at 26 for four and he was ninth out at 250. He shared partnerships with Gus Logie and Malcolm Marshall of 74 and 61, to put his side into an overwhelmingly strong position from which they won by 217 runs, with Marshall completing match figures of 11 for 89.

His memorable display on a pitch on which only seven batsmen out of 22 managed double figures twice in the match was accomplished with a bad hand. 'The ball either squatted or flew, and after I got a knock, my hand hurt every time the ball missed the sweet spot of the bat. I concentrated as hard as I have ever done, and it was one of my best innings for the team.'

His time at the crease was officially 352 minutes - 37 minutes longer than he batted for what he is certain is 'the innings of my life' in which he scored almost double the runs.

> I have to pick Georgetown, even though it was a good pitch, because I have never played an innings like it before which had such an effect on the opposition. The Australians were after us, and came to Georgetown 3-1 up in the one-day series, and they had the better of the first Test at Sabina Park. We played the final one-day game at the Bourda three days before the second Test, and they beat us easily again, so their morale was sky-high.
>
> We had not beaten them on that ground since 1965, and a win looked unlikely when they scored 348 and got Gordon Greenidge LBW for two in the middle session of the second day. I did not plan to play the way I did, although I woke feeling good. Some days you do, and some you don't, but I started to fancy it a lot as soon as I took guard. The bat started to sing, and the attacking fields soon went. Allan Border set one-day fields for me with deep sweepers, but I still hit them where I wanted. It is funny when you really get going like that. You feel as though you can do anything, and all sorts of shots just flow.
>
> I knew if I could play a really big one, I would demoralise them and that's what happened. Desmond was also going well, and at the close of play we were 226 for one, and on the way towards taking charge, providing I could carry on next morning. I started the third day on 114, and piled it on even more. At lunch we had added 81 and I scored 68 of them.

It seems that Mike Whitney and Merv Hughes caught most of the flak, sharing combined figures of 48-8-196-0, but even Craig McDermott went for over three runs an over, and 37.5 overs from Greg Matthews brought him three for 155. It was savage stuff, and *Wisden* is in no doubt of its effect upon Australia. 'The spectacular and sudden shift of the balance of power clearly stunned the Australians, and they showed little fight thereafter, with the result they were almost beaten by an innings.' The extravagantly billed series as one to settle the World Championship was thus settled in just over five hours batting of sheer brilliance.

It was undoubtedly the individual highlight of a bad-tempered series which brought charges and counter-allegations of racial abuse and sledging of such vehemence that they shocked hard-bitten cricketers and journalists alike. Tony Cozier says, 'Above all else, what should have been a compelling advertisement for cricket was ruined by the obvious acrimony between the teams. This manifested itself time and again in verbal altercations on the field, and the rancour was transmitted by the television cameras which, for the first time, were transmitting live, ball-by-ball coverage back to Australia from the Caribbean.

A BLAZING HOOK PLAYED DURING RICHARDSON'S 182 IN GEORGETOWN IN 1991.

(ALLSPORT/BEN RADFORD)

'After the final Test, the umpires were moved to report to the West Indies Board on the abusive language used in the middle by certain players, and even the two Boards became involved in a succession of verbal exchanges.'

Referring to the cricket, Cozier says that Richardson's performance in Georgetown was enough on its own to earn him the Man of the Series award, without account being taken of his unbeaten 104 in the first Test at Kingston, or a brilliant 99 in the fourth Test at Bridgetown.

Few players were not drawn into the on-field bickering, with allegations from both sides of racial undertones, but Richardson's natural dignity enabled him to stand above behaviour he could barely understand, let alone tolerate. He was not one of the players who joined in the appeal against Dean Jones when the Australian left his crease after failing to hear the call of 'no ball' when he was bowled and was promptly run out. The law is quite specific - he should not have been given out, but Richardson still does not understand how the incident developed: 'I could not do it. How can you when a man leaves his crease believing he is out?'

He has a natural dignity which sits well on a man who is full of the right sort of national pride. It burns within, but never consumes - unlike some others. His batting style is similarly distinctive. As proved by his favourite innings, he can bludgeon with the best, but his bat is more a flashing blade - even a rapier. His square-cutting is exquisite, and his pulling and hooking are full of authority, despite a habit he shares with Viv Richards. Neither man has ever batted in a helmet and neither man has paid a physical price for an act of bravery or bravado - or is it simply a statement of courage based on a self-confidence in pure ability that few batsmen possess?

Significantly, Richardson uses an unusual word to explain why his Georgetown innings was so special. Considering the flashpoint level of the relationships between two teams who clearly wanted to teach each other a lesson - and preferably a humiliating one - it would be understandable if Richardson had chosen a more meaningful phrase or word than 'demoralise'. Yet that is enough for him:

I set out to demoralise, and I did just that. I know it was a good pitch - perhaps it played low - but I have never played a better or more important big innings. I name it as my best because of its effect on the Australians and the series.

Richie Benaud agrees: 'It was a wonderful exhibition, and nobody could bowl to him. Most top batsmen have a purple patch, perhaps for a couple of hours, but Richie just got better and better for over five hours. It was a privilege to watch and commentate upon, and it definitely swung the match and the series.'

Allan Border also admitted that the game was won and lost because of Richardson's innings, and its effect upon the scoring rate. West Indies' final score of 569 from 153.5 overs gave the home attack extra time in which to bowl Australia out for a second time on a docile pitch, and the game finished with three hours to

WEST INDIES V AUSTRALIA (2ND TEST)

PLAYED AT BOURDA, GEORGETOWN, GUYANA, ON 23, 24, 25, 27, 28 MARCH 1991.
TOSS: AUSTRALIA. RESULT: WEST INDIES WON BY TEN WICKETS.

AUSTRALIA

	FIRST INNINGS		SECOND INNINGS	
M.A.Taylor	lbw, b Patterson	0	lbw, b Ambrose	15
G.R.Marsh	c Hooper, b Patterson	94	b Walsh	22
D.C.Boon	c Dujon, b Marshall	7	c Dujon, b Marshall	2
A.R.Border*	b Marshall	47	c Dujon, b Marshall	34
D.M.Jones	b Marshall	34	run out	3
M.E.Waugh	c Dujon, b Patterson	71	c Richards, b Ambrose	31
G.R.J.Matthews	c Dujon, b Ambrose	1	c Dujon, b Marshall	16
I.A.Healy†	run out	53	run out	47
C.J.McDermott	lbw, b Patterson	1	c Dujon, b Patterson	4
M.G.Hughes	b Ambrose	0	c Patterson, b Walsh	21
M.R.Whitney	not out	1	not out	0
Extras	b 6, lb 8, w 2, nb 23	39	b 17, lb 6, w 2, nb 28	53
		348		248

	O	M	R	W	O	M	R	W
Ambrose	31.4	9	64	2	24	5	44	2
Patterson	24	1	80	4	14	5	47	1
Walsh	24	2	81	0	23	4	55	2
Marshall	23	3	67	3	15	2	31	3
Hooper	13	3	37	0	18	6	35	0
Richards	1	0	5	0	4	2	13	0

FALL OF WICKETS
1-3, 2-24, 3-124, 4-188, 5-237, 6-238, 7-339, 8-346, 9-346, 10-348
1-32, 2-43, 3-67, 4-73, 5-130, 6-161, 7-172, 8-187, 9-241, 10-248

WEST INDIES

	FIRST INNINGS		SECOND INNINGS	
C.G.Greenidge	lbw, b McDermott	2	not out	5
D.L.Haynes	c Waugh, b Border	111	not out	23
R.B.Richardson	lbw, b McDermott	182		
C.L.Hooper	c Waugh, b Matthews	62		
I.V.A.Richards*	b Matthews	50		
A.L.Logie	c Healy, b Border	54		
P.J.L.Dujon†	lbw, b Border	29		
M.D.Marshall	not out	22		
C.E.L Ambrose	b Border	0		
C.A.Walsh	b Border	1		
B.P.Patterson	lbw, b Matthews	15		
Extras	b 5, lb 13, nb 23	41	lb 2, nb 1	3
		569	(0 wickets)	31

	O	M	R	W	O	M	R	W
McDermott	36	2	114	2	4	1	10	0
Whitney	28	4	103	0				
Matthews	37.5	6	155	3				
Hughes	20	4	93	0	3.5	0	19	0
Waugh	2	0	18	0				
Border	30	11	68	5				

FALL OF WICKETS
1-10, 2-307, 3-353, 4-443, 5-444, 6-529, 7-530, 8-530, 9-532, 10-569

Umpires: C.E.Cumberbatch and C.R.Duncan

spare. Seldom has a Test match changed so dramatically before the halfway stage. At lunch on the second day, Australia were 328 for six, and well on the way towards an impregnable position. By lunch on day three, they were already five runs in arrears and had only taken two wickets. The balloon was pricked - and all by one of the most ferocious innings ever played in Test cricket.

It was that batting dynamism which prompted Yorkshire to sign Richardson for the 1993 season. The most traditional of county clubs dictated his choice of headgear - forbidding his trademark wide-brimmed floppy hat, but they will never make him wear a helmet.

His disinclination to shelter behind the anonymity of a grill in his first decade in Test cricket says a great deal about a man who is taking the powerful West Indies side through the 1990s in an admirably mannerly fashion. If more Test captains had his instinctive grasp of the dividing line between acceptable and unacceptable aggression, the recently introduced system of International Cricket Council-appointed match referees would quickly be dropped. Richardson is a perfect example of a man who has learned to combine courtesy and innate sportsmanship with aggression.

JACK RUSSELL

55 on the fourth and fifth days of the fourth Test between West Indies and England at Bridgetown, Barbados, 8 and 10 April 1990.

Russell's defiant half-century came in five hours and nine minutes, and took his side to the brink of a draw, before he became the first of four wickets in 25 deliveries for Curtly Ambrose with the second new ball. Russell went in to bat the night before as second nightwatchman at 15 for three, and was sixth out at 166. When England lost their last wicket and the match, fading light would not have allowed more than half an hour's further play, which illustrates how close Russell's heroic innings came to ensuring England at least a share of a series they were to lose in Antigua. *Wisden* said of his efforts: ' The stirring defiance of Russell and Smith on the final day will live in the memory as long as the earlier centuries from Best, Lamb and Haynes.'

Robert Charles Russell was born on 15 August 1963 in Stroud. He made his first appearance for Gloucestershire in 1981, was capped in 1985 and, at the end of the 1992 English season, he had played in more than 250 first-class games and taken 651 victims behind the stumps, and stood second in the county wicketkeepers' list behind Bruce French. He had then scored 7334 runs at 27.06. Acknowledged from the mid-1980s to be the best wicketkeeper in county cricket, Russell's Test debut was delayed until 1988, allegedly because of batting considerations. Ironically, he was nightwatchman in his first innings at Lord's against Sri Lanka, and seemed to prove his point with 94 scored in 4½ hours.

Despite a career-best unbeaten 128 in the 1989 Old Trafford Test against Australia, he has been omitted from the England side on several occasions because of the same batting considerations that delayed his debut, and his omission from the 1993 tour of India, together with that of David Gower, resulted in a special meeting of MCC members when a vote of no-confidence in the England selectors was defeated only because of the postal proxy vote. His individualistic style of batting has brought him success at all levels, which makes the view of the selectors a curious one.

For a man who is a natural fighter, and who applies himself rigorously to every detail of his cricket, the choice of his most memorable innings simply had to be one of those rearguard actions he so often leads for county and country.

The innings of my life has to be my 55 at Bridgetown, when I batted for over five hours as nightwatchman, to try to save the fourth Test in 1990. We should have won in Trinidad, but the light ran out when a win would have put us 2-0 up in the series with two games to play.

Russell is referring to the Trinidad Test, two weeks earlier, when *Wisden* commented on 'the cynical time-wasting of the West Indies'. In that game their delaying tactics slowed down the pace of play spoiling what had been, until then, a magnificent match. Russell was five not out at the end of a session of 100 minutes in which the West Indies bowled 17 overs out of a supposed mandatory minimum of 30.

'KEEP GOING - WE MUST KEEP GOING.' AS SMITH AND RUSSELL DID FOR TEN HOURS BETWEEN THEM FOR 95 RUNS - AN EPIC EFFORT WHICH NARROWLY FAILED TO SAVE THE TEST BY 30 MINUTES.

(ALLSPORT/ADRIAN MURRELL)

Regarding the fourth Test, the little wicketkeeper says: 'Once we had had 446 put past us after we put them in, all we could do was to play for a draw, but even the hope of that seemed to have disappeared soon after the start of our second innings on the fourth evening.'

England had been on the rack throughout the game under the acting captaincy of Allan Lamb - his decision to field first had ignored history. The previous two England captains made the same decision at the Kensington Oval, with Ian Botham's side losing in 1981 by 298 runs, and David Gower's team going down five years later by an innings and 30 runs. Not only have nine visiting captains in recent years failed to win after deciding to field first, neither has any Test captain in history managed to win there since Bob Wyatt led England to victory in a freak Test match in a rain-affected game in 1935.

Lamb's hope of bowling the West Indies out with a four-man attack comprising Malcolm, Small, DeFreitas and Capel seemed the height of optimism. So it proved, with 164 from Best and 70 from Richards ensuring an overall run-rate of well over three runs per over. Lamb did his best to redeem himself with his second hundred of the series, and his sixth against the West Indies, and with the obdurate Smith, he helped to add 193 for the fourth wicket.

At 268 for three, England were not in trouble, but the relentless West Indies pace attack wore down the last seven wickets for 90, and the remainder of the third and fourth days brought some time-wasting tactics from England which might have been marginally less obvious than those at Trinidad, but which were still unsavoury. *Wisden* commented: 'Amid the great and good, there was bad and downright ugly. England indulged in time-wasting every bit as blatant, if not as theatrical, as the West Indies in the previous Test. The tactics reduced the over-rate to a funereal 11 per hour.'

Haynes scored 109, his fourth century against England and his 13th for the West Indies, before Richards declared and the temperature of the game boiled over in the final few overs of the fourth day. Larkins completed a pair in three balls, and with Bailey the centre of a controversial dismissal that resulted in litigation between the umpire and the BBC cricket correspondent, Russell padded up as the first nightwatchman, Small, went in to bat with the score 10 for two.

On the same score, another roar greeted another wicket - Small was the first of four LBWs for Ambrose,

WEST INDIES V ENGLAND (4TH TEST)

PLAYED AT KENSINGTON OVAL, BRIDGETOWN, BARBADOS, ON 5, 6, 7, 8, 10 APRIL 1990.
TOSS: ENGLAND. RESULT: WEST INDIES WON BY 164 RUNS.

WEST INDIES

	FIRST INNINGS		SECOND INNINGS	
C.G.Greenidge	c Russell, b DeFreitas	41	lbw, b Small	3
D.L.Haynes	c Stewart, b Small	0	c Malcolm, b Small	109
R.B.Richardson	c Russell, b Small	45	lbw, b DeFreitas	39
C.A.Best	c Russell, b Small	164		
I.V.A.Richards*	c Russell, b Capel	70	(4) c Small, b Capel	12
A.L.Logie	c Russell, b Capel	31	(5) lbw, b DeFreitas	48
P.J.L.Dujon†	b Capel	31	(8) not out	15
M.D.Marshall	c Lamb, b Small	4	(7) c Smith, b Small	7
C.E.L.Ambrose	not out	20	c Capel, b DeFreitas	1
I.R.Bishop	run out	10	not out	11
E.A.Moseley	b DeFreitas	4	(6) b Small	5
Extras	lb 8, nb 18	26	lb 12, w 1, nb 4	17
		446	(8 wickets declared)	267

	O	M	R	W	O	M	R	W
Malcolm	33	6	142	0	10	0	46	0
Small	35	5	109	4	20	1	74	4
DeFreitas	29.5	5	99	2	22	2	69	3
Capel	24	5	88	3	16	1	66	1

FALL OF WICKETS
1-6, 2-69, 3-108, 4-227, 5-291, 6-395, 7-406, 8-411, 9-431, 10-446
1-13, 2-80, 3-109, 4-223, 5-228, 6-239, 7-239, 8-239

ENGLAND

	FIRST INNINGS		SECOND INNINGS	
A.J.Stewart	c Richards, b Moseley	45	c Richards, b Ambrose	37
W. Larkins	c Richardson, b Bishop	0	c Dujon, b Bishop	0
R.J.Bailey	b Bishop	17	c Dujon, b Ambrose	6
A.J.Lamb*	lbw, b Ambrose	119	(6) c Dujon, b Moseley	10
R.A.Smith	b Moseley	62	(7) not out	40
N.Hussain	lbw, b Marshall	18	(8) lbw, b Ambrose	0
D.J.Capel	c Greenidge, b Marshall	2	(9) lbw, b Ambrose	6
R.C.Russell†	lbw, b Bishop	7	(5) b Ambrose	55
P.A.J.DeFreitas	c and b Ambrose	24	(10) lbw, b Ambrose	0
G.C.Small	not out	1	(4) lbw, b Ambrose	0
D.E.Malcolm	b Bishop	12	lbw, b Ambrose	4
Extras	b 14, lb 9, w 3, nb 25	51	b 8, lb 9, w 1, nb 15	33
		358		191

	O	M	R	W	O	M	R	W
Bishop	24.3	8	70	4	20	7	40	1
Ambrose	25	2	82	2	22.4	0	45	8
Moseley	28	3	114	2	19	3	44	1
Marshall	23	6	55	2	18	8	31	0
Richards	9	4	14	0	10	5	11	0
Richardson					2	1	3	0

FALL OF WICKETS
1-1, 2-46, 3-75, 4-268, 5-297, 6-301, 7-308, 8-340, 9-340, 10-358
1-1, 2-10, 3-10, 4-71, 5-97, 6-166, 7-173, 8-181, 9-181, 10-191

Umpires: D.M.Archer and L.H.Barker

and Russell joined Stewart with the famous Oval now like a bull ring. They hung on, and were able to enjoy the unusual luxury of a rest day after four, instead of three, days. How did Russell spend his day? Boating perhaps, surfing or snorkelling?

I sat in my room relaxing and thinking of how I was going to play. A whole day for England to survive, but I was determined to lie down and die to avoid losing the lead we had done so much to deserve in Jamaica and Trinidad. I remember, before play started, someone said to me: 'If you get 30 I'll buy you a pint, and if you bat all day I'll get you a pub.'

I said nothing, because I thought I would have done something if I could last an hour. I had no interest in scoring runs - even ten would have done me. I decided to take it step by step. Firstly, play for the drinks intervals and then, if I survived, play for lunch. Alec Stewart got out 20 minutes before lunch, and when Robin Smith came in, I had really wound myself up in a way I find hard to describe. Every ball was like a little battle all of its own. Bowlers like Curtly Ambrose, Ian Bishop, Malcolm Marshall and Ezra Moseley are always at you and, with us having no chance of winning, I was always surrounded by close catchers.

I felt absolutely brilliant when I was not out at lunch. Robin batted for over five hours in the first innings, and I have always loved batting with him. He's like me - he enjoys a battle, and that was what it was becoming. We didn't talk a lot, but helped each other to concentrate. I squirted a few runs, in between ducking and weaving at all the short stuff I was getting. Malcolm went round the wicket, then back over - and it encouraged me that I had forced him to try everything he knew.

The noise from the crowd was unbelievable - and I noticed some Union Jacks to the left. People there were cheering me on, as it began to dawn on them, as well as the West Indies, that we might actually save it. When we got to tea, I was dehydrated and had some tea and honey and lay down, because I had to keep my concentration going. Mickey Stewart and 'Goochie' were full of encouragement, but by then I really was tired.

When we went out for the last session, I remember geeing myself up after every ball. I would walk away towards square-leg and talk out loud to myself, and Gus Logie and Des Haynes could not stop laughing at short-leg. I didn't care - it was my way of making myself concentrate, and I knew I was becoming a real pain in the backside to them when Desmond hit me on the head with the ball in fun.

We got through the next hour, but I knew the crunch would be when they took the second new ball. Curtly came on and I told myself that he would be bound to get a bit more bounce - so what did he do? He got it through shin height and down went my off-stump. As I went off, I remember waving to our supporters thinking that we would still save it. We were 166 for six, but by using two nightwatchmen, we still had Nasser Hussain, David Capel and Phil DeFreitas to come before Devon.

We also knew they would never complete the last 20 overs because of the light, and with Robin there, I just thought we would make it. In the end, Curtly was too good, but I shall never forget all the emotion of as fierce a day's play as I've known.

I wrote in the *Birmingham Post*: 'A brilliant bowling performance by Curtly Ambrose of eight for 45, including a spell of four wickets in his first 25 deliveries with the second new ball, won the fourth Test match for the West Indies. The last wicket did not fall until 5.15pm and, as the light goes in Barbados by 5.45pm, England got within half an hour of securing an improbable draw.

'Ambrose struck with his second delivery, by torpedoing Russell with a wicked delivery which never left the ground, and he then swept aside Hussain, Capel and DeFreitas, all LBW.'

Wisden summed the game up thus: 'After the rest day, it was plain that either Lamb or Smith, or probably both, had to be at his best to save the game. In the event it was Smith, unbeaten with 40 and extending his batting time in the game to 11 hours who held up the West Indies in company with the marvellously game Russell.'

'Marvellously game' - that is the perfect phrase to sum up the effort of England's wicketkeeper, who caused those Union Jacks to be waved with such pride for most of the final day's play. No batsman could have sold himself more dearly, and it was a shame for him that the draw slipped away, despite 'the innings of his life'. Five hours and nine minutes of defiance that will live with the player and everyone who was at the Kensington Oval on 10 April 1990.

MIKE 'M.J.K.' SMITH

182* on the third day of the County Championship match between Gloucestershire and Warwickshire at Stroud, 2 June 1959.

Warwickshire needed 318 to win - the highest score of the game - on a turning pitch against one of the best spin attacks in county cricket. Smith's unbeaten 182 was scored from 252 runs while he was at the wicket, and was Warwickshire's only score of over 50 in the match. The next highest individual scored in the first three innings of the match was 53 from Graveney.

Michael John Knight Smith, OBE, was born on 30 June 1933 in Westcotes, Leicestershire, for which county he played 28 times between 1951 and 1955. After National Service, he had a brilliant three-year career at Oxford in which, uniquely, he scored hundreds in each Varsity match - 201* in 1954, 105 in 1955 and 117 in 1956 - to establish a record aggregate for those Lord's games of 477 runs. He joined Warwickshire in 1956 but, because of an enforced period of qualification, did not make his Championship debut until 1957.

He was club captain for 11 seasons, in addition to which he captained England in 25 of his 50 Tests, winning five and losing only three. His first appearance was in 1958 against New Zealand, and his final Test was against Australia in 1972. His England record was ordinary - 2278 at an average of 31.63, although his three hundreds in 78 innings could have been more, with four of his 11 fifties being scores of 96, 98 and 99 twice.

'M.J.K.', as he was, and is, universally known in cricket, is the fifth most prolific English batsman since the Second World War, with his aggregate of 39,832 runs putting him behind Boycott, Graveney, Amiss and Cowdrey. His heavy run-scoring also made him one of only five batsmen in that period to top 3000 runs in a season. Compton, Edrich, Hutton and Alley were the other four, and Smith's aggregate of 3245 in 1959 is the 11th highest in a list of 28 instances of 3000 runs being scored in the history of cricket in an English season.

As Smith also topped 2000 runs in a season five times, the choice of his innings in 1959 at Stroud marks it as something special, particularly as no more unassuming man has played first-class cricket, and he invariably understated the merit of his contributions for club and country. A rare double international - he played rugby against Wales at Twickenham in 1956 - he was also an outstanding fielder, with 593 catches including 422 for Warwickshire, still a club record.

His third season at Edgbaston was his best, bringing his first hundred for England, and his positive leadership taking Warwickshire to fourth place in the Championship after 13 victories and only five drawn games. Smith was occasionally accused of defensive captaincy, with an over-reliance on pace at the expense of spin, but the innings he has chosen was played in a match which proved otherwise.

I have to pick the Stroud innings, because it brought a win that nobody ever thought was on. The pitch was a slow turner and they had Mortimore, Allen and Cook. I lost the toss and, although Roley Thompson bowled well, their score of 257 was a good one. Nobody was ever really 'in' on the pitch, and only Tom Graveney managed a fifty.

We got in terrible trouble with Cook and Mortimore whistling us out after Jim Stewart (43) and 'Billy' Ibadulla (38) helped us recover to 80 for three. Then it started - nobody else reached double figures and when Thompson went in at number ten, we were 100 for eight and still needed eight to avoid the follow-on. With due respect to him and Ossie Wheatley, we were odds against saving it, especially as we had just lost five wickets for 20. It's not often that a ninth-wicket partnership of seven turns a match, but this one did. It left us needing one more run when Wheatley batted and, although we didn't know it then, when he scored it, the opportunity to win the game was created.

There have been several instances of a side winning after following-on, but I didn't think we would add to the list.

Smith had only one specialist spinner at Stroud, off-spinner Basil Bridge, and, although the 21-year-old took a career-best eight for 66 to bowl out the home side for 175, the Warwickshire side thought that their chances of scoring 318 on the last day were so remote as to be non-existent.

Gloucestershire skipper Tom Graveney remembers: 'I couldn't bat in the second innings because of an elbow I'd injured the game before when walking out on to the Derby ground, but I really believed we had got more than enough runs anyway.'

Smith continues the story:

When I went in to bat at 66 for two, I never gave a thought to winning the game. It was just a matter of approach and I decided there was no point in dying in the hole, because I thought that a score of 320 was not a proposition.

Their three spinners were all class bowlers, and the ball was now turning a lot. Tom Cartwright was a good player of spin and we put on 65 for the third wicket, but when he was LBW to Cook and Ibadulla got out quickly, we were 144 for four and had only two front-line batsmen to come in. By this time, it was a matter of just playing and seeing what would happen, but we were still long odds against.

The famous Smith penchant for the on-side was now in evidence, and the Gloucestershire players started to become uneasy. Tony Brown recalls: 'We didn't bowl badly, but whereas we were always on top of everybody else, "M.J.K." seemed to be playing a different game. The Stroud ground was narrow, with short square boundaries, and Mike just played a miraculous innings. I reckon we would have won 999 games out of 1000 from that position, yet in the end we lost it comfortably.'

Joined by all-rounder Alan Townsend, Smith was now at his most clinical. He hit five sixes and 28 fours in a stay of four hours, and his domination of the last day's dramatic events was such that the normally free-scoring Townsend had to fight for his life to score 24 in a fifth-wicket partnership of 134. Townsend says: 'It was just a big battle for the rest of us. I did not dare take any chances once it became clear that Mike was so much in charge. Think of it: three spinners who had played for England, and here he was hitting them all over the place. They all got clobbered, yet their final figures don't show it.'

Townsend is right. Only Brown and Allen conceded marginally over three runs per over, yet Gloucestershire, under the acting captaincy of Arthur Milton, bowled 113 overs before the game was won and lost. And that in the face of one of the fiercest successful onslaughts ever mounted in county cricket. Of the last 187 runs scored following the dismissal of Cartwright at 131 for three, a mere 33 were scored by other

MIKE SMITH, KNOWN AS THE
MOST PROLIFIC LEG-SIDE
BATSMAN IN POST-WAR
COUNTY CRICKET, OPENS THE
FACE FOR AN OFF-DRIVE.
(PATRICK EAGAR)

batsmen. Although there have been similar instances of one batsman dominating the scoring, it has seldom happened on such a pitch, and is a testimony to Smith's ability to pepper the leg-side.

Not that he could not play off-side strokes. He could, but knew that he was stronger on the 'working man's' side of the wicket, and the legislation, introduced that year, which limited the number of leg-side fielders to five increased a mastery of spin bowling which had already made him a batsman to fear in county cricket.

Opposing acting-captain Milton says: 'He gave a half chance to long-on, and that was it. There was one other incident I remember. He tried to lap a ball from Sam Cook and some of our players thought he'd got a touch on to his pad, which I caught at short-leg. He said to me, "I'm afraid you'll have to appeal for that, Arthur." We didn't, because that was how we played it then, and I have to say I'm still glad we didn't, otherwise we would have missed seeing one of the best innings on a turning pitch I have ever seen. The ground isn't there any more, but every time I pass the area, I think back to Mike and what he did to us.'

Having already mentioned one aspect of the county game of the 1950s - the gentlemanly acceptance of one player's word by another - a study of the over-rates of that time highlights another. The match ended half an hour early, despite which the Gloucestershire attack bowled 113 overs, including 40 overs of seam, and the aggregate number of overs bowled in the three days was 357.1, including 196 overs of seam.

Townsend again: 'Of all the innings I ever saw, that one stands out in my memory. It was just survival to me, while the captain helped himself at the other end as though it was a benefit match. It was a great knock, and one which no other player in the game thought was possible.'

Smith played many memorable innings in a career which lasted for 24 years and encompassed 1091 visits to the crease, but it is small wonder that he ignored his double hundreds against Cambridge, Worcestershire and Natal. The latter innings was scored out of a total of 300, and bears comparison with the Stroud performance but, ever the team man, 'M.J.K.' chose the performance that brought a competitive win for his side against all the odds.

Of all post-war England captains, he is the one against whom no player ever said a bad word. He led sides to South Africa, Australia and India and never lost a series. For his county, he led them to final Championship placings of fourth, third, fourth, second and sixth in 1959, 1962, 1963, 1964 and 1966, in which latter year he brought to Edgbaston the Gillette Cup for the first time.

GLOUCESTERSHIRE V WARWICKSHIRE (COUNTY CHAMPIONSHIP)

PLAYED AT STROUD, ON 30 MAY, 1, 2 JUNE 1959.
TOSS: GLOUCESTERSHIRE. RESULT: WARWICKSHIRE WON BY FOUR WICKETS.

GLOUCESTERSHIRE

	FIRST INNINGS		SECOND INNINGS	
D.M.Young	b Thompson	13	c Cartwright, b Bridge	17
C.A.Milton	lbw, b Thompson	2	b Bridge	27
R.B.Nicholls	c Thompson, b Wheatley	35	c Smith, b Bridge	3
T.W.Graveney*	b Cartwright	53	absent hurt	-
D.G.Hawkins	c Fox, b Cartwright	13	c Thompson, b Ibadulla	52
J.B.Mortimore	c Fox, b Ibadulla	28	c Cartwright, b Bridge	13
D.A.Allen	c Fox, b Thompson	39	c Ibadulla, b Bridge	21
A.S.Brown	b Thompson	28	b Bridge	0
D.R.Smith	c Fox, b Thompson	29	c Wolton, b Bridge	12
B.J.Meyer†	c Cartwright, b Thompson	0	not out	6
C.Cook	not out	4	b Bridge	14
Extras	b 9, lb 2, nb 2	13	b 1, lb 9	10
		257		175

	O	M	R	W	O	M	R	W
Wheatley	34	7	75	1	10	2	17	0
Thompson	29.4	7	74	6	12	3	15	0
Townsend	9	2	19	0				
Cartwright	23	6	61	2	1	0	6	0
Ibadulla	10	4	15	1	20	7	61	1
Bridge					30	9	66	8

FALL OF WICKETS
1-12, 2-17, 3-83, 4-116, 5-123, 6-159, 7-210, 8-240, 9-240, 10-257
1-25, 2-37, 3-65, 4-95, 5-123, 6-123, 7-137, 8-161, 9-175

WARWICKSHIRE

	FIRST INNINGS		SECOND INNINGS	
N.F.Horner	c Nicholls, b Brown	1	b Mortimore	20
W.J.Stewart	c Brown, b Cook	43	b Smith	30
T.W.Cartwright	b Smith	3	lbw, b Cook	40
M.J.K.Smith*	c Milton, b Smith	3	not out	182
K.Ibadulla	c Meyer, b Cook	38	c and b Mortimore	2
A.V.Wolton	c Brown, b Cook	4	c Milton, b Mortimore	4
A.Townsend	b Cook	0	c Milton, b Mortimore	24
W.B.Bridge	lbw, b Mortimore	3	not out	3
J.G.Fox†	c Brown, b Mortimore	6		
R.G.Thompson	c Graveney, b Cook	4		
O.S.Wheatley	not out	4		
Extras	b 6	6	b 10, lb 1, w 2	13
		115	(6 wickets)	318

	O	M	R	W	O	M	R	W
Smith	23	8	44	2	25	9	61	1
Brown	15	5	36	1	15	2	46	0
Cook	17.3	13	13	5	31	11	89	1
Mortimore	10	5	16	2	29	12	64	4
Allen					13	4	45	0

FALL OF WICKETS
1-3, 2-22, 3-26, 4-80, 5-96, 6-96, 7-100, 8-100, 9-107, 10-115
1-43, 2-66, 3-131, 4-144, 5-278, 6-288

Umpires: J.B.Bowes and T.W.Spencer

Now chairman of Warwickshire and one of a panel of referees appointed by the International Cricket Council, Smith continues to serve a game which he has graced for over 40 years. His philosophy in cricket, whether in victory or defeat, is perfectly summed up by this memory of his favourite innings. 'It was a matter of taking it as it came. Suddenly I was fifty and then a hundred, and we could have a go at winning the game. In the end, time never came into it, and it ended up quite a nice day.'

ROBIN SMITH

148* on the second and third days of the second Test between England and West Indies at Lord's, 21 and 22 June 1991.

Replying to a West Indies first innings total of 419, England were in trouble at 60 for four when Smith joined his captain, Graham Gooch, who was soon bowled by Walsh. That left Smith with the responsibility of steering his side past the follow-on mark of 220. Overnight he was 23 not out and, in front of a full house on Saturday, the Hampshire man scored a magnificent unbeaten 148 against a hostile attack, spearheaded by Ambrose. He gave an almost flawless exhibition of resolute defence, interspersed with some typically ferocious square-cuts and drives.

It was his fifth and highest hundred for England, and the first against West Indies. In a stay of nearly seven hours, he was given solid support by Russell and Pringle in partnerships for the sixth and seventh wickets of 96 and 89 respectively, and his innings helped England to add 270 for the last five wickets. Rain on the fourth and fifth days ensured the draw that Smith's innings merited and, as a result, England went to Trent Bridge, still 1-0 ahead after two Tests.

Robin Arnold Smith was born on 13 September 1963 in Durban, the younger brother of Chris, who he followed into the teams of Northlands High School, South African Schools, Natal, Hampshire and England. After playing for Natal at the age of 17, he decided to become 'English' by virtue of British parents and residential qualification, and made his debut for Hampshire in 1982. Essentially a front-foot batsman of muscular build, he soon developed an ability to square-cut with an explosive power which rivalled that of his county colleague, West Indies opener Gordon Greenidge.

Elevation to Test status was considered so inevitable by his elder brother that a substantial bet with a bookmaker was struck about Smith Junior playing 50 Tests, and collecting day could be in 1994, with 40 caps already in the cupboard at the start of the Ashes series in England in 1993. He had then scored 2954 runs at

A SHOW OF RAW POWER ON
THE WAY TO AN UNBEATEN
148 AGAINST THE WEST
INDIES AT LORD'S IN 1991.
(PATRICK EAGAR)

an average of 49.19, which is especially outstanding considering that half of his Tests had been against West Indies and Australia - ten against each country.

Doubts were expressed about his ability to cope mentally with Test cricket, but he has dispelled those with a series of innings for England which have relied upon concentration and courage, as much as a technique which is so heavily dependent upon playing forward that it sometimes gets him into trouble. His tendency to commit himself too early means that he has to play around, instead of alongside his front leg, but his outstanding record makes him one of the most effective batsmen in world cricket.

He is one of few cricketers whose career average is several points lower than in Test cricket (44 compared with 49), with the real proof that he is the man for a big occasion coming from his ratio of innings per century - one in eight for his country and one in 12 for his county.

His final choice of a hundred at Lord's in front of a Saturday crowd as 'the innings of my life' is unsurprising, but what other innings did he consider?

There were two. I might have played better at Trent Bridge in 1989 against Australia when I scored 101 and we were always in trouble. I went in at one run for two wickets, and was sixth out at 172, but it did not affect the result of the game - we followed-on and lost inside four days. The other innings really counted, because it helped win a Benson and Hedges Cup quarter-final against Worcestershire in 1988, and of course we went on to reach our first-ever Lord's final when we beat Derbyshire by seven wickets.

Wisden quotes Smith as saying that it was 'the most satisfying innings of my career', so it must have run his unbeaten 148 pretty close. On a lively New Road pitch which offered extravagant movement and variability of bounce to the quicker bowlers, Smith's unbeaten 87 rescued his side from the perils of 84 for six and 114 for seven, with partners Jefferies and Cowley contributing 25 out of the last 86 runs. Dilley, Radford and Newport would surely have won the game for Worcestershire but for Smith.

It is nice to have a few innings to pick from, but my final choice was really a formality. You can't ask for more than to score a big hundred against the best fast bowlers in the world. And as Lord's is my favourite ground for atmosphere and sense of occasion, to do so well in front of a capacity Saturday crowd made it the highlight of my career.

The first session of the third day was crucial, but after Smith survived a catch to Logie off Ambrose, and Russell also escaped the clutches of the same bowler-fielder combination when a lob off the shoulder of the bat went square, while Logie was two yards too straight, the England recovery got under way.

The sixth-wicket pair batted well with a sensible mixture of attack and defence and they took the score to 180, just before lunch, when Russell was caught at the wicket off Hooper for 46. The partnership was the start of an England recovery built around Smith's innings which, in the day's middle session, blossomed from a good one into a genuine tour-de-force.

His ability to fight it out, ball by ball, without a break in concentration, was a source of inspiration to his lower-middle order colleagues, to whom he pays this generous tribute.

Jack Russell played beautifully, and he took the pressure off me on Saturday morning while I settled in. At one stage I went 30 minutes without scoring, but it didn't get to me because of how well he batted. As for 'Pring', I've never seen him play better.

Smith deserved the high praise heaped on him from all quarters. David Frith wrote: 'Smith played one thrilling stroke after another in an innings which was to grow in size and technical quality to match Gooch's in the Headingley Test. The Hampshire man's strength injected hooks and square-cuts with a power which bordered on the supernatural, and seldom if ever can Lord's have witnessed such speed of the ball through the covers.'

Not that the West Indies bowlers were ever conquered. In the morning session alone, they beat the outside edge a dozen times, but 76 from 27 overs gave the home side a lifeline to which they clung successfully throughout the rest of the Smith-led recovery. He had one more lucky escape when he was 73. He edged one from Marshall between Richards and Hooper in the slips, with Marshall's growing frustration not helped by neither man offering a hand. The score was then 207 for six and the huge crowd indulged in their own public countdown to the follow-on avoidance figure of 220, and roared Pringle home off the final run of a three he hit off Ambrose.

Ambrose promptly let Smith have four bouncers in five deliveries to invite a gentle word from umpire Barry Meyer, but the Hampshire man was not fussed - he has the admirable ability to consider such tactics as part and parcel of the modern game, and he brought the crowd to their feet with his hundred off the 199th ball he faced. On television, Richie Benaud said: 'That is quite a comeback after what happened in Australia [238 in eight completed innings with a highest score of 58] - it is a great innings.'

Referring to Smith's poor tour of Australia, Ray Illingworth commented that he believed Smith was standing still longer than at any time in his career, which meant he was in much greater control of his whereabouts vis-à-vis off stump, and thus could decide more safely on what to leave alone. Geoff Boycott called it 'a stupendous performance and a big psychological breakthrough.'

I wrote at the time: 'Smith is a man of great contrasts. In the middle, he oozes confidence from a thickset, muscular frame which generates enormous power in his strokes. He is unflinching against the most intimidatory bowling, and never complains about the sort of overdose of bouncers he received in Antigua, when he sustained both a broken finger and a badly bruised cheek. Yet, off the field, he is diffident to the point of shyness, and he only agreed to be interviewed on television by Tony Lewis if the interview would not be used if, in his opinion, it went wrong. It did not and, as he did when batting, he did himself full justice.'

One of his last strokes was his most thrilling - a square-cut off Walsh to the Grandstand boundary, which brought this from Benaud: 'There were two men behind square on the boundary... I tell you it went like a rocket and neither had a chance. Worth paying your money just to see that.'

ENGLAND V WEST INDIES (2ND TEST)

PLAYED AT LORD'S, LONDON, ON 20, 21, 22, 23 (NO PLAY), 24 JUNE 1991.
TOSS: WEST INDIES. RESULT: MATCH DRAWN.

WEST INDIES

	FIRST INNINGS			SECOND INNINGS		
P.V.Simmons	c Lamb, b Hick	33	lbw, b DeFreitas	2		
D.L.Haynes	c Russell, b Pringle	60	not out	4		
R.B.Richardson	c DeFreitas, b Hick	57	c Hick, b Malcolm	1		
C.L.Hooper	c Lamb, b Pringle	111	not out	1		
I.V.A.Richards*	lbw, b DeFreitas	63				
A.L.Logie	b DeFreitas	5				
P.J.L.Dujon†	c Lamb, b Pringle	20				
M.D.Marshall	lbw, b Pringle	25				
C.E.L.Ambrose	c and b Malcolm	5				
C.A.Walsh	c Atherton, b Pringle	10				
I.B.A.Allen	not out	1				
Extras	b 3, lb 7, nb 19	29	lb 2, nb 2	4		
		419	(for 2 wickets)	12		

	O	M	R	W	O	M	R	W
DeFreitas	31	6	93	2	3	2	1	1
Malcolm	19	3	76	1	2.5	0	9	1
Watkin	15	2	60	0				
Pringle	35.1	6	100	5				
Hick	18	4	77	2				
Gooch	2	0	3	0				

ENGLAND

	FIRST INNINGS		
G.A.Gooch*	b Walsh	37	
M.A.Atherton	b Ambrose	5	
G.A.Hick	c Richardson, b Ambrose	0	
A.J.Lamb	c Haynes, b Marshall	1	
M.R.Ramprakash	c Richards, b Allen	24	
R.A.Smith	not out	148	
R.C.Russell†	c Dujon, b Hooper	46	
D.R.Pringle	c Simmons, b Allen	35	
P.A.J.DeFreitas	c Dujon, b Marshall	29	
S.L.Watkin	b Ambrose	6	
D.E.Malcolm	b Ambrose	0	
Extras	lb 1, nb 22	23	
		354	

	O	M	R	W
Ambrose	34	10	87	4
Marshall	30	4	78	2
Walsh	26	4	90	1
Allen	23	2	88	2
Hooper	5	2	10	1

FALL OF WICKETS
1-90, 2-102, 3-198, 4-322, 5-332, 6-366, 7-382, 8-402, 9-410, 10-419
1-9, 2-10

FALL OF WICKETS
1-5, 2-6, 3-16, 4-60, 5-84, 6-180, 7-269, 8-316, 9-353, 10-354

Umpires: B.J.Meyer and K.E.Palmer

The innings won for Smith the *Evening Standard* Cricketer of the Month award, but his immediate reaction after the match was: 'Lord's is now in the past tense. And it will be until September when I sit down and watch it on video with a beer.' What he saw was an innings which changed the shape of the Test match and was, according to Frith, 'an innings which, for quality and significance, probably entered the top 20 of England's 73 Test centuries at Lord's since 1884.'

Smith might not have been born in England but, like Mike Gatting and the late Ken Barrington who were, he walks in to bat as though the Union Jack is pinned to his chest: a man of pride and a batsman of considerable ability and courage.

GARRY SOBERS

163* on the fourth and fifth days of the second Test between England and West Indies at Lord's, 20 and 21 June 1966.

Sobers came in at 91 for four, and was joined by his cousin, David Holford, four runs later with their side perilously placed. They were nine runs ahead with two days remaining, and England were heavy odds-on to win the game and square the five-match series, having lost at Old Trafford by an innings and 40 runs. The sixth-wicket related pair then shared an unbroken partnership of 274 - still the highest for the West Indies for that wicket against all countries. Sobers scored 163 not out and Holford 105 - his only Test hundred - as England failed to take another wicket in nearly four full sessions.

It was the sixth of Sobers' ten hundreds against England, half of which were scores over 150. He inspired his partner and his side to draw the game, and the West Indies won the next two Tests at Trent Bridge and Headingley.

Sir Garfield St Aubrun Sobers was born on 28 July 1936 in St Michael, Barbados, with an extra finger on each hand that had to be removed soon after his birth. A wonderful athlete, he played for his island at golf, soccer and basketball as well as cricket, which was always his first love. He made his Test debut at the age of 17 and, within four years, made the record Test score of 365 not out against Pakistan at Kingston in February 1958 in what was his 17th Test match and 29th innings. It was also the first of 26 hundreds for the West Indies and, when he played his 93rd and final Test in Trinidad in April 1974, he had broken many records at Test level, and even more for the three first-class sides for which he played, Barbados, Nottinghamshire and South Australia.

His figures are well known - 8032 Test runs at an average of 57.78, and 28,315 first-class runs at 54.87 with one of his 86 hundreds coming, on average, every seven innings. It is a magnificent record, but that is not even the half of it. He took 235 Test wickets and 1043 in all, with a versatile mix of seam and both sorts of spin never seen before in top cricket. To complete the picture of the greatest all-rounder in the history of the game, he took 109 Test catches and 407 in all first-class cricket, mostly at short leg or slip.

He dazzled players and spectators alike, all over the world, but never to greater effect than in a three-year period in the early 1960s when he became the first cricketer to score 1000 runs and take 50 wickets for South Australia in their ten Sheffield Shield matches. Astonishingly enough, he repeated the feat the following year, and two years later succeeded Frank Worrell as captain of the West Indies. He led the side for a then record 39 times, setting as E.W.Swanton says, 'an example on the field which never faltered.'

He joined Nottinghamshire in 1968 and served them well for seven seasons, but the physical strain of his versatility began to take its toll and he retired in 1974, 20 years after making his Test debut as a slow left-arm bowler against Len Hutton's side at Sabina Park.

That was in April 1954 and, after missing West Indies' next Test on the same ground against Australia 12

months later, the hugely talented 18-year-old was selected a fortnight later for the Trinidad Test to start a record run for his country of 85 consecutive appearances. Coincidentally, that run ended on the same Queen's Park Oval, Port-of-Spain, in April 1972 against New Zealand. Border, Gavaskar and Viswanath subsequently passed his mark, but no other cricketer has done so. His Test batting average still remains the highest among post-war batsmen who have scored more than 3000 runs and, of those who topped 2000 runs, Graeme Pollock is the only one with a higher average.

The true all-rounder is good enough to play for his country as a batsman if he does not bowl, and vice versa, and that is why Sobers stands head and shoulders above any other all-round cricketer who ever lived. Only the best fully appreciates the best, which makes praise from Bradman something to cherish. Of an innings of 254 played by Sobers in Melbourne for the Rest of the World XI in 1972, Bradman said: 'I believe it to be, probably, the best innings ever played in Australia. The people who saw it have enjoyed one of the historic events of cricket. They were privileged to have such an experience. Without a chance, 254 runs in 376 minutes. What more can be said?'

Bradman found something more. He supplied a commentary on a film of the innings in which he analysed the Sobers technique. Back swing, footwork, use of wrists and follow-through drew from 'The Don' that he was 'describing a genius'. Surely, therefore, this was 'the innings of my life'?

No, although it was a good one. Bradman was not at Lord's in 1966 - that is why he rates Melbourne. I thought about one other before I settled for Lord's. It was also against England, and again we drew the game after being in deep trouble before I got runs. It was at Sabina Park in 1968, and John Snow's seven for 49 made us follow-on.

It was an explosive Test, featuring a bottle-throwing riot on the fourth day and the 75 minutes lost was made up on an extra sixth day. When Sobers walked in on a pair - Snow had dismissed him first ball for the second successive innings in which he had bowled to him - his side was still 59 behind. If that was not trouble enough, the riot quickly followed.

The crowd did not like the decision which gave Basil Butcher out, caught down the leg-side by Jim Parks off Basil D'Oliveira, and the bottles came over at the same time as David Holford walked in to join me.

We went off and agreed to make up the time. At the end of that day we were 258 for five - only 25 on but it was such a poor pitch, I thought we had a chance. I finished with 113 not out, and I remember I dare not take a risk and went from 88 to 100 with 12 singles. In the end I declared and left England 159 in what turned out to be 39 overs. What a match it turned out to be! We got four out for 19 that night - I got Boycott and Cowdrey and Wes and Charlie got Edrich and Barrington. Gibbs got three more next morning when the pitch really was bad, but they held on at 68 for eight.

Michael Manley's assessment of that performance was: 'The wicket looked like a nightmare and played only slightly less badly. Sobers, on a "king pair", was nearly caught first ball and D'Oliveira dropped a return catch when he was seven. Thereafter, he put his head down and in six hours of masterful defence steered the West Indies to 391 for nine. He then took the new ball and in the first over bowled Boycott and had Cowdrey LBW in three balls. Those who saw the Sobers declaration on the fifth evening were put in mind of some knight of old throwing down the gauntlet - the gesture, all fierce defiance, relieved at the margins by a delicious trace of the imp. Thereupon he proceeded to bowl like the devil incarnate.'

Angel or devil? It all depended on whether you played with or against a man who C.L.R.James memorably described as 'a West Indian cricketer, not merely a cricketer from the West Indies.' That was written in 1969, as was this crafted piece of praise: 'Sobers exceeds all I have ever seen or read of.'

However, I still go for Lord's in 1966, because we were in so much trouble. I know it was a much better pitch than Sabina Park, but the match situation was desperate. We were gone at 95 for five, with only the wicketkeeper and three bowlers to come. I remember telling David Holford to treat the game as though he was back in Bridgetown at the Oval. I knew he could bat, and it was just a matter of talking to him and encouraging him all the time.

His temperament was ideal, calm and orderly, and I knew the crowd would not affect him. The England fielders crowded him but, surprisingly, when I was on strike they dropped back. It was Cowdrey's first game of the series as captain, having taken over from Mike Smith, and his defensive fields were aimed at giving me the single to bowl at David. I made no effort to shield David, nor did I ever make an effort to shield any of my partners, unless perhaps it was number eleven.

Cowdrey explained his tactics thus: 'The reason I did not encircle Sobers with close fielders as soon as he came in was that I knew him. Had I surrounded him, he could not possibly have played naturally, and the last thing I wanted was for him to steel himself into getting his head down.' Some you win and some you lose, and Cowdrey lost that battle of the captains. Holford says: 'In the space of an hour, Garry realised we could save it, and batted on and on.'

By the close of play - well over two sessions - they had added 193, with Sobers on 121 and Holford 71, and the West Indies were 202 ahead, and neither England's three main seamers - Jones, Higgs and Knight - nor the spin of Titmus could make a breakthrough. The game was not quite safe - it needed another session, which the cousins batted through next morning to add 81 before Sobers declared to leave England needing 284 in four hours. Not even a magnificent unbeaten 126 from Milburn could threaten a win which, in truth, the heroics of Sobers and Holford deserved to deny them.

Manley said: 'The Lord's Test provided one of those opportunities for greatness. The partnership between Sobers and Holford was one of the epics of Test cricket. Holford was the sort of batsman of whom fifty might be expected at a pinch, but not the sort of grinding innings needed if Sobers was to make enough runs while consuming the clock and putting the game beyond England's reach.'

Sobers concludes:

The innings was the most satisfying of my life, similar to my 150 on the same ground in 1973, which was my last Test hundred. The innings which always pleased me were those where I had to play in a restrained way - when I had to play in conditions which suited the fielding side.

I was less satisfied with innings on good pitches when the batting side had all the advantages. I made ten hundreds against England, five in the West Indies and five in England. The two at Lord's were the best, with the 1966 effort the best of all.

ENGLAND V WEST INDIES (2ND TEST)

**PLAYED AT LORD'S, LONDON, ON 16, 17, 18, 20, 21 JUNE 1966.
TOSS: WEST INDIES. RESULT: MATCH DRAWN.**

WEST INDIES

	FIRST INNINGS		SECOND INNINGS	
C.C.Hunte	c Parks, b Higgs	18	c Milburn, b Knight	13
M.C.Carew	c Parks, b Higgs	2	c Knight, b Higgs	0
R.B.Kanhai	c Titmus, b Higgs	25	c Parks, b Knight	40
B.F.Butcher	c Milburn, b Knight	49	lbw, b Higgs	3
S.M.Nurse	b D'Oliveira	64	c Parks, b D'Oliveira	35
G.St A.Sobers*	lbw, b Knight	46	not out	163
D.A.J.Holford	b Jones	26	not out	105
D.W.Allan†	c Titmus, b Higgs	13		
C.C.Griffith	lbw, b Higgs	5		
W.W.Hall	not out	8		
L.R.Gibbs	c Parks, b Higgs	4		
Extras	b 2, lb 7	9	lb 8, nb 2	10
		269	(5 wickets declared)	369

	O	M	R	W	O	M	R	W
Jones	21	3	64	1	25	2	95	0
Higgs	33	9	91	6	34	5	82	2
Knight	21	0	63	2	30	3	106	2
Titmus	5	0	18	0	19	3	30	0
D'Oliveira	14	5	24	1	25	7	46	1

ENGLAND

	FIRST INNINGS		SECOND INNINGS	
G.Boycott	c Griffith, b Gibbs	60	c Allan, b Griffith	25
C.Milburn	lbw, b Hall	6	not out	126
T.W.Graveney	c Allan, b Hall	96	(6) not out	30
K.F.Barrington	b Sobers	19	(3) b Griffith	5
M.C.Cowdrey*	c Gibbs, b Hall	9	(4) c Allan, b Hall	5
J.M.Parks†	lbw, b Carew	91	(5) b Hall	0
B.L.D'Oliveira	run out	27		
B.R.Knight	b Griffith	6		
F.J.Titmus	c Allan, b Hall	6		
K.Higgs	c Holford, b Gibbs	13		
I.J.Jones	not out	0		
Extras	b 7, lb 10, nb 5	22	b 4, lb 2	6
		355	(4 wickets)	197

	O	M	R	W	O	M	R	W
Sobers	39	12	89	1	8	4	8	0
Hall	36	2	106	4	14	1	65	2
Griffith	28	4	79	1	11	2	43	2
Gibbs	37.3	18	48	2	13	4	40	0
Carew	3	0	11	1				
Holford					9	1	35	0

FALL OF WICKETS

1-8, 2-42, 3-53, 4-119, 5-205, 6-213, 7-252, 8-252, 9-261, 10-269
1-2, 2-22, 3-25, 4-91, 5-95

FALL OF WICKETS

1-8, 2-123, 3-164, 4-198, 5-203, 6-251, 7-266, 8-296, 9-355, 10-355
1-37, 2-43, 3-67, 4-67

Umpires: J.S.Buller and W.F.F.Price

Like Botham in this book, it is interesting that two of the most destructive batsmen of their time have plumped for an innings which called for something other than all-out attack.

If there is a common thread which links some of the chosen innings in this book, it is that 13 of them were played at Lord's. No player graced the ground more than Sobers. In five Test matches he batted nine times and was only once dismissed in single figures. In six completed innings he scored 571 runs at an average of 95.16. The innings of his life? More like the ground of his life.

GRAHAM STEVENSON

Stevenson became the ninth number
eleven in the history of cricket to score a hundred, and only the third to
do so in Championship cricket. He came in to bat at 143 for nine, and
scored 115 out of a last-wicket partnership with opener Geoffrey Boycott
of 149. Boycott was favourite to carry his bat, but was bowled, sweeping
at occasional leg-spinner Asif Din. It was one of two first-class hundreds
scored by Stevenson, and an innings that turned a likely Yorkshire defeat
into a subsequent victory. His innings lasted for 130 minutes, and he hit
three sixes and 15 fours. The partnership broke the previous record
Yorkshire tenth-wicket stand - one of 148 between Lord Hawke and David
Hunter in 1898.

Graham Barry Stevenson was born on 16 December 1955 in Ackworth. He joined Yorkshire in 1973 and, after 14 seasons for his native county, he was released to join Northamptonshire in 1987, at the end of which season he retired at the age of 31. A strongly built all-rounder, he never fulfilled the promise that earned selection on two major tours - Australia and India in 1979-80, and West Indies in 1980-81. He played in two Tests, the Golden Jubilee game in Bombay in 1979, and the fourth Test in the West Indies at St John's, Antigua, in 1981, when Boycott saved the game with an unbeaten 104. In a career which was interrupted by injuries, he played 188 first-class games, taking 488 wickets at an average of 28.84, and scoring 3965 runs at 20.33.

A likeable, enthusiastic cricketer, Stevenson was one of Boycott's three favourite cricketers - Ian Botham and David Bairstow were the others - so it is fitting that two cricketers of such a widely contrasting nature should share a day that was highlighted by Stevenson's 'innings of my life'.

Boycott says: 'I was always close to Graham. We were brought up in the same area, and I was captain of Yorkshire when he first played. He is a smashing lad, and he and Bairstow could always make me laugh. He was a strong lad, stronger than most people think, but he was like Ian Botham in many respects. He could hit the ball a country mile, without much backlift. He had such a short hitting area, but his strength carried him through. He was also a difficult batsman to set a field for, because he could hit inside-out into areas where a fielding captain could not believe he would need anyone. He had such a lot of ability, it was a pity we didn't see him make the most of it often enough. That's why that day at Edgbaston was so special - for him, for me and for the Yorkshire team.

'The pitch was not easy - a slow seamer with an inconsistent bounce, and although we bowled Warwickshire out for 158, we were on the wrong end of it when Graham joined me at 143 for nine, with Gladstone Small having taken seven of the wickets, and Bob Willis the other two. I was 50, and it had been a huge struggle all the way.'

Warwickshire were well on top when the visitors were 108 for eight an hour before lunch on the second

---

WARWICKSHIRE V YORKSHIRE (SCHWEPPES COUNTY CHAMPIONSHIP)

PLAYED AT EDGBASTON, BIRMINGHAM, ON 19, 20, 21 MAY 1982.
RESULT: YORKSHIRE WON BY NINE WICKETS.

WARWICKSHIRE

	FIRST INNINGS		SECOND INNINGS	
D.L.Amiss	c Bairstow, b Stevenson	39	c Boycott, b Old	75
T.A.Lloyd	b Stevenson	12	b Old	5
A.I.Kallicharran	b Sidebottom	11	c Bairstow, b Sidebottom	8
G.W.Humpage†	b Boycott	4	c Sidebottom, b Old	18
P.R.Oliver	c Hartley, b Boycott	16	b Stevenson	9
Asif Din	c Athey, b Old	13	c Boycott, b Old	5
P.A.Smith	c Bairstow, b Old	15	c Boycott, b Sidebottom	16
G.C.Small	b Old	22	(9) c Bairstow, b Old	5
R.G.D.Willis*	b Stevenson	12	(10) not out	2
J.Cumbes	c Lumb, b Sidebottom	4	(8) c Sharp, b Old	0
W.Hogg	not out	0	c Bairstow, b Sidebottom	8
Extras	b 2, lb 3, w 1, nb 4	10	lb 5, w 2, nb 8	15
		158		166

	O	M	R	W	O	M	R	W
Old	20	7	52	3	27	8	76	6
Stevenson	18	5	41	3	9	2	30	1
Sidebottom	15.1	4	30	2	21.3	7	34	3
Boycott	6	1	15	2	4	0	10	0
Carrick	5	1	10	0	2	1	1	0

FALL OF WICKETS

1-21, 2-43, 3-58, 4-87, 5-92, 6-114, 7-121, 8-148, 9-158, 10-158
1-7, 2-21, 3-50, 4-77, 5-94, 6-148, 7-148, 8-152, 9-156, 10-166

YORKSHIRE

	FIRST INNINGS		SECOND INNINGS	
G.Boycott	b Asif Din	79	not out	21
R.G.Lumb	lbw, b Small	1	lbw, b Small	4
C.W.J.Athey	lbw, b Small	0	not out	5
K.Sharp	c Smith, b Willis	0		
S.N.Hartley	c Amiss, b Willis	7		
D.L.Bairstow†	c Humpage, b Small	30		
P.Carrick	lbw, b Small	0		
J.P.Whiteley	c Humpage, b Small	1		
A.Sidebottom	c Humpage, b Small	13		
C.M.Old*	b Small	27		
G.B.Stevenson	not out	115		
Extras	b 5, lb 4, w 7, nb 3	19	lb 2, nb 1	3
		292	(1 wicket)	33

	O	M	R	W	O	M	R	W
Willis	23	4	71	2	2	0	3	0
Small	29	7	68	7	7	0	13	1
Hogg	7	0	41	0	6.3	2	14	0
Cumbes	20	8	34	0				
Asif Din	12	4	27	1				
Smith	5	0	32	0				

FALL OF WICKETS

1-2, 2-2, 3-9, 4-35, 5-89, 6-89, 7-91, 8-108, 9-143, 10-292
1-26

Umpires: R.Julian and M.J.Kitchen

---

day. The players knew that, as Boycott was unlikely to dominate on such a pitch, all they had to do to obtain a small but important first-innings lead was to dismiss tailenders Chris Old and Graham Stevenson. Old, who was to join Warwickshire the next year, hit 27 out of 35 for the ninth wicket. Then came Stevenson, who came in to bat hoping he might score a few, but realising that Boycott looked certain to carry his bat.

When I left the dressing-room, our players were getting ready to bowl and field - just the sort of thing to encourage the last man in such difficult conditions. I didn't have any instructions as such, so what happened in the next couple of hours was as much a surprise to me as it was to everyone else.

Boycott comments: 'I had to talk to him and encourage him, especially against Willis and Small, because Graham was much happier against medium pace and spin. I tried to take as much of Willis as I could, but whenever Graham was on strike, I would be down the pitch telling him "steel yourself". I know Bob Willis heard me because he just smiled.'

Stevenson might have been uncomfortable against pace, but he laid the foundations down for one of the most remarkable innings ever played by a number eleven by injuring Willis's bowling hand when he tried to intercept a 'Stevenson Rocket', after which the train roared away from the station. 'He couldn't grip the ball properly after that, and with Gladstone having had a long spell, things suddenly seemed to get easier.'

My report of the drama in the *Birmingham Post* said: 'As comebacks go, this was of 22-carat quality. Stevenson gave Boycott a start of over three hours and 50 runs, but although the Test opener only scored 29 in the partnership of 149, without his marathon effort, Yorkshire would have finished well over 100 short of their final total of 292. Their stand broke the previous tenth-wicket record for Yorkshire, and was the highest last-wicket partnership scored against Warwickshire. Stevenson came in to bat as the only obstacle between

Boycott and a not out, after Small had dismissed Sidebottom, caught behind the wicket, and then bowled Old for a well-struck 27.

NO PHOTOGRAPH EXISTS OF A STEVENSON DEFENSIVE STROKE. *(PATRICK EAGAR)*

'At 143 for nine and Boycott on 50, the odds against Stevenson outstaying him were enormous, but very quickly the improbable took shape. Stevenson climbed into Hogg - his first six was a contemptuous flick off a short ball over the longer Rea Bank mid-wicket boundary, and he was off and running. In just over an hour before lunch he reached 50, and he took just the same time after the interval to complete a marvellous hundred.

'All the time the fascinating prospect existed that when he got out, an opening batsman was going to carry his bat for an appreciably lower total than that scored by the number eleven, and if that is not a record, it should be.'

Stevenson remembers:

It all happened so quickly, with everything I tried coming off. I had already got a Championship hundred for Yorkshire higher up the order, but it seems more special when the last man in scores runs. I flashed past Geoffrey in the 70s, and he was terrific. He gave me my head, but I think he started to fancy a few runs himself when they brought Asif Din on. I hadn't given a chance, and he came to me and said, 'Now don't try to hit him into Birmingham. You look OK against the rest, so I'll keep you away from Asif.' He did just that, and kept on trying to get the strike.

Back to the *Birmingham Post*: 'When Asif Din was brought on - perhaps belatedly - he was treated with more respect from the hard-hitting Stevenson than any other bowler, before the tale of the tail took its most unexpected twist. Boycott essayed a sweep against Din, and after 340 minutes was bowled for a masterly 79,

115 OUT OF 149 FOR THE 10TH WICKET. STEVENSON WAS THE THIRD NUMBER 11 TO SCORE A COUNTY CHAMPIONSHIP HUNDRED, AFTER A.FIELDER OF KENT AND T.P.B.SMITH OF ESSEX. (*BIRMINGHAM POST AND MAIL*)

leaving the history-making number eleven on 115 - his highest-ever score. As Stevenson might have said, and probably did, "If only I had a reliable partner at the other end."'

What Stevenson does say is: 'He was really sloughed at getting out, and I don't blame him. He had helped me no end out there, and then got out in a way that was completely unlike Geoff.'

Boycott, understandably, has a slightly different version. 'I geed him up against the quicks by trying to frighten him about what I would say if he backed away and got out. I reckon I scared him more than the bowlers did. Once he got going, I left him alone, because I didn't want to tell him to think. Once he did that, he'd be knackered. In the end, I couldn't get a run while he was whopping it everywhere.'

My personal memory, which did not go into the *Birmingham Post*, was of Boycott, still on one knee as he contemplated the horror of his dismissal, while the players and umpires were leaving the field and the motor-roller was at least 30 yards on the field to do its between-innings work. It was only then that life came back into those run-filled legs.

The last word must go to Boycott, who played an important part in the events of one of the most remarkable turnabouts ever seen in County Championship cricket. 'His innings won us the match, and showed what a good cricketer Graham was. What a shame that he soon became a forgotten man, and left Yorkshire when he was only 30. He had such talent, but even more important, he was such a great lad to have in the dressing-room.'

Even number elevens have a particular innings they rate as their best, but Stevenson is one of only a handful who can point proudly to a hundred as 'the innings of my life'.

ALEC STEWART

69 on the third and fourth days
of the second Test between England
and Pakistan at Lord's, 20 and
21 June 1992.*

Stewart's unbeaten 69 out of England's second innings total of 175 was the sixth instance of an England player batting throughout an innings. He was only the second such batsman not to score a hundred - Geoffrey Boycott was the other - and his fighting innings not only kept his side in the game, it came within a whisker of being a match-winning effort. Needing 138 to win, Pakistan were in desperate trouble at 18 for three and 95 for eight, before their talented fast bowlers, Wasim Akram and Waqar Younis, took advantage of injuries to Phillip DeFreitas and Ian Botham, and England's three-man attack finally conceded defeat at the end of a day's play the like of which has rarely been seen at Lord's, and certainly never before on the Sabbath. A crowd of over 25,000 were transfixed for 6½ hours in which they saw 17 wickets fall in 79 overs while 264 runs were scored, mostly against and through attacking field-placings used by captains who were encouraged by the bowlers' success. Stewart went from his overnight 21 to 69, and was one of only eight batsmen to reach double figures that day.

Alec James Stewart was born on 8 April 1963 in Merton, Surrey, and followed father Michael into county and Test cricket. He first played for Surrey in 1981 and, having won his county cap in 1985, he was appointed club captain in 1992. His first appearance for England was in the historic game at Kingston in February 1990, and he was at the crease when Wayne Larkins made the winning hit to register England's first win against the West Indies in 16 years and 30 Tests. Always an attractive county batsman, his selection for England in his first 26 Tests before the start of the 1993 summer was often swayed by wicketkeeping considerations, with England's tour of India and Sri Lanka in early 1993 clouding the issue of his definitive role in the side. He captained England to defeats in Madras and Sri Lanka. His Test average of 39 - half a point more than his first-class career average - would be even higher but for failures when he kept wicket. He is naturally reluctant to refuse any request from the selectors, but the evidence of his first three years in international cricket suggests that he, and the England side, will gain more than they will lose if he is allowed to concentrate exclusively on batting. He still only averages a hundred every 16 visits to the crease, but the fact that he averages close to 40 suggests that the ratio will improve if his developing maturity is allowed to ripen naturally.

Being a relatively late arrival on the international scene - Gooch, Gatting, Gower, Atherton, Fairbrother and Hick all made their debuts at an earlier age - it was predictable that the Surrey captain would choose an innings for England as the best of his life, and he narrowed it down to three.

My 190 at Edgbaston in the first Test against Pakistan was a starter, because it ensured that we got out of the game with a draw, but I have to take into account the attack and the pitch. Wasim did not play and Waqar was not at full throttle after injury. Also, it was a slow pitch and, once I got in, there weren't too many problems. Then there was my 148 at Christchurch in early 1992 - it was the first time I had opened for England, and I nearly batted all day - but I have to go for a smaller score under more difficult conditions and in a much tighter match situation.

The second Test against Pakistan at Lord's was different in every way to the one at Edgbaston, and that is why I picked my second innings when I carried my bat for 69. I had a good match with 74 in the

first innings, when Graham Gooch and I put on 123 for the first wicket, but you are never out of the wood against Wasim and Waqar. They swing the old ball more than the new and, sure enough, Waqar nailed Allan Lamb, Ian Botham, Chris Lewis and Phil DeFreitas in a marvellous spell of 9-1-34-4. He was lethal, with two unplayable yorkers to 'Both' and Chris. I

GOOD FOOTWORK, WITH THE BACK FOOT HALFWAY BETWEEN THE CREASE AND STUMPS.
(PATRICK EAGAR)

have seen him do it so many times for Surrey that it was no real surprise that we had to settle for 255 instead of at least a hundred more.

At 228 for three, Pakistan looked sure to take a stranglehold on the match on the third day, but Devon Malcolm, DeFreitas and debutant Ian Salisbury took the last seven wickets for 65, and England were well placed at the end of the third day at 52 for one - an overall lead of 14 - with Stewart on 21 and nightwatchman Salisbury on one.

It was honours even, except that England were in the hands of their batsmen to give them a winning chance, now that injuries to DeFreitas and Botham meant that the home side's attack would be severely depleted in the final innings of the match. Stewart comments:

I knew that the pre-lunch session on Sunday would be vital. The pitch was reasonable but, against Pakistan, that is only half the battle. Wasim and Waqar swing it so much that you are never 'in'. Somehow we had to get a lead, and I set out to concentrate as hard as possible on squeezing every possible run.

Stewart's resolute defence was matched, for the first hour, by Salisbury until he was given out LBW to Akram - at best a marginal decision - and then for all-too-brief periods by Hick (11), Lamb (12) and Lewis (15). Before the latter was bowled by Younis, a score of 174 for six with an overall lead of 136 promised a final target of around 200. With Lewis, Russell and DeFreitas to support Stewart, whose apparent impregnability highlighted his colleagues' technical deficiencies against the swinging ball, this seemed a reasonable bet. Then came Lewis's dismissal by Waqar.

HOW TO EVADE THE BOUNCER. THE HEAD IS STILL, AND THE EYES HAVE WATCHED THE BALL THROUGHOUT. (PATRICK EAGAR)

Almost single-handedly, Stewart had clawed his side into a reasonable position, with 69 runs out of 147 off the bat, and seemingly the power to add - until Akram steamed in to take the last three wickets in four balls, and leave Stewart looking, as the editor of the *Wisden Cricket Monthly*, David Frith, neatly put it, 'like a man who was the sole survivor of a particularly nasty plane crash.'

He had survived one difficult chance to wicketkeeper Moin Khan off Akram after lunch when 58 but, otherwise, his judgement was flawless, and fully justified the verdict of a man whose praise of Stewart Junior is, understandably, less readily forthcoming than of most players. The possibility of nepotism between the former England team manager and his son has been aired too many times by too many people. There are two schools of thought - the facile view is that father favours son. However, the other one, which holds greater credibility, is that, because of the relationship, Alec Stewart had to prove something extra to deflect charges of favouritism. Put another way, Stewart had to be more equal than other candidates.

Not reluctantly, but only after careful consideration, did Senior offer this comment on Junior's performance at Lord's: 'It was the innings in which Alec came of age as a Test player. It is no surprise he chose that knock as the innings of his life because, although his 190 at Edgbaston was a more enjoyable innings and showed how well he can play once he gets in, at Lord's he had to temper what he wanted to do according to the needs of the side. It was an object lesson in playing the swinging ball, and also he still got down the pitch to Mushtaq because he could read him. There were several patches when he had to fight it out, but he never allowed three world-class bowlers to dominate him in what was becoming a match situation of ever-increasing tension, and it was so nearly a match-winning innings. It was a great team knock.'

Frith's report for *Wisden Cricket Monthly* said this: 'It was a match to rank with the Lord's classics of 1953 and 1963. Three times England were in command and three times they were forced to relinquish their grasp.

An immense amount of credit was earned by Alec Stewart. Cool and straight-batted, he had survived a couple of early shaves as Waqar and Akram almost found his stumps, but he seemed galvanised by the disasters occurring regularly at the other end. He was never either intimidated into strokelessness or tempted into a reckless rescue bid, for such an endeavour against this bowling would have been futile.

'He carried his bat through the innings, the first to do so for England at Lord's, thus winning another campaign medal of note. For just over four hours he had resisted while a famous collapse took place, his longest-lasting partner being the unlikely Salisbury.'

Stewart's only regret about the game is that England lost it: 'It would have been perfect if we'd won, because it was such a battle all through that fourth day. The ball swung all the time, and you have to be pleased when you score runs against world-class bowling.'

England captain Graham Gooch makes the same point: 'It was a super innings, because it was against

ENGLAND V PAKISTAN (2ND TEST)

PLAYED AT LORD'S, LONDON, ON 18, 19, 20, 21 JUNE 1992.
TOSS: ENGLAND. RESULT: PAKISTAN WON BY TWO WICKETS.

ENGLAND

	FIRST INNINGS			SECOND INNINGS	
G.A.Gooch*	b Wasim	69		lbw, b Aqib	13
A.J.Stewart	c Miandad, b Asif	74		not out	69
G.A.Hick	c Miandad, b Waqar	13	(4)	c Moin, b Mushtaq	11
R.A.Smith	c sub (Rashid Latif), b Wasim	9	(5)	b Mushtaq	8
A.J.Lamb	b Waqar	30	(6)	lbw, b Mushtaq	12
I.T.Botham	b Waqar	2	(7)	lbw, b Waqar	6
C.C.Lewis	lbw, b Waqar	2	(8)	b Waqar	15
R.C.Russell†	not out	22	(9)	b Wasim	1
P.A.J.DeFreitas	c Inzamam, b Waqar	3	(10)	c Inzamam, b Wasim	0
I.D.K.Salisbury	hit wicket, b Mushtaq	4	(3)	lbw, b Wasim	12
D.E.Malcolm	lbw, b Mushtaq	0		b Wasim	0
Extras	b 6, lb 12, nb 9	27		(b 5, lb 8, nb 15)	28
		255			175

	O	M	R	W	O	M	R	W
Wasim	19	5	49	2	17.4	2	66	4
Aqib	14	3	40	0	12	3	23	1
Waqar	21	4	91	5	13	3	40	2
Mushtaq	19.1	5	57	2	9	1	32	3
Asif	3	3	0	1	1	0	1	0

FALL OF WICKETS

1-123, 2-153, 3-172, 4-197, 5-213, 6-221, 7-232, 8-242, 9-247, 10-255
1-40, 2-73, 3-108, 4-120, 5-137, 6-148, 7-174, 8-175, 9-175, 10-175

PAKISTAN

	FIRST INNINGS			SECOND INNINGS	
Aamir Sohail	c Russell, b DeFreitas	73		b Salisbury	39
Ramiz Raja	b Lewis	24		c Hick, b Lewis	0
Asif Mujtaba	c Smith, b Malcolm	59		c Russell, b Lewis	0
Javed Miandad*	c Botham, b Salisbury	9		c Russell, b Lewis	0
Salim Malik	c Smith, b Malcolm	55		c Lewis, b Salisbury	12
Inzamam-ul-Haq	c and b Malcolm	0		run out	8
Wasim Akram	b Salisbury	24		not out	45
Moin Khan†	c Botham, b DeFreitas	12		c Smith, b Salisbury	3
Mushtaq Ahmed	c Russell, b DeFreitas	4		c Hick, b Malcolm	5
Waqar Younis	b Malcolm	14		not out	20
Aqib Javed	not out	5			
Extras	b 4, lb 3, nb 7	14		b 2, lb 5, w 1, nb 1	9
		293		(for 8 wickets)	141

	O	M	R	W	O	M	R	W
DeFreitas	26	8	58	3				
Malcolm	15.5	1	70	4	15	2	42	1
Lewis	29	7	76	1	16	3	43	3
Salisbury	23	3	73	2	14.1	0	49	3
Botham	5	2	9	0				

FALL OF WICKETS

1-43, 2-123, 3-143, 4-228, 5-228, 6-235, 7-263, 8-271, 9-276, 10-293
1-6, 2-10, 3-18, 4-41, 5-62, 6-68, 7-81, 8-95

Umpires: B.Dudleston and J.H.Hampshire

the best two swing bowlers in the world, and the biggest test of any batsman is to score runs against the best bowlers when conditions are in their favour. Alec did that, and nearly helped to win us the game.'

Stewart looks set for a successful Test career, but only if England make up their mind about how best to use his versatility. He has proved that he can adapt to the demands of batting in the first three, but it is a damaging policy to pick him to keep wicket and then allow the toss to decide where he bats. He is a good enough wicketkeeper, but he and any alternative specialist glove-man must not suffer because of other players' shortcomings which have resulted in too many fudged selections concerning one of the cleanest striking batsmen England have. His attitude on the field has attracted criticism, but his naturally abrasive approach merely needs fine tuning. A late developer, his best is yet to come - providing he is treated properly by the England selectors. Some batsmen never seem 'in' no matter how long they bat. Stewart is not one of these, as he proved at Lord's in what he proudly claims is 'the innings of my life'.

STEVE WAUGH

177 on the second and third days
of the first Test between England
and Australia at Headingley, 9 and
10 June 1989.*

Waugh, playing in his 27th Test match and with his place in danger, went in to bat at 273 for four, and played a wonderful, cultured innings of 177 not out to register his first Test hundred, and take his side to 601 for seven. It was an innings which removed all doubts about his international future, as he proved by starting the 1993 Ashes series in England with 52 caps at the age of 28. It also helped Australia pull off an unexpected win, which set the tone for a series in which England lost four home Ashes Tests for only the second time since the Second World War. His innings was a model of orthodoxy, and he hit 24 fours off 242 deliveries in a stay of five hours and nine minutes.

Stephen Rodger Waugh was born on 2 June 1965, a twin brother to Mark, in Canterbury, New South Wales, and played his early cricket for the Bankstown club in Sydney. His all-round skills soon brought a first-class debut against Queensland at Brisbane at the age of 19, and a Test debut a year later at Melbourne against India, in what was only his tenth first-class match. He was, understandably, a slow starter at this level, scoring 113 in this first nine innings, including 74 against New Zealand at Christchurch, but seven wickets for 152 in the same five Tests kept him in the side for the next two home series in 1986-87 against India and England. He was moved up and down the order to try to help his development, and innings against England of 71 at number three and 79 not out at seven, followed by 73 at six were enough to convince the selectors that he would make a Test cricketer.

There was a school of thought that his all-round abilities were more suited to one-day cricket, and an excellent World Cup campaign in India in 1987 - 167 runs at an average of 55.66 and 11 wickets - seemed to prove the point. Twin brother Mark was soon pressing hard for Test recognition but, ironically, when the call came in the fourth Test against England at Adelaide in 1991, he replaced Steve, whose unbroken sequence of 42 Tests from debut thus ended under circumstances that must have strained family loyalty to the limit. The brothers finally created history three months later in Port-of-Spain by playing in the same team, and the twins have also played in English county cricket. Steve played 18 Championship games for Somerset in 1987 and 1988, and scored eight hundreds in 28 innings to make an even bigger mystery of why he had scored only two previous first-class hundreds, and still had not reached three figures for Australia.

His entry into English domestic cricket was not planned, and came, after four games for Somerset in 1987, because of a back injury sustained by Martin Crowe in May 1988. Waugh was playing in the Birmingham League for Smethwick when he was summoned to Southampton on 1 June. He arrived at lunch, and went in at number seven with his side in trouble at 106 for five. His unbeaten 115 helped Somerset recover to 308, and was the start of a sequence of scores which brought him 1000 runs from his first 11 completed innings. Like many other overseas cricketers, English cricket provided the ideal finishing school for a young man whose entry into international cricket was precipitated at a much too early stage of his career by the retirement of Dennis Lillee, Greg Chappell and Rod Marsh, and the defection of a 'rebel' touring party to South Africa under the captaincy of Kim Hughes.

Batting regularly at number four - a luxury denied him in his own country - he discovered the pleasant

PERFECTION. GOOD STRIDE, SOFT HANDS AND STILL HEAD.

(PATRICK EAGAR)

habit of compiling hundreds, and it was Sod's Law that he would make the final breakthrough in Test cricket in the country in which he finally matriculated. After his hugely successful part-season for Somerset in 1988, he followed a disappointing tour of Pakistan - 92 in five innings and two wickets for 308 in the three Tests - with a couple of near misses against the West Indies. He scored 90 and 91 in the first two Tests at Brisbane and Perth, but 120 in the next four innings meant that his place was again in question when Australia arrived in England to try to regain the Ashes - something no Australian side had done since 1934.

Waugh scored 185 in his five first-class innings of the tour before the crucial first Test at Headingley, and was worried.

I knew that my position in the side was in question leading up to the Test, and that increased the normal pressure of playing in an Ashes Test. I had passed fifty only three times in six previous Tests against England, and that first Test hundred seemed as though it would never come.

David Gower won the toss after, against all his better instincts, omitting John Emburey and handicapping himself with a four-man pace attack. He further compounded the decision by putting Australia in to bat. The pitch was a reasonable batting one by previous Headingley standards, and some shoddy bowling helped the tourists to 207 for three at the end of a day shortened by 40 minutes because of bad light. The anxious Waugh watched Mark Taylor, Allan Border and Dean Jones help themselves in shared partnerships for the third and fourth wickets of 117 and 99, before Taylor was LBW to Foster, the best of a poor home attack, for 136.

As Waugh walked out for his date with destiny, he must have wondered whether there was more

ENGLAND V AUSTRALIA (1ST TEST)

PLAYED AT HEADINGLEY, LEEDS, ON 8, 9, 10, 12, 13 JUNE 1989.
TOSS: ENGLAND. RESULT: AUSTRALIA WON BY 210 RUNS.

AUSTRALIA

	FIRST INNINGS		SECOND INNINGS	
G.R.Marsh	lbw, b DeFreitas	16	c Russell, b Foster	6
M.A.Taylor	lbw, b Foster	136	c Broad, b Pringle	60
D.C.Boon	c Russell, b Foster	9	lbw, b DeFreitas	43
A.R.Border*	c Foster, b DeFreitas	66	not out	60
D.M.Jones	c Russell, b Newport	79	not out	40
S.R.Waugh	not out	177		
I.A.Healy†	c and b Newport	16		
M.G.Hughes	c Russell, b Foster	71		
G.F.Lawson	not out	10		
G.D.Campbell	} did not bat			
T.M.Alderman	}			
Extras	lb 13, w 1, nb 7	21	b 2, lb 5, w 9, nb 5	21
	(7 wickets declared)	601	(3 wickets declared)	230

	O	M	R	W	O	M	R	W
DeFreitas	45.3	8	140	2	18	2	76	1
Foster	46	14	109	3	19	4	65	1
Newport	39	5	153	2	5	2	22	0
Pringle	33	5	123	0	12.5	1	60	1
Gooch	9	1	31	0				
Barnett	6	0	32	0				

FALL OF WICKETS
1-44, 2-57, 3-174, 4-273, 5-411, 6-441, 7-588
1-14, 2-97, 3-129

ENGLAND

	FIRST INNINGS		SECOND INNINGS	
G.A.Gooch	lbw, b Alderman	13	lbw, b Hughes	68
B.C.Broad	b Hughes	37	lbw, b Alderman	7
K.J.Barnett	lbw, b Alderman	80	c Taylor, b Alderman	34
A.J.Lamb	c Boon, b Alderman	125	c Boon, b Alderman	4
D.I.Gower*	c Healy, b Lawson	26	c Healy, b Lawson	34
R.A.Smith	lbw, b Alderman	66	c Border, b Lawson	0
D.R.Pringle	lbw, b Campbell	6	c Border, b Alderman	0
P.J.Newport	c Boon, b Lawson	36	c Marsh, b Alderman	8
R.C.Russell†	c Marsh, b Lawson	15	c Healy, b Hughes	2
P.A.J.DeFreitas	lbw, b Alderman	1	b Hughes	21
N.A.Foster	not out	2	not out	1
Extras	b 5, lb 7, w 1, nb 10	23	b 4, lb 3, nb 5	12
		430		191

	O	M	R	W	O	M	R	W
Alderman	37	7	107	5	20	7	44	5
Lawson	34.5	6	105	3	11	2	58	2
Campbell	14	0	82	1	10	0	42	0
Hughes	28	7	92	1	9.2	2	36	3
Waugh	6	2	27	0				
Border	2	1	5	0	5	3	4	0

FALL OF WICKETS
1-35, 2-81, 3-195, 4-243, 5-323, 6-338, 7-392, 8-421, 9-424, 10-430
1-17, 2-67, 3-77, 4-134, 5-134, 6-153, 7-153, 8-166, 9-170, 10-191

Umpires: J.W.Holder and D.R.Shepherd

pressure in trying to consolidate a wonderful start, or in going in to rescue his side from a poor position. Failure in that situation would probably not be regarded so seriously as one on a good pitch against a moderate attack, with a good score already on the board.

I knew I had to get in and make it count. I wanted a hundred, and a big one, but I had to get on with it. I had a bit of a shaky start, but once I got through that, everything seemed to hit the middle of the bat.

So much so that the first two sessions of the second day were worth 120 and 114, with that much-prized first hundred coming off only 124 deliveries, and the magical three figures were reached with his 16th four - a square-drive played with typical wristy authority.

It was a refreshing display of old-fashioned orthodoxy, with grip, stance, backlift and footwork impeccably correct, and all on show under a lovely green, baggy cap: no helmet, no standing with feet apart and bat held aloft like a baseballer ready to repel boarders, and no early commitment of feet before the line and length could be picked up. Waugh showed what a simple exercise batting can be. You stand still, you watch the ball and, if it is over-pitched you drive, and if it is short you pull or cut. There were no frills, no superfluous movement; it was batting at its purest and best.

Wisden said, 'Waugh reminded many spectators of a bygone age, despatching the ball stylishly through the gaps, and timing his forcing strokes so well that he brought an effortless quality to the proceedings.'

Waugh shared partnerships with Jones, Healy, and Hughes of 138, 30, and 147, and played with a rare authority which mocked the absence of a Test hundred in his previous 26 Tests. David Frith wrote: 'His patent joy at scoring a hundred quickly gave way to renewed determination. He passed 150 on a sunlit evening, justifying, as far as one can tell, Bill O'Reilly's comparison with Stan McCabe in terms of physique and cleanliness of strokeplay. Waugh's unbeaten 177 was his highest in first-class cricket, and his lofty position in the world game was confirmed beyond question.'

Waugh says, 'It put the side in a comfortable position and possibly a winning one after consolidating our good work on the previous day.' It was the pace of his innings which did as much as anything to set up a winning position, because the 373 runs scored from 92 overs on the second day created sufficient time - just - for Australia to win the match on the fifth day, even though it was an awful batting display by England which handed them the game, and the initiative for the series. On the final day, the home batsmen had to survive 83 overs to draw the game on a pitch which was still good, but collapsed to Alderman, Hughes and Lawson so abjectly that the tourists needed only 55.2 overs to take ten wickets, the last seven of which went for 57 runs.

LOVELY SQUARE CUT, WITH GOOD WEIGHT DISTRIBUTION AND USE OF THE CREASE. SMALL WONDER THAT ENGLAND DID NOT DISMISS WAUGH UNTIL THE THIRD TEST IN 1989, BY WHICH TIME HE HAD SCORED 393 RUNS. (ALLSPORT/ADRIAN MURRELL)

Having broken through, Waugh followed up with an unbeaten 152 in the next Test at Lord's, and was dismissed only four times in the six-match series in which he scored 506 runs and topped the averages with 126.50.

So 'the innings of my life' became 'the series of my life', thus repaying a faith in class shown by the Australian selectors. Their rich reward was proof that orthodoxy and a feeling for tradition still have a big part to play in the modern game.